# Images of America
# Newaygo County
## 1850–1920

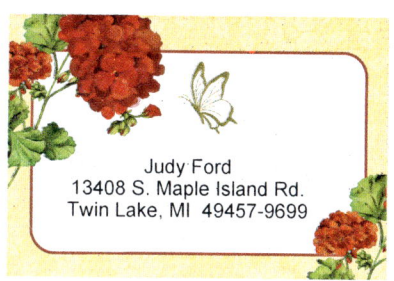

Judy Ford
13408 S. Maple Island Rd.
Twin Lake, MI 49457-9699

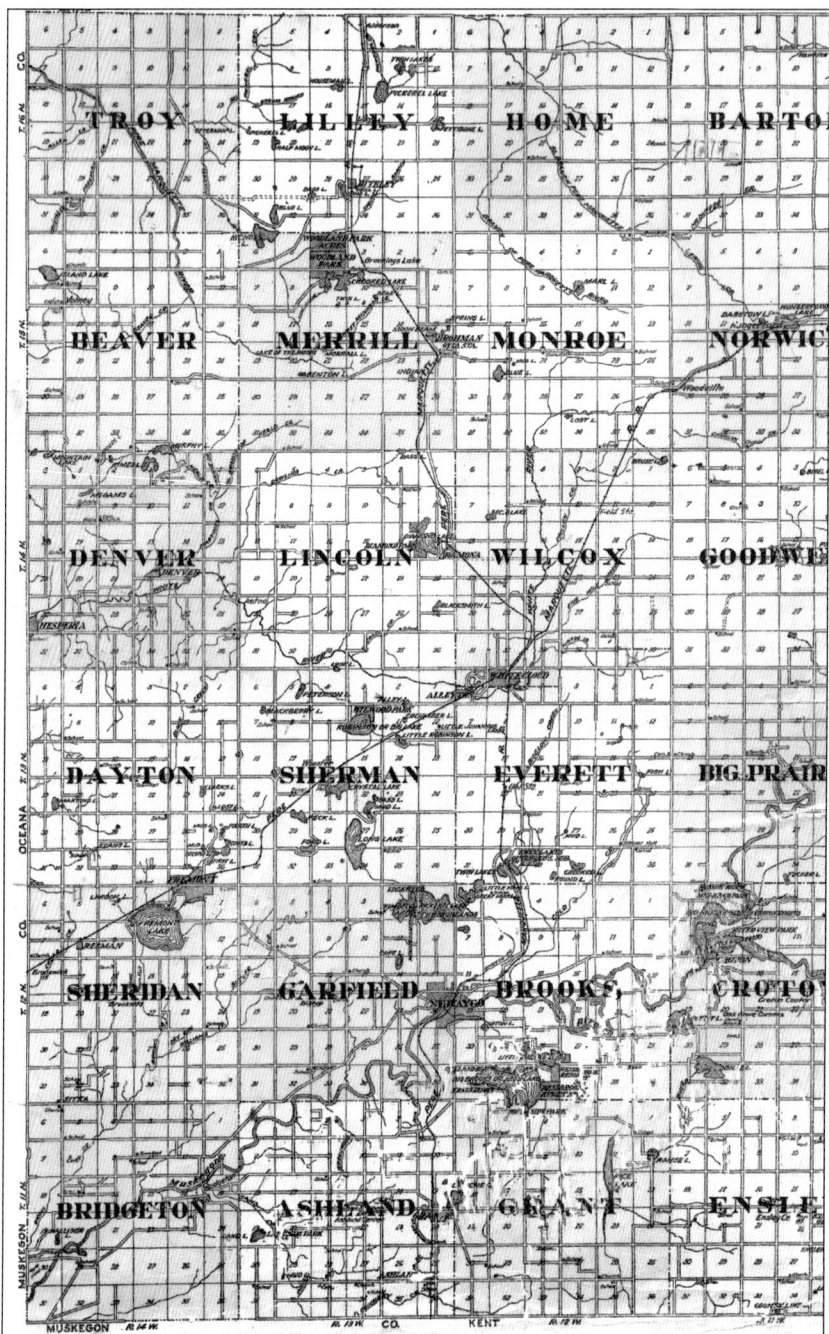

Newaygo County formed in 1840 from parts of Mackinac County and Oceana County. Newaygo County owes its beginning to the lumbering industry. In 1836, the Native Americans had given up title to the lands in what is now Newaygo County, and the territory was to be thrown open to settlers. This Newaygo County map dates from 1900.

*On the cover*: Please see page 12. (Courtesy of Newaygo County Society of History and Genealogy.)

# IMAGES of America
# NEWAYGO COUNTY
## 1850–1920

Newaygo County Society of
History and Genealogy

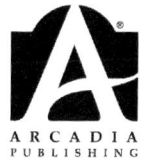

ARCADIA
PUBLISHING

Copyright © 2006 by Newaygo County Society of History and Genealogy
ISBN 978-0-7385-4115-0

Published by Arcadia Publishing
Charleston, South Carolina

Printed in the United States of America

Library of Congress Catalog Card Number: 2006934712

For all general information contact Arcadia Publishing at:
Telephone 843-853-2070
Fax 843-853-0044
E-mail sales@arcadiapublishing.com
For customer service and orders:
Toll-Free 1-888-313-2665

Visit us on the Internet at www.arcadiapublishing.com

# Contents

| | | |
|---|---|---|
| Acknowledgments | | 6 |
| Introduction | | 7 |
| 1. | The White Pine Era Begins | 9 |
| 2. | The Logging Trains Arrive | 27 |
| 3. | The Power of the River | 33 |
| 4. | Early Settlements | 39 |
| 5. | Four Seasons of Family Fun | 81 |
| 6. | The Melting Pot | 89 |

# ACKNOWLEDGMENTS

This book was made possible by the efforts of the Newaygo County Society of History and Genealogy and its hope to preserve the history of Newaygo County. Many of the photographs are courtesy of the society's collection. Special thanks go to the following individuals for allowing use of photographs from their personal collections: M. Scott Rumsey, Terry Wantz, Sandra Vincent, Toni Rumsey, and Keith Bassett.

The layout for the book was developed by Sandra Vincent, Joyce Pearson, and Toni Rumsey. Many references from the 1884 *Portrait and Biographical Album of Newaygo County* were used as a guideline in developing this book.

# INTRODUCTION

The county of Newaygo was originally a part of Kent County; once it was established on its own, it contained two townships, Brooks on the west side and Newaygo on the east side. By 1882, the 21st township of Goodwell was established, and after that the last three, Lilley, Merrill, and Home, rounded out the county's 24 townships. There are four rivers that flow through the county. The Muskegon River flows northeast to southwest through the county; the White River rises northeast in the center of the county and flows westward. The northeast corner has the south branch of the Pere Marquette River, and the southern part has the Rogue River flowing southward. A number of lakes and streams are found throughout.

Many of Newaygo County's earliest settlements were based around the rivers. The rivers were a great source of natural power for the establishments and a major attraction for the logging industry. Settlers came to the county and began transporting logs in these streams and rivers as early as 1836. Primitive roads were cut. Dams and mills were soon built, which began the business of industry here. The earliest settlements were at Croton and Newaygo. As early as 1853, the county had four sawmills: Croton, Brooks, Merrill, and Smith. By 1884, there were an estimated 100 sites.

As the original towns were built, there were also connecting establishments that provided stopovers for mail routes and stagecoaches. As people purchased land and started farms around these establishments, schools, churches, and stores were being built. These provided the feeling of community for the farmers. The establishments were named and several generations of families would eventually raise their children in these areas.

Newaygo County participated in the Civil War. During the whole war, the county contributed about 300 men to fight.

By 1882, the county had established school districts in townships with 94 schools, the majority being wood-frame houses. There were nine townships and 13 school district libraries.

Railroads were a desired mode of transportation to bring in stock and market goods, raise property values, and promote immigration to the area. The first passenger train to run from Newaygo was on September 11, 1872. The first train from Grand Rapids to Newaygo held 300 people and a brass band. The railroad tracks were then expanded north to Morgan (White Cloud). By 1873, a line connecting Muskegon to Big Rapids was in existence, and the stations between these towns were located in Newaygo County: Fremont, Alleyton, White Cloud, Woodville, Lumberton, and Hungerford. Much to the dismay of Hesperia, no tracks were laid to connect it to its fellow towns in Newaygo or Oceana County.

As soon as the county was formed and the townships laid out, the need for government arose and thus came roads, buildings, more settlers, physicians, dentists, storekeepers, and businesses. The county was growing and many new needs had to be met to accommodate the growth.

The Newaygo County Society of History and Genealogy hopes to give you a glimpse of life during these early years and to allow you to envision the efforts and pride of the Newaygo County pioneers.

# One
# THE WHITE PINE ERA BEGINS

In 1836, when a group of capitalists from Chicago journeyed up the Muskegon River looking for new ventures, they hired Mitchell Charloe (Charleau), a French trader, to guide them. The Pennoyer brothers were with them, and they built the first sawmill in the county at the mouth of a small creek that was to become the village of Newaygo. Logging reached its height during the winter of 1882–1883, bringing new population to Newaygo County and helping to build and develop a new county.

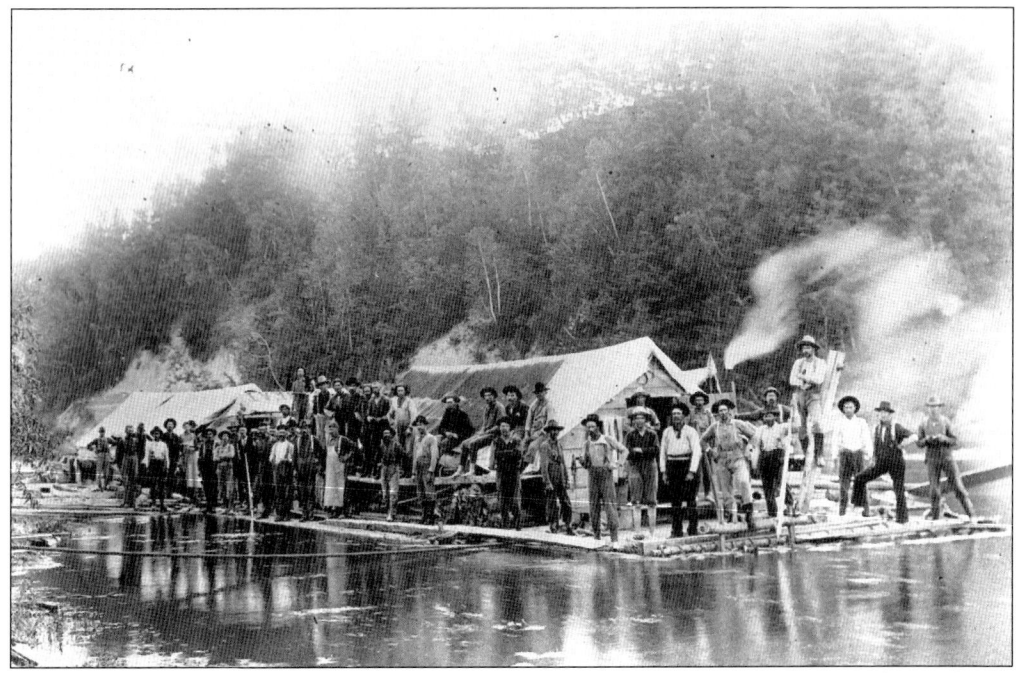

The log drivers employed by the Muskegon Boom Company are pictured here at their home during a drive in 1886. Their craft is tied up between Newaygo and Croton. The drive usually ended at Sand Creek holding pond, where the crews were paid off. From Maple Island, a solid mass of logs extended 12 miles downstream to the sorting pens at the mouth of the Muskegon River.

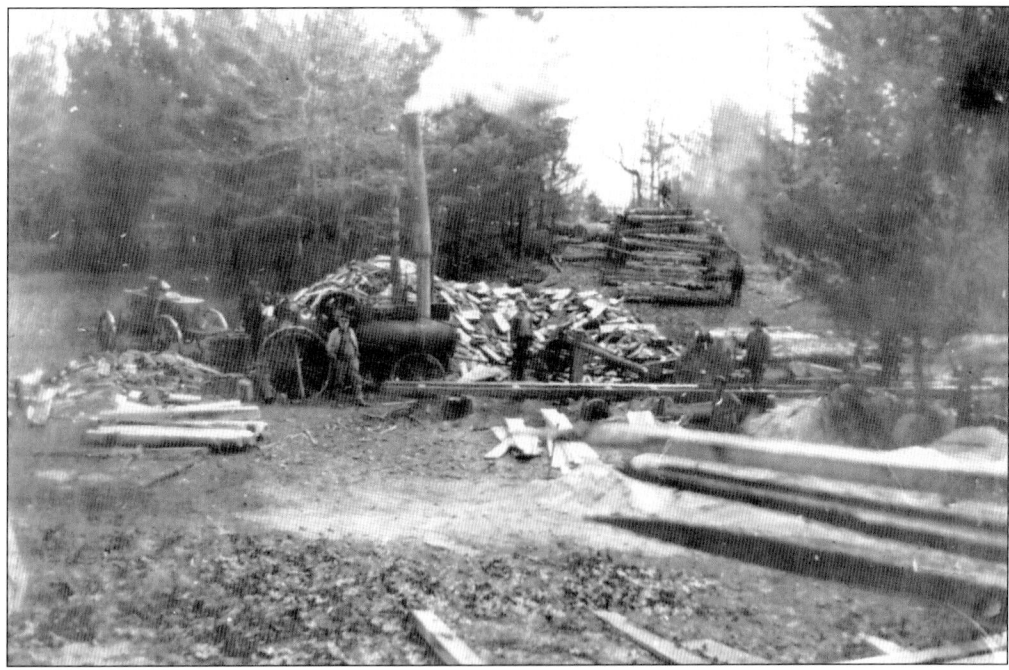

C. Gifford is cutting up pine sawlogs into timbers for construction work on the Hardy Dam Railroad. The trees, located in the southwestern part of the northeastern portion of section 3 in Brooks Township, were blown down during the fall storm of 1929. Note the big pile of slab wood.

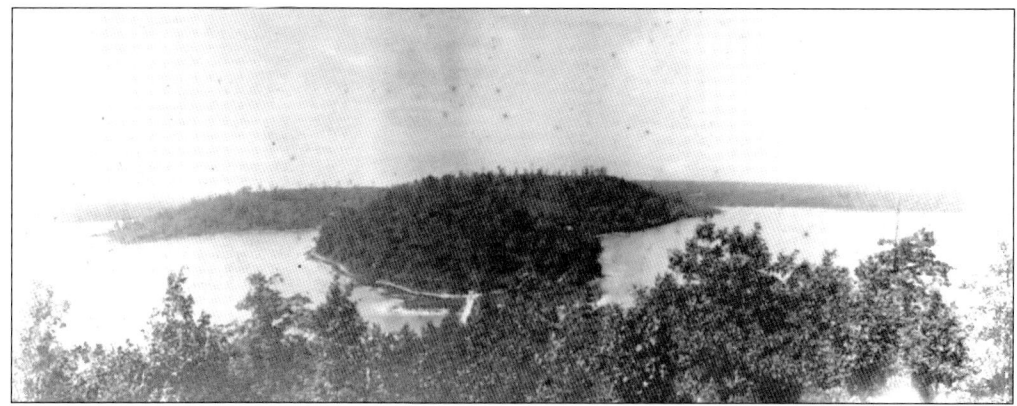

The Newaygo Lakes were a part of the Ryerson-Hills logging area in the 1870s and 1880s. Later marl from the lakes was used to make cement. The area became a famous summer resort, which was platted by H. W. Sawyer in the 1900s. Note the swing bridge over the channel between Emerald (left) and Sylvan Lakes.

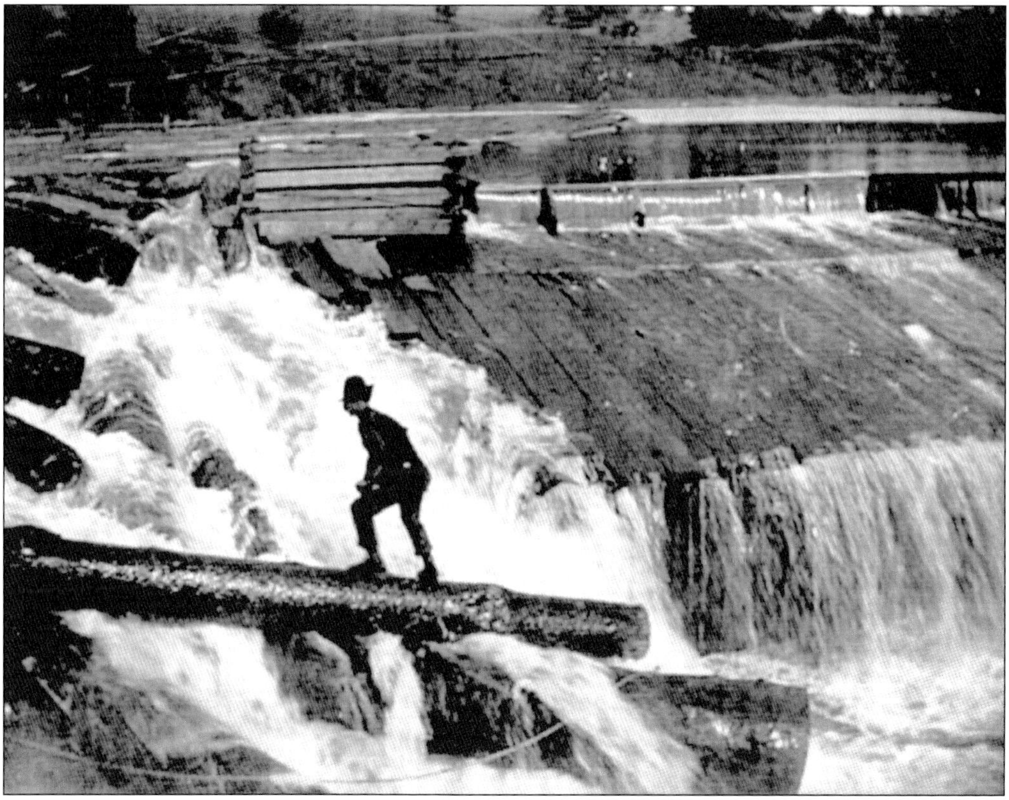

Nicholas Rossiter, first-generation son of Irish immigrants Jeremiah Rossiter and Bridget (Furlong) Rossiter, lived two miles northeast of Hesperia by Daly School. He was a logger on the rivers, particularly in Newaygo County. This photograph is believed to have been taken on the Muskegon River near Croton. Nicholas and wife Ethel (Gilbert) Rossiter raised their children in Hesperia, and most of them chose to live in the area. Many descendants still live in the area, but the Rossiter name has not survived.

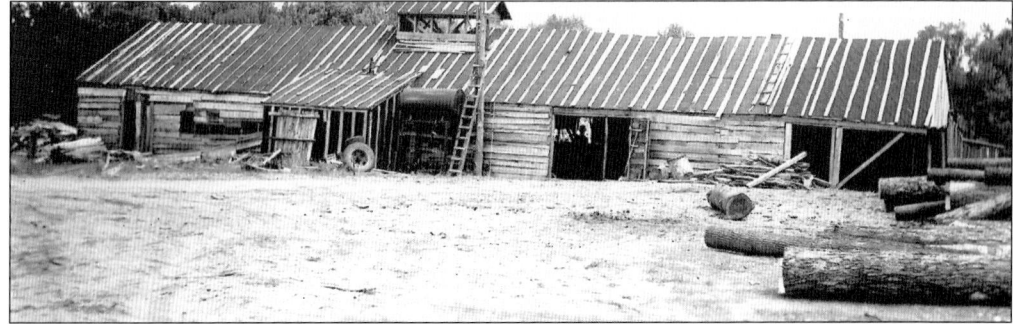

During the lumber era, many mills were located in the wooded areas near the village of Hesperia. The community of Huber was located three miles north and one mile east of Hesperia. Typical of communities around 1900, there was a school, cemetery, Seventh-Day Baptist church, general store, pickle station, and dairy center located at Huber. Many farmers established farms in the late 1800s and early 1900s in the area. Eventually the businesses closed, and most were gone by 1930. The only evidence left of this village in 2006 is the tiny cemetery and local residents who can still claim they were born in Huber.

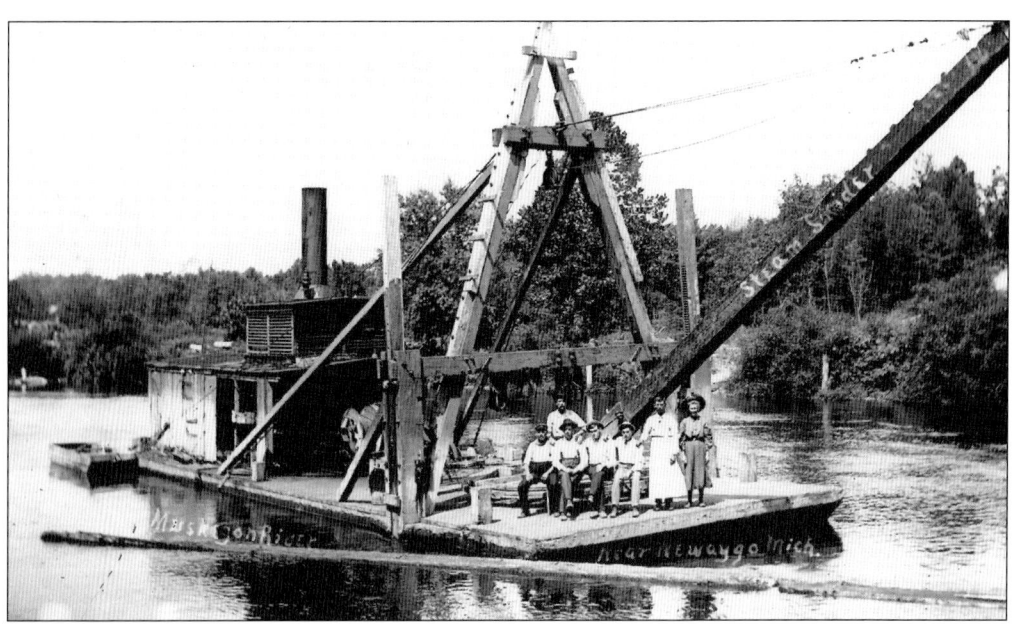

Steam skidders operated on the Muskegon River and its surrounding lakes. This skidder was operated by steam to pull up sunken logs off the lake or river bottom. This picture was taken on the Muskegon River, between the high banks above Bridgeton. To this day, there are many logs and deadheads (or logging marks) still found on the bottom of the waterways.

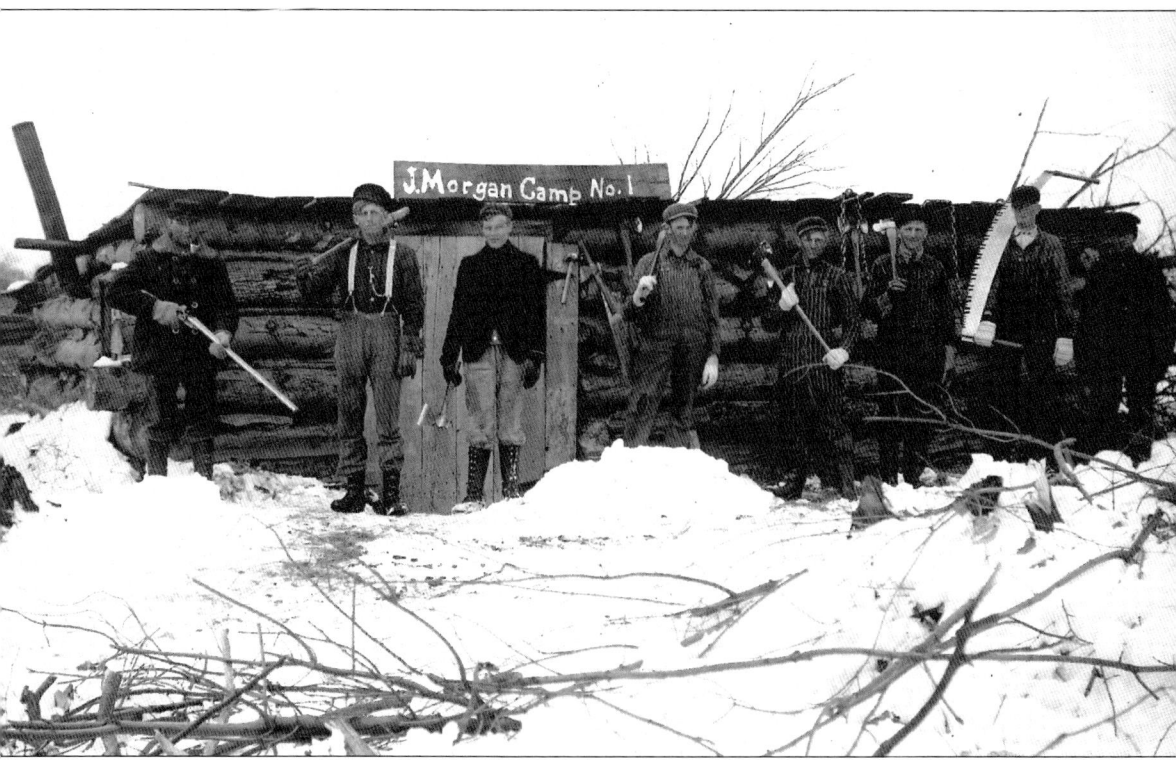

James L. Morgan formed the James L. Morgan Lumber Company in 1877. It built a mill at the northeast corner of White Cloud where Route 88 crosses the White River. The Wilcox logging company had a camp in White Cloud and another on section 3, Everett.

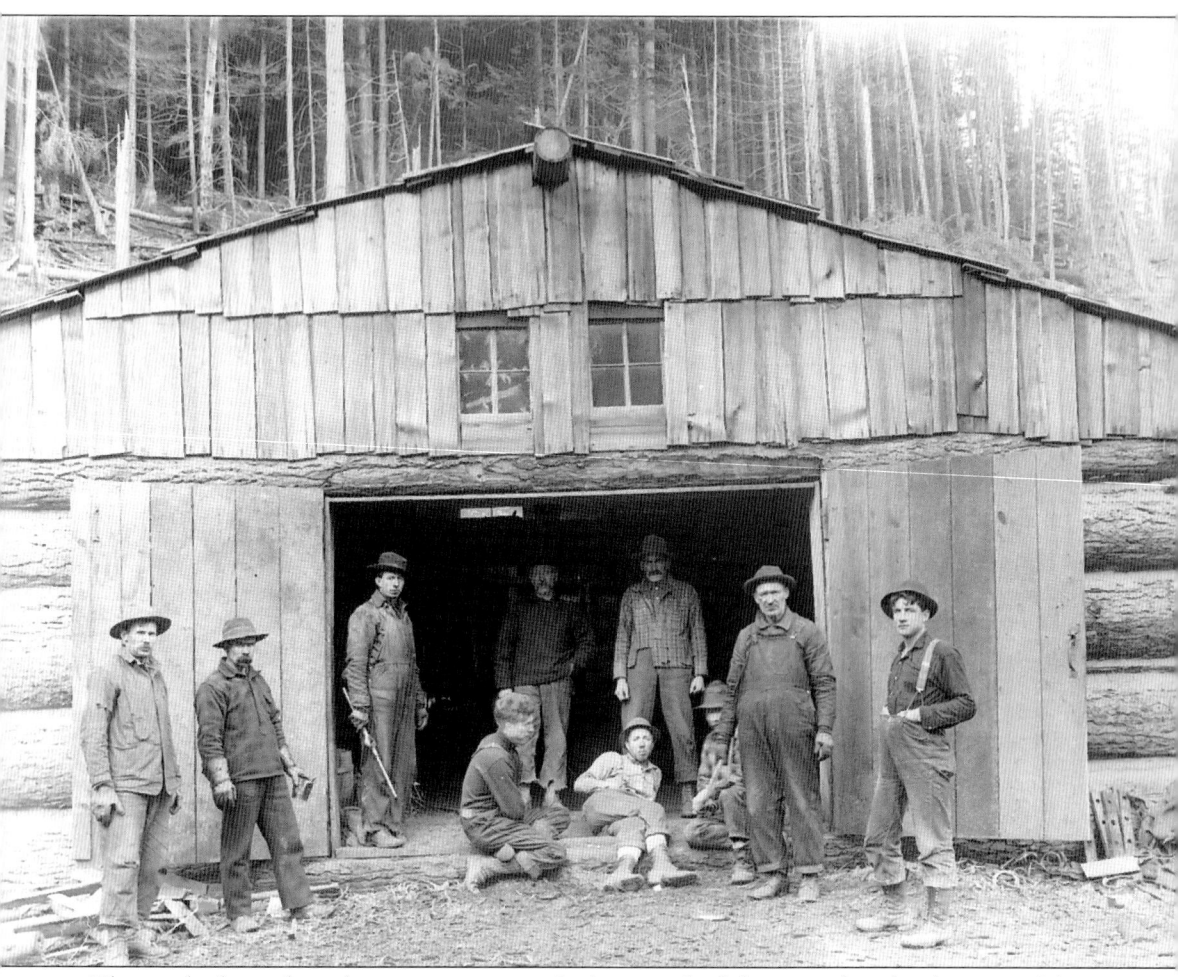

The methods used in this operation were fairly typical of those used in level terrain. Men, working in pairs, sawed down the trees with two-man crosscut saws and cut them into suitable lengths, usually 16 feet, seldom utilizing the trunk above the lowest limbs. By this time, however, with timber getting scarce, they were less particular and often took logs that were crooked or knotty if shingle (16 inch) or lath (48 inch) bolts could be scavenged from them. Also, they took such hardwoods as hard maple, for pails, and oak, for furniture. After this came the swamper. His job was to clear away brush and improvise temporary roads so that the skidder, with his oxen or horses, could drag the logs into yards for temporary piling on skids. Then trucks, trams, or sleighs could easily reach them for conveyance to the mill or river.

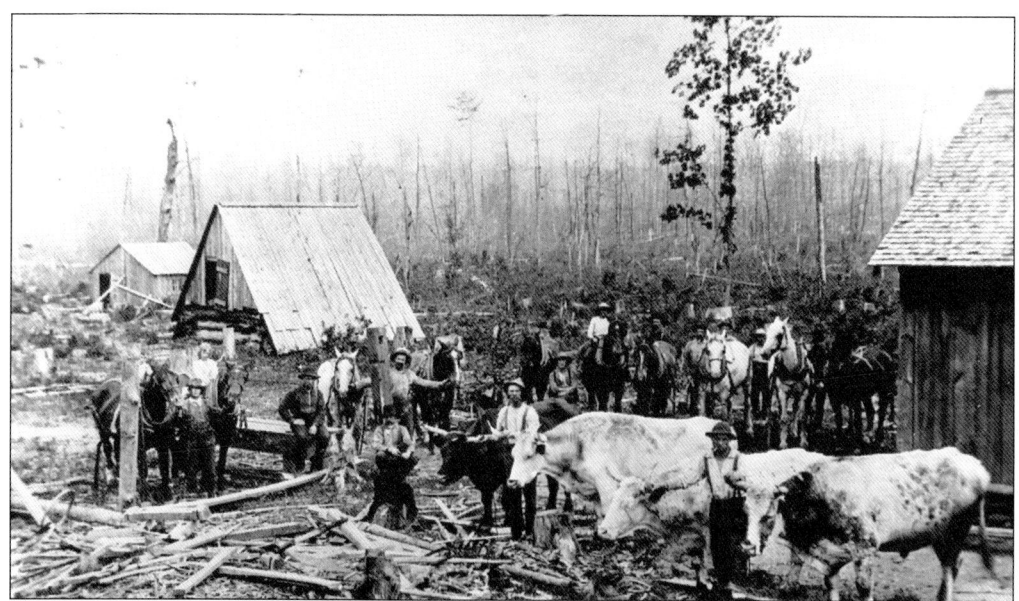

Oxen were used as well as horses to pull the logs out of the woods. They did not travel as fast as the horses, but the lumbermen found they were steady and did not startle as easy as the horses did. They could pull heavy loads and were often used as food if one was injured.

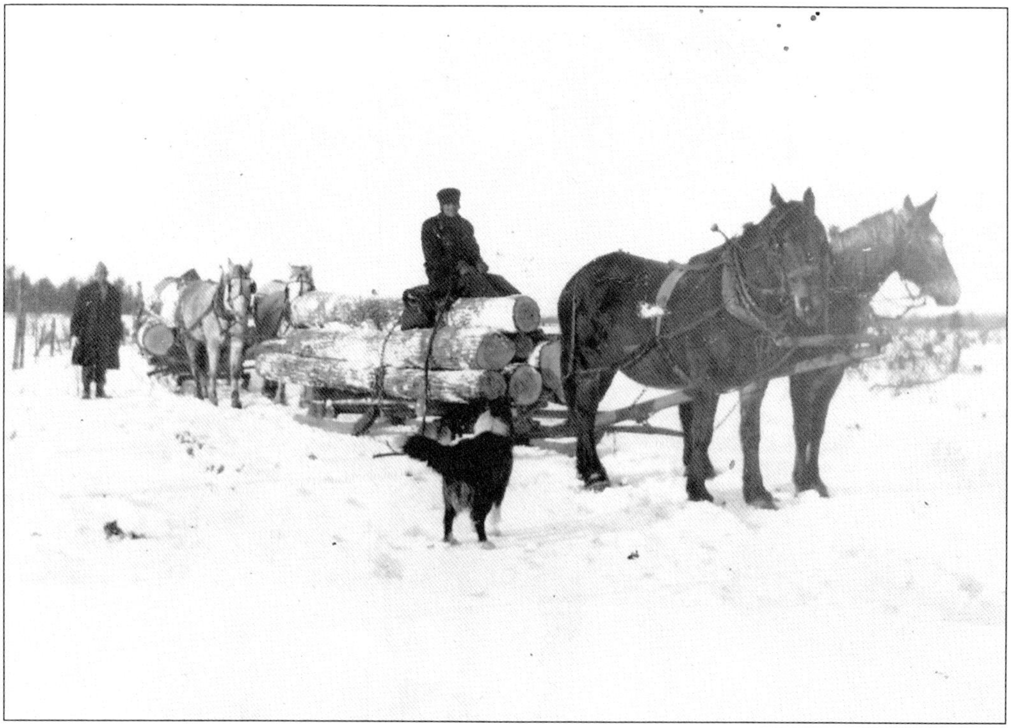

Timber was cut mainly during the winter when the ground was frozen and snow allowed for easier hauling. Awaiting the spring thaw and rain, the logs were piled along the river, ready to be dumped in when the high waters came. By building a series of small dams every few miles, pools were created, and logs could be washed from one to another until they reached larger waters.

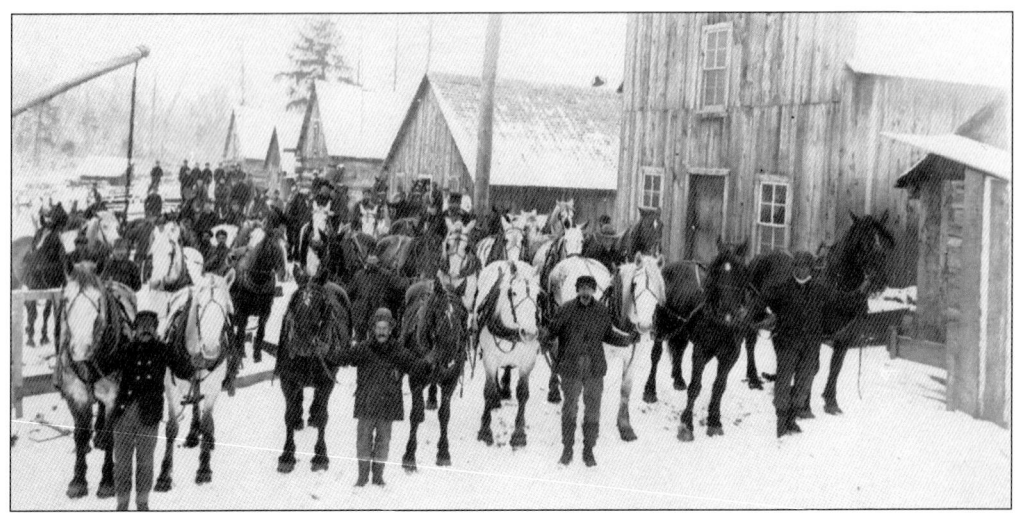

Mills sprang up rapidly. By 1880, Newaygo County had 26 sawmills. Most of the mills' equipment was mechanized by 1888. Production was increased greatly, with one mill just north of White Cloud producing 88,000 feet of lumber a day and employing over 350 men. The life of the men working in the camps and mills was a hard one. In return for 14 hours or more of work, they received $1 plus "found," which meant they received three meals and a place to sleep. Many camps did not pay the men until spring when the season ended. Clothing for the men consisted of heavy long underwear, flannel shirts and pants, and two or three pairs of wool socks. High leather boots with rubber soles were worn, along with a bright mackinaw to finish the outfit. The weather could be quite cold out in the woods during those long winter days.

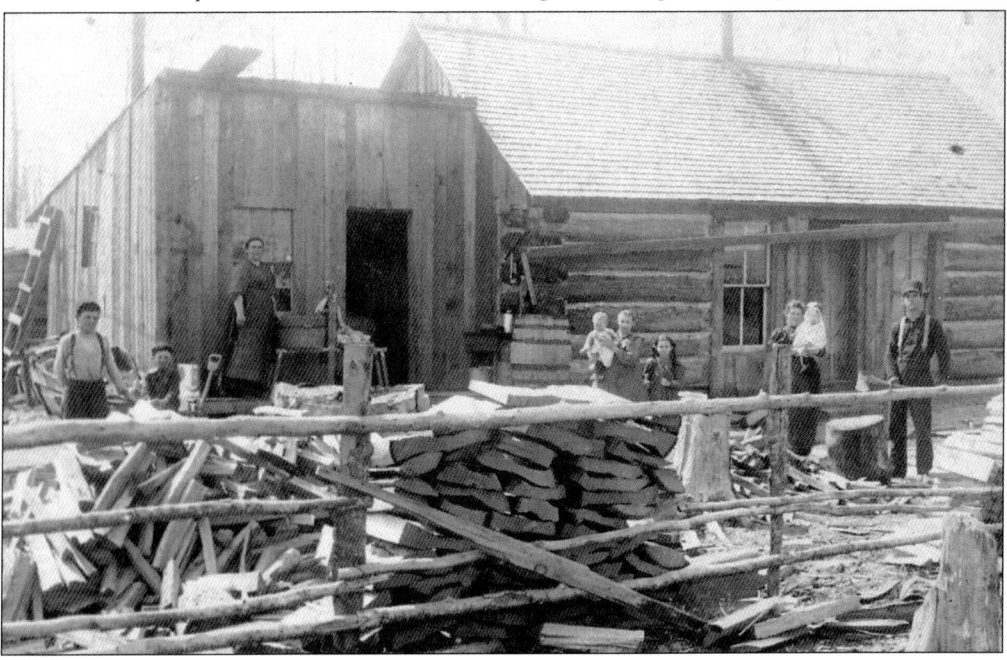

In 1882, Benjamin Whitney erected a shingle mill near Volney to cut shingles for E. L. Gray. Some women joined their husbands in the woods, as settling into a new life was often hard and isolated. Volney became an active settlement and had its own post office from 1880 to 1909. The town once had a general store, boardinghouse, and saloon.

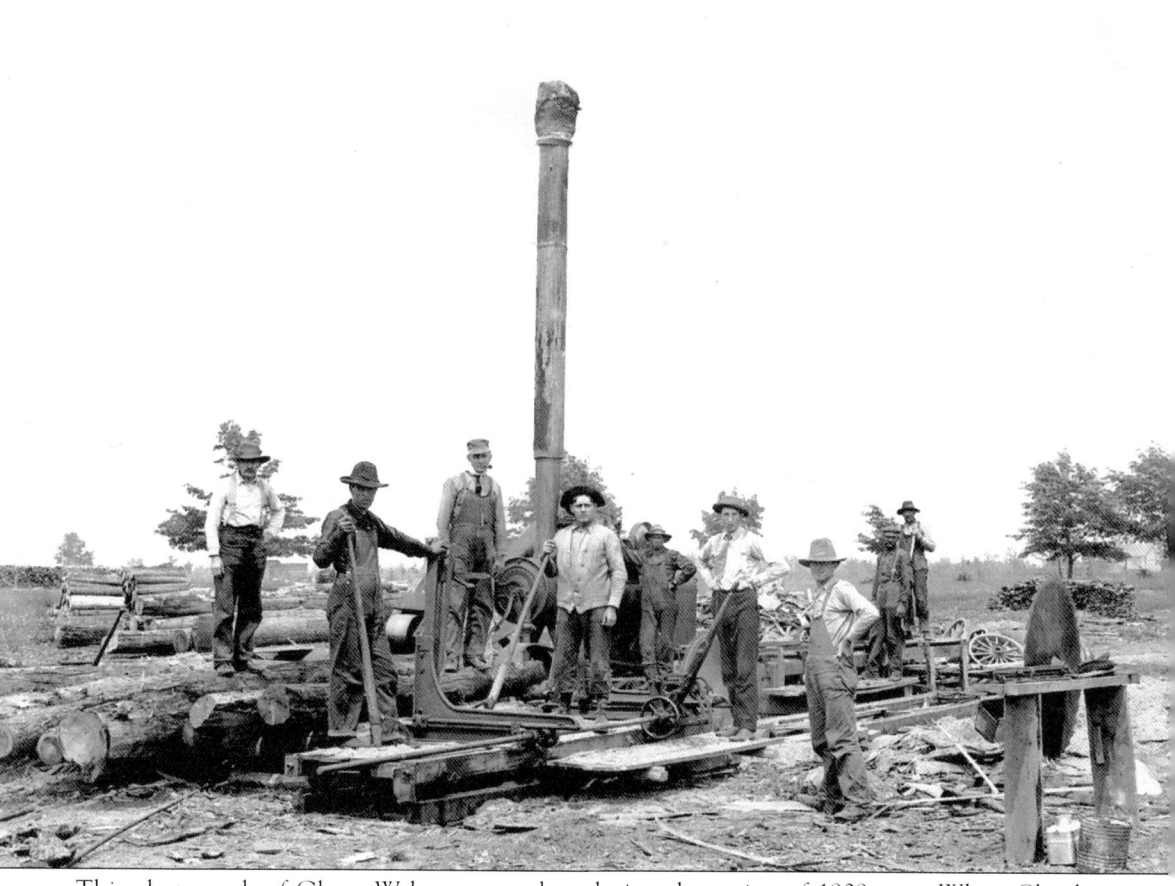

This photograph of Glenn Webster was taken during the spring of 1909, near White Cloud at Lafaham's Mill. Many of the settlements in Newaygo County were attributed to the lumber industry. The greatest periods of prosperity in the early days coincided with the rise and fall of the lumber interests. Lumbering operations and its increasing demands for workers determined the patterns of settlements throughout the county.

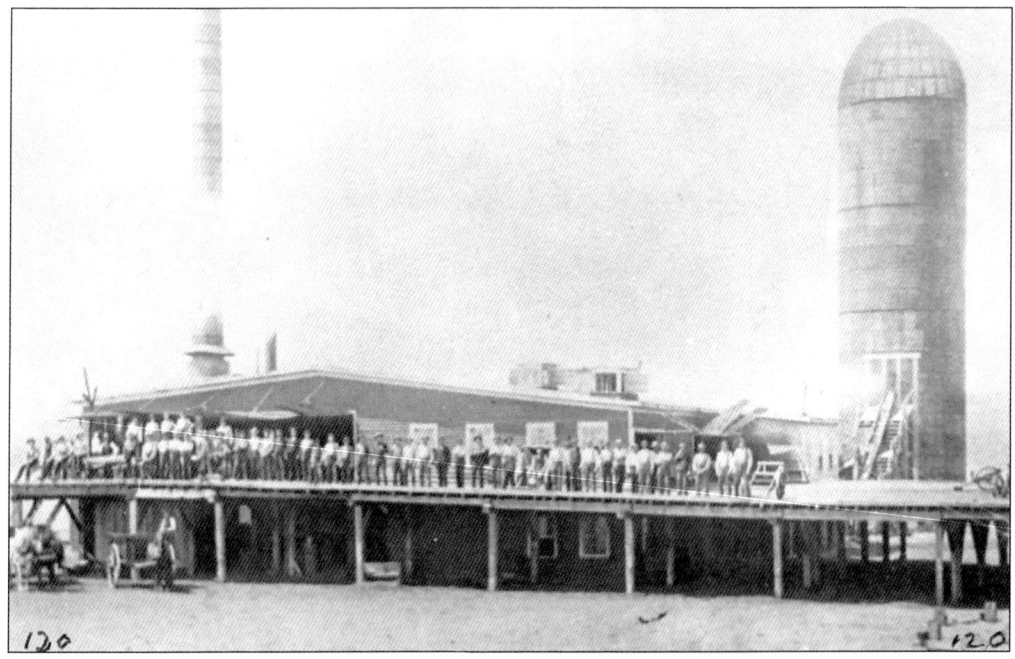

Ryerson and Hills sawed the lumber and did its own business. The mill was on Muskegon Lake, like all mills on sawmill row along the shoreline, and was supplied for the most part by logs rafted in from the sorting pens above the mouth of the Muskegon River, mainly Newaygo County.

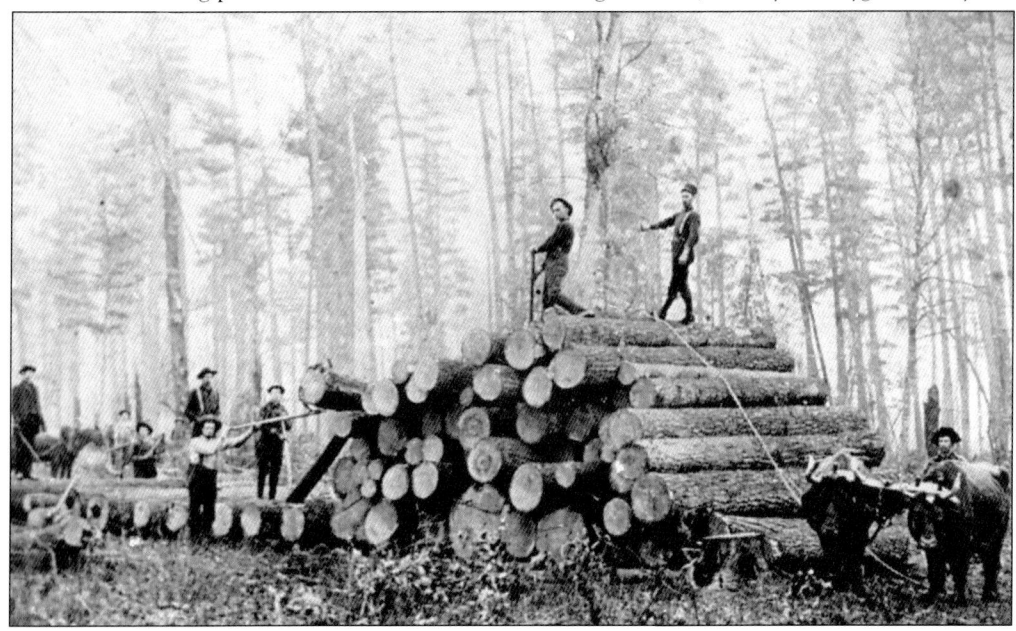

Lumbermen are decking logs in the woods and are part of Cooks Camp Grawn, Sailor's crew, on the Gidding's tract south of Brooks Lake for the Converse Manufacturing Company in Newaygo, makers of fine furniture. Pictured are, from left to right, the following: the scaler, with his scale, standing on the log at far left; Bill Anderson with marking hammer; a Mr. Wagner, whose cant hook sticks in the log; Len Cook standing on logs; George Crofoot on the top deck; an unidentified lumberman; and Everett Crofoot with the oxen.

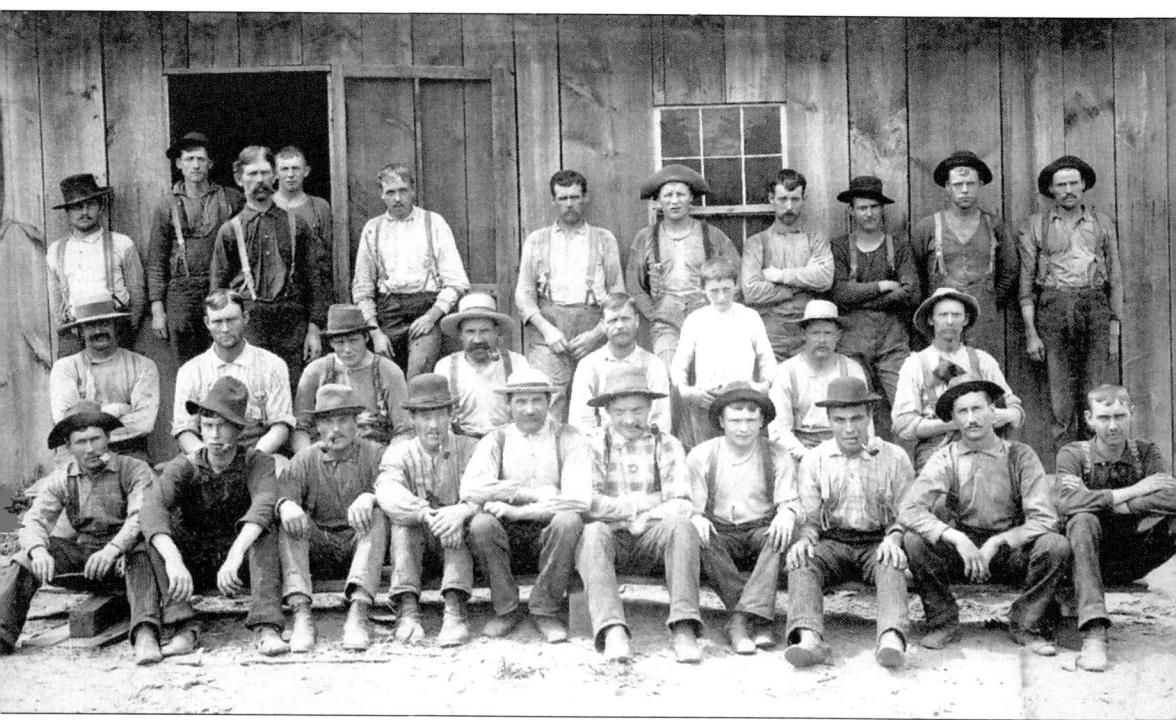

The Giddings Pine No. 1 Lumber Camp was one of two camps built by Giddings Pine in the area of the Hess, Brooks, and Rice Lakes. A tramway was constructed over which logs were hauled to the Muskegon River near High Rollaway. Erastus Sailors, father of Dave Sailors, was well known hereabouts for many years because of his woods activities. He was woods boss and foreman; Lewis Cook, also from Everett Township, was foreman of the other camp.

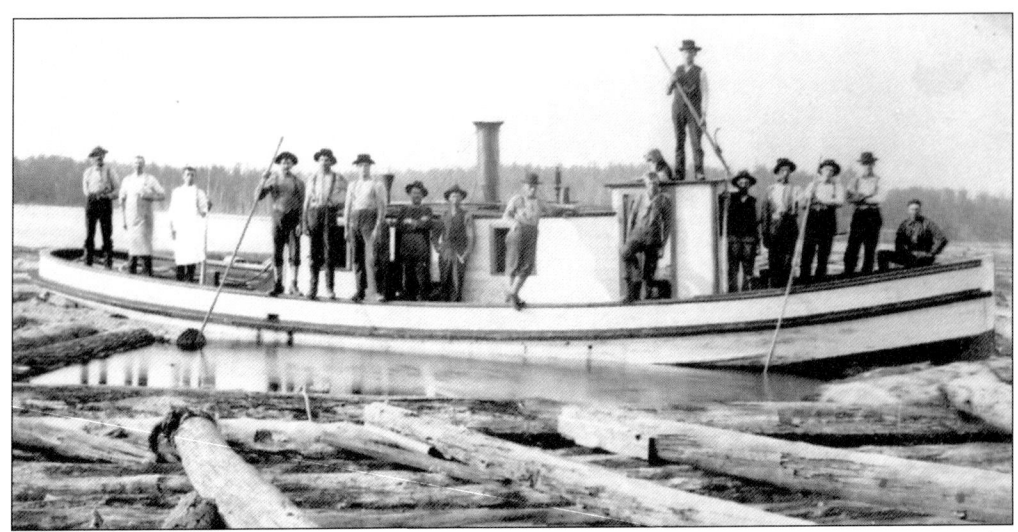

The tub boat plied the waters of Pickeral and Marl Lakes in the late 1870s and 1880s. The *Newaygo Republican* of October 30, 1878, quotes, "William Kimball has placed an engine on a flat boat and is now towing logs through Pickeral Lake and the two Marl lakes. The idea is a novel one, and original, and by this plan several miles of trucking are saved."

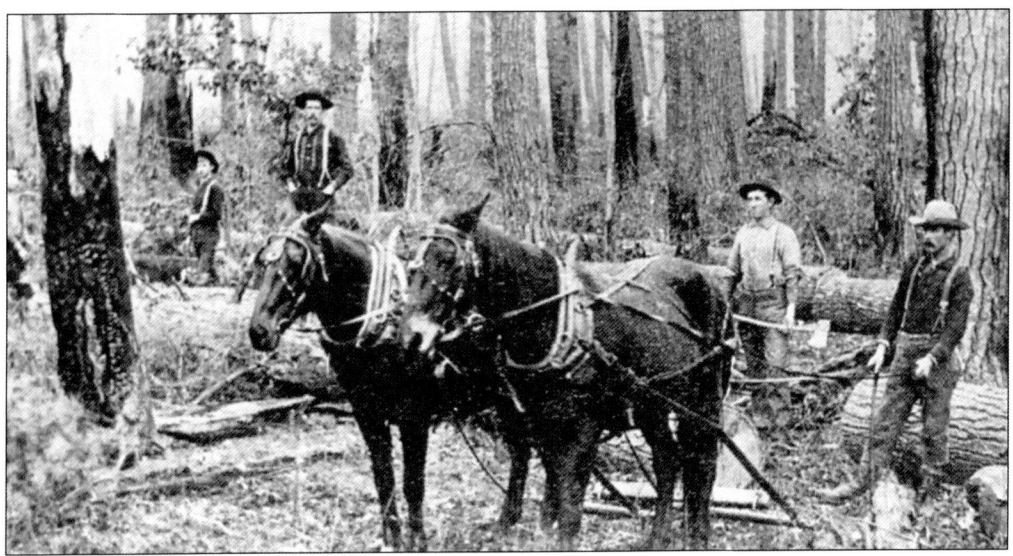

While logging east of Hess Lake, the following are pictured from left to right, skidding out logs for the decking crew: Art Alverson and Art Crofoot with saw, swamper John Cochrane, and skidder Ed Cook. This is on Gidding's tract in the 1890s, the last of the big holdings of virgin pine. The logs were hauled to the river over a tram road.

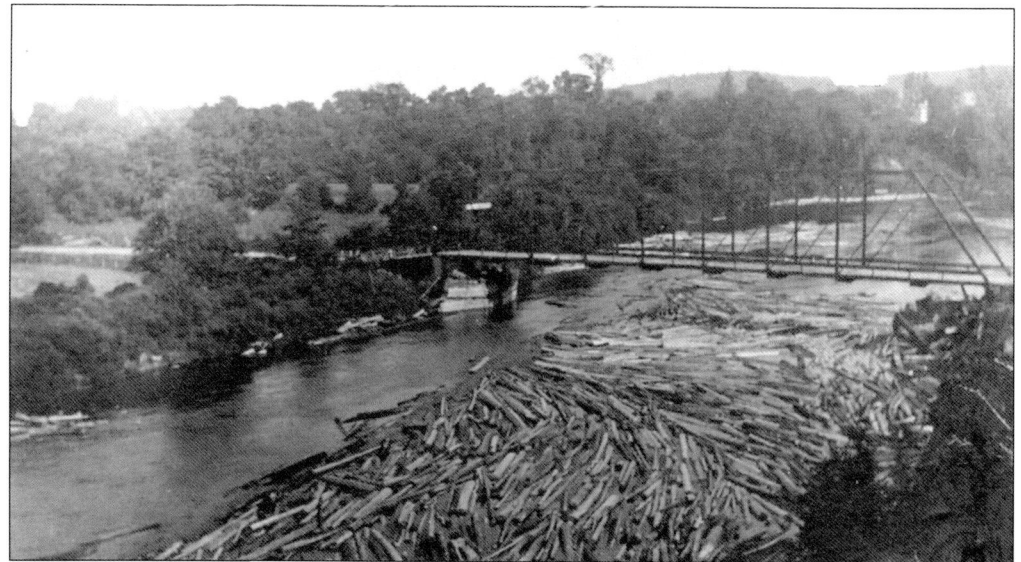

A logjam built up at the bridge that crossed the Muskegon River at Croton during the 1890s. This road enters Croton from the west, then turns right and crosses over the flow from the Little Muskegon Pond, and continues to Howard City. Homes at the upper right corner on the high ground are near the Congregational church.

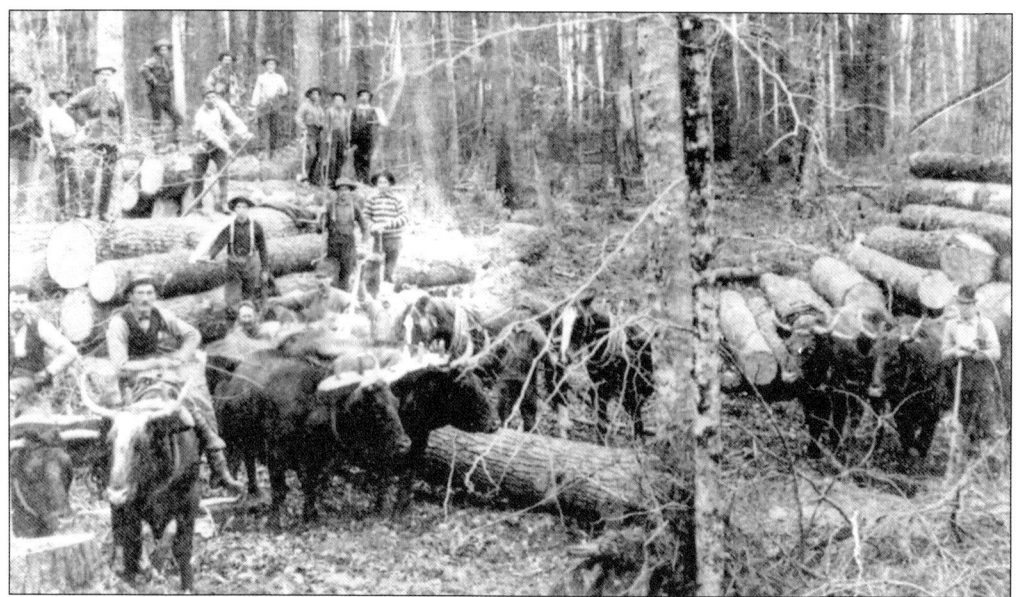

Loggers from D. P. Clay lumber camp, south of Hess Lake, are pictured here. Sailor's crew, 1888, includes Jim Berry, center, yoke of oxen; Bob Bly with Fid Cooper's team; Smith with Sailor's oxen; and Billy Brown, right, with axe.

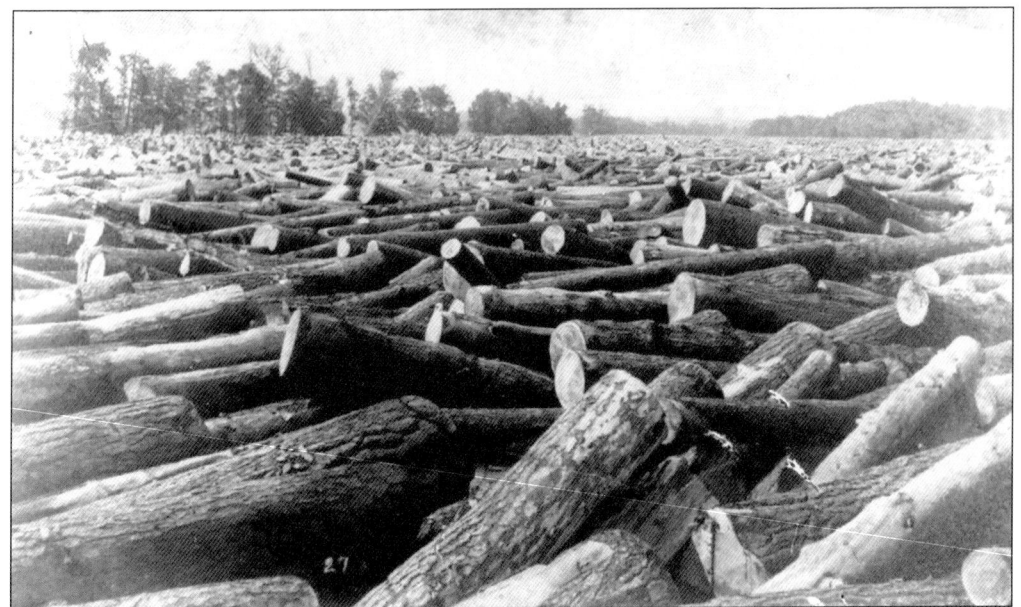

The river between Mitchell rollaway below Big Rapids and Bridgeton kept the log men alert to prevent the logs from jamming due to its winding course. This was especially true between Newaygo and Croton, where a special crew was employed to patrol the riverbank to watch the logs and keep them running free. Driving logs was hazardous work, which drew young and adventurous men.

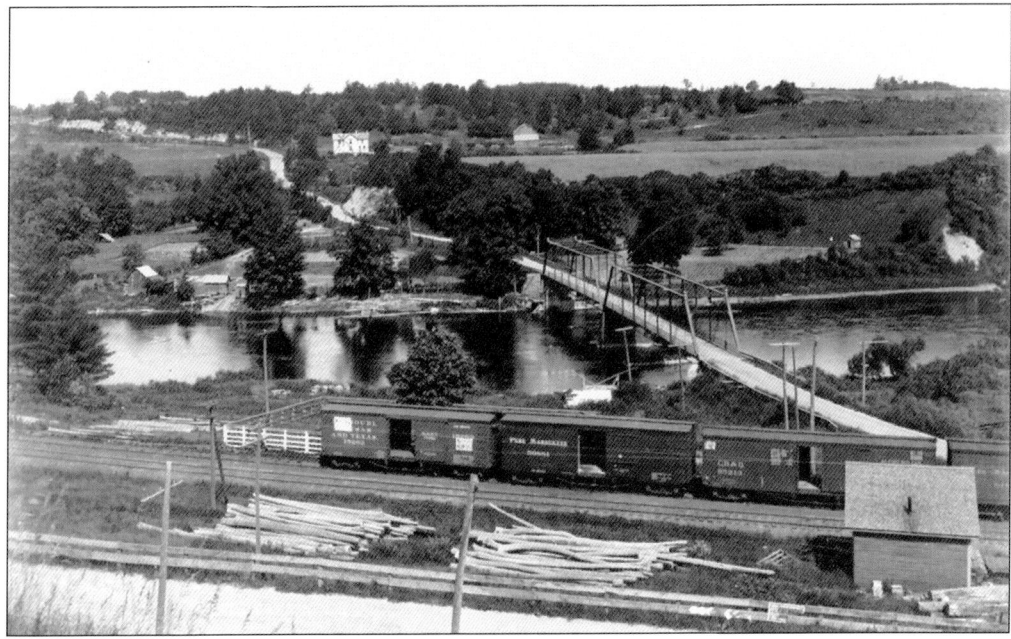

John H. Wood came to Newaygo in the 1860s and engaged in the lumbering business. He was a man dedicated to the temperance movement, and the hill in front of his home (the large white house) was called "Whiskey Wood." The house was also known as the Aliki Bowers Place. This view was taken from the top of Price Hill looking north. Newaygo Lower Bridge is in the center with utility poles and handcar house is in foreground.

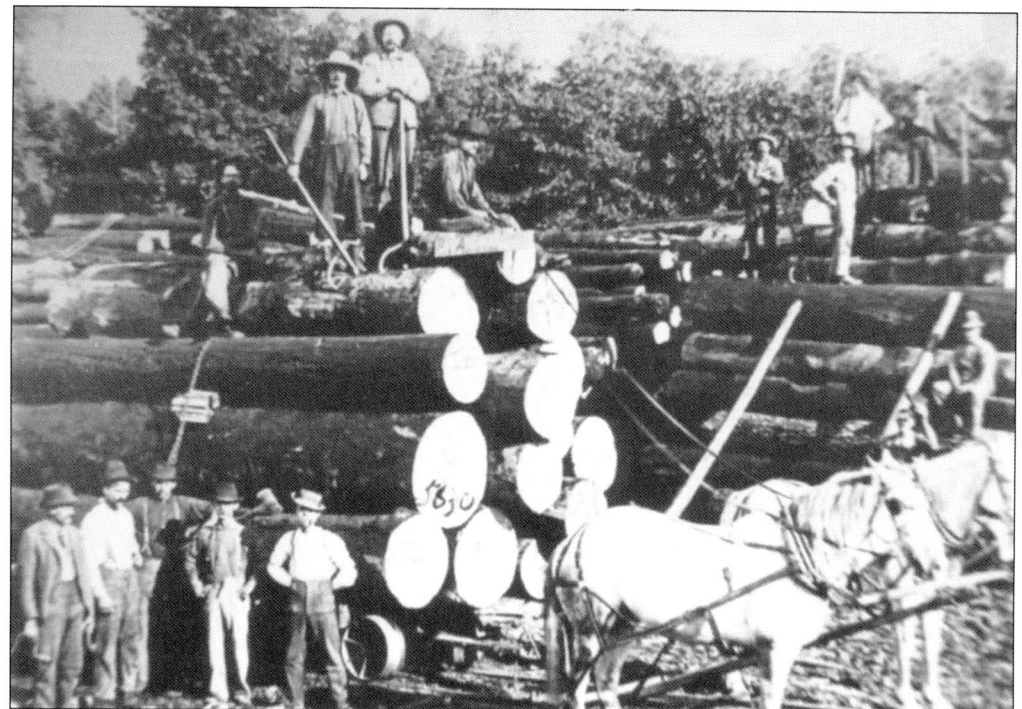

This is said to have been the largest load of logs loaded on the Frank Squires farm, southwest of Grant in 1903. Log marks and lumber records were stored in the courthouse, along with land records and other statistics.

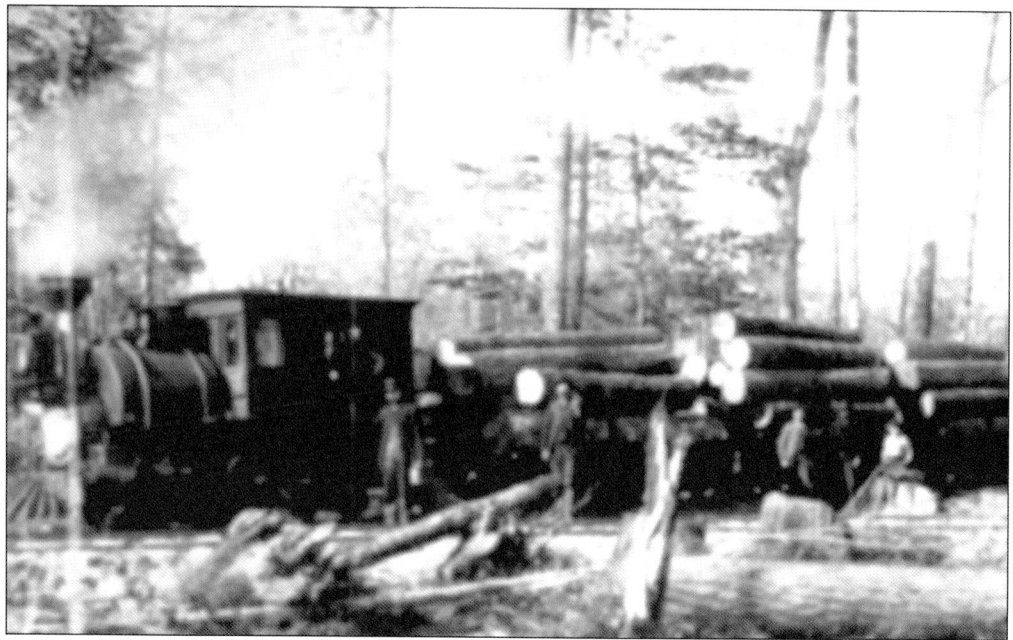

Shown here is the Sisson and Lilly log train around Pettibone Lake around 1890. The engineer, oilcan in hand, was a man by the name of Oaks. According to different sources of information, both George E. Sisson and Francis Lilly had narrow- and wide-gauge lines.

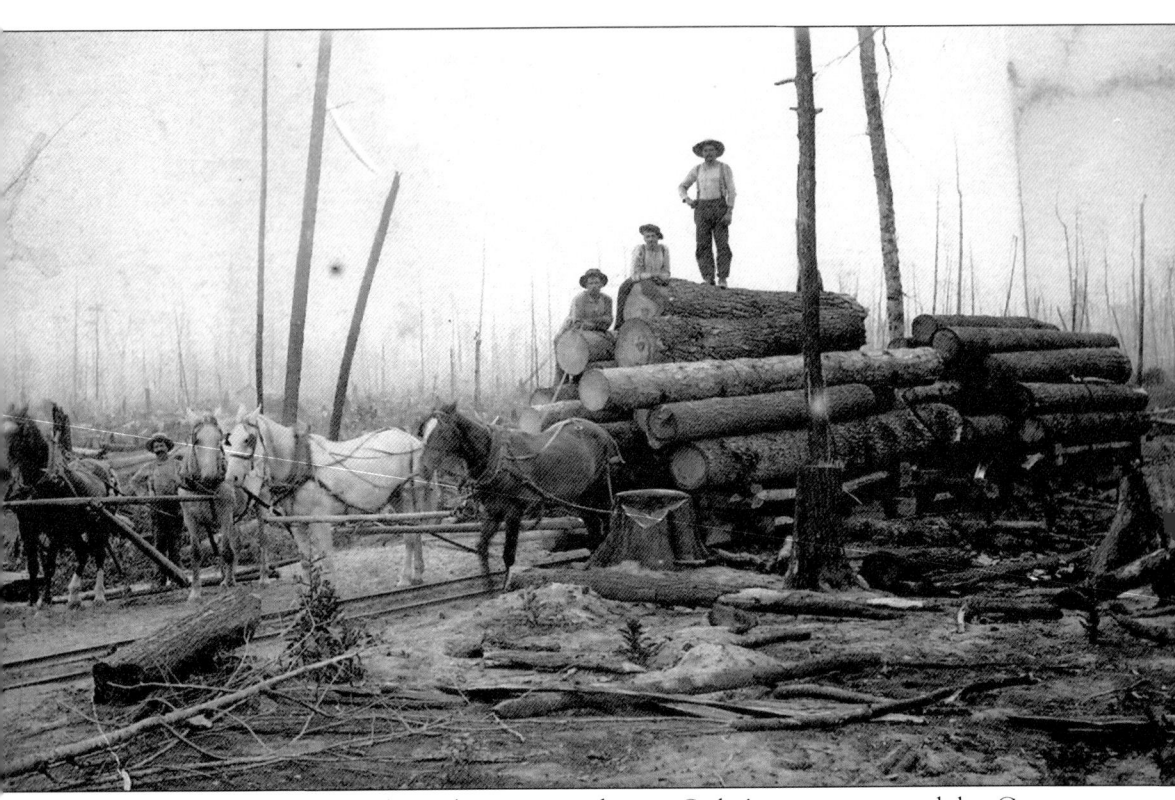

A work team is shown along the tram road near Sailor's camp, operated by Converse Manufacturing Company from 1889 to 1890. The road ran on the east side of Brooks Lake, in the Giddings tract that was the last of the virgin pine. The long neck yoke on the horses made it possible for them to travel on the outside of the rails.

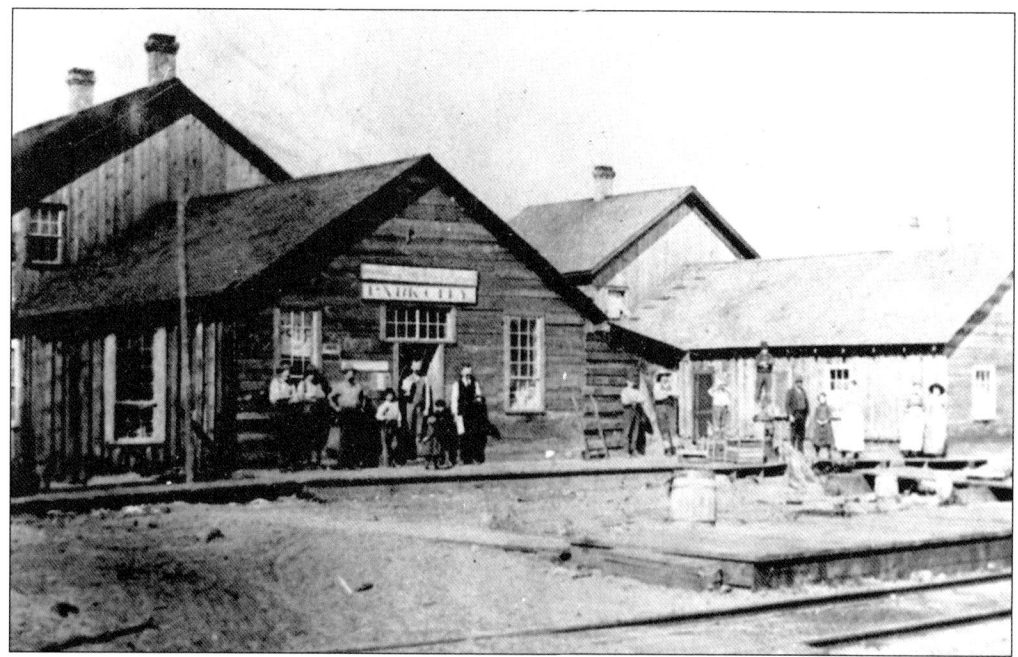

Park City served as a regional center for lumber cutting, sorting, and transporting in Newaygo County during the last decades of the 19th century. As in most flourishing lumber communities, the new townspeople constructed a modest schoolhouse where their children could be educated. The school in Park City was typical of country schools in Michigan. Built by local craftspeople with local materials, the structure provided a small entryway, a cloakroom, and a single schoolroom.

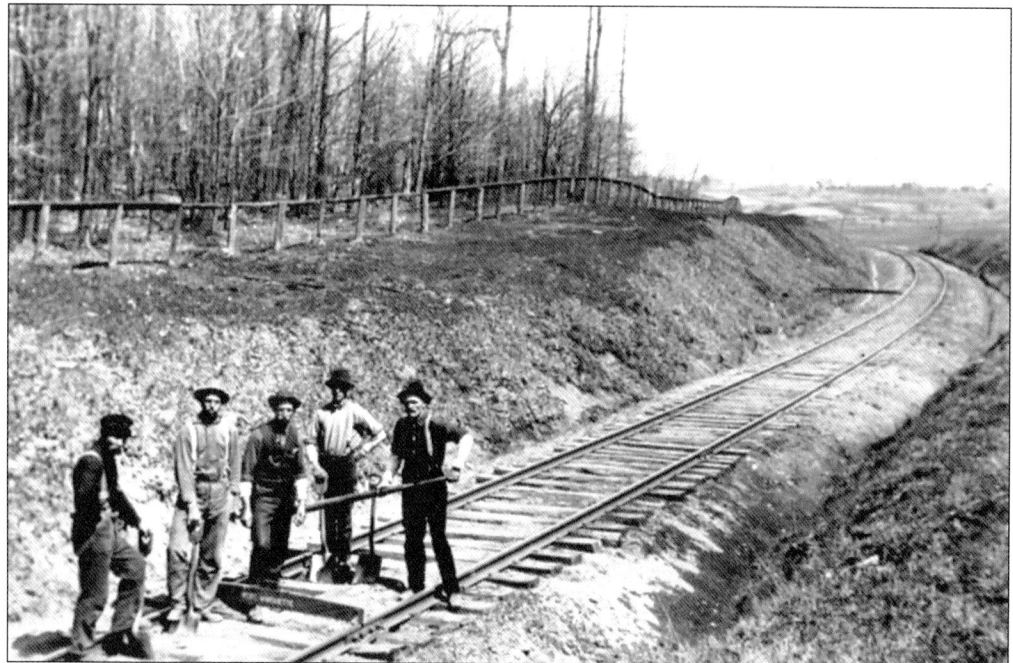

Here a crew is repairing tracks at the big curve about a mile east of Fremont, in Sherman Township near Windmill Gardens.

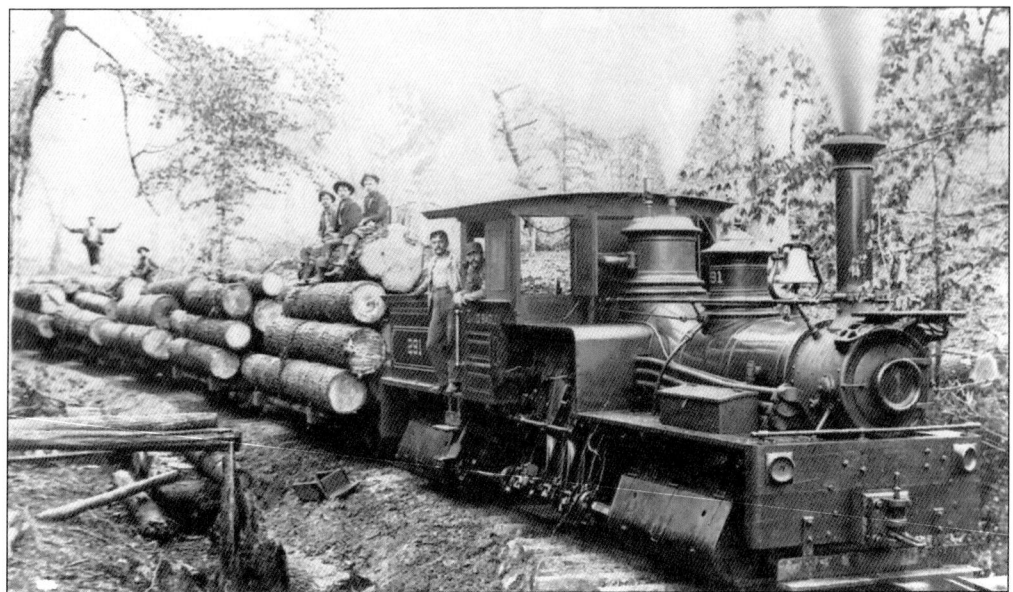

The Shay locomotive hauled logs belonging to Ryerson Hills to the railroad trestle that was built over the water on the north shore of Pickeral Lake near Newaygo. Mose Bell was the engineer. This photograph was taken in 1888. The introduction of the logging railroad changed lumbering methods. It made possible both the lumbering of area that could not be reached from the streams and the cutting of hardwoods that could not be floated down the river.

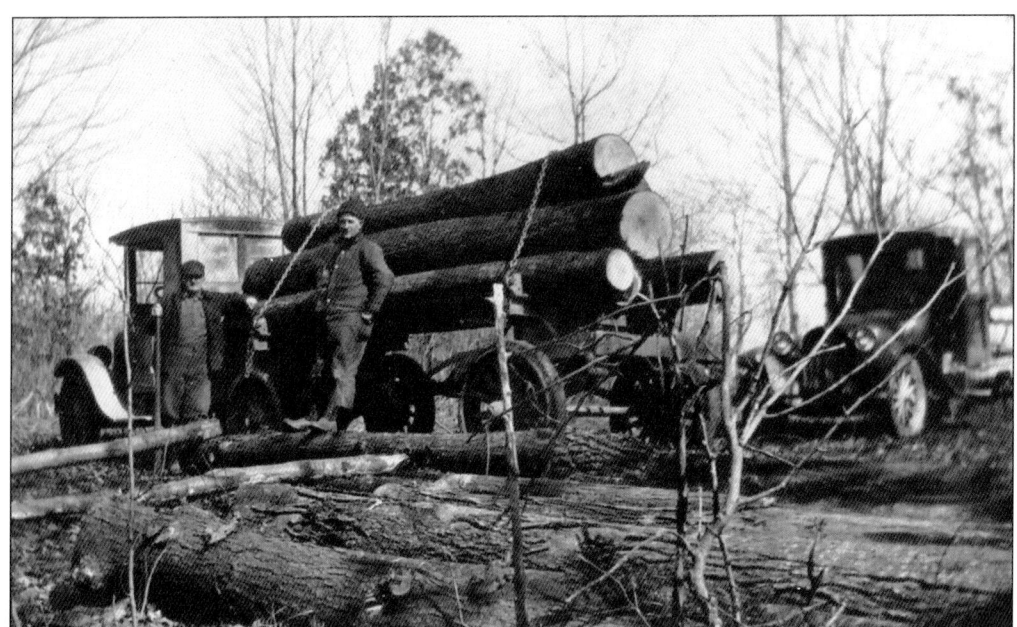

With the automobile came an easier and more rapid way to transport the logs to the mill. This photograph is of the Hills Family Lumbering operation located south of Fremont.

# Two

# The Logging Trains Arrive

In 1870, several businessmen undertook the task of bringing the railroad to Newaygo County. They had to raise $125,000 for the construction cost to Newaygo, of which $50,000 was needed to pay the contractor. The amount needed was quickly raised, and a balance of $75,000 was soon needed. During the 1872 winter, 9 million feet of logs were shipped to Grand Rapids over the new railroad at the rate of 100,000 feet a day. Most were shipped from Wonderly's Camp in Ashland City, two miles south of Grant Station. These were the first log trains in Michigan.

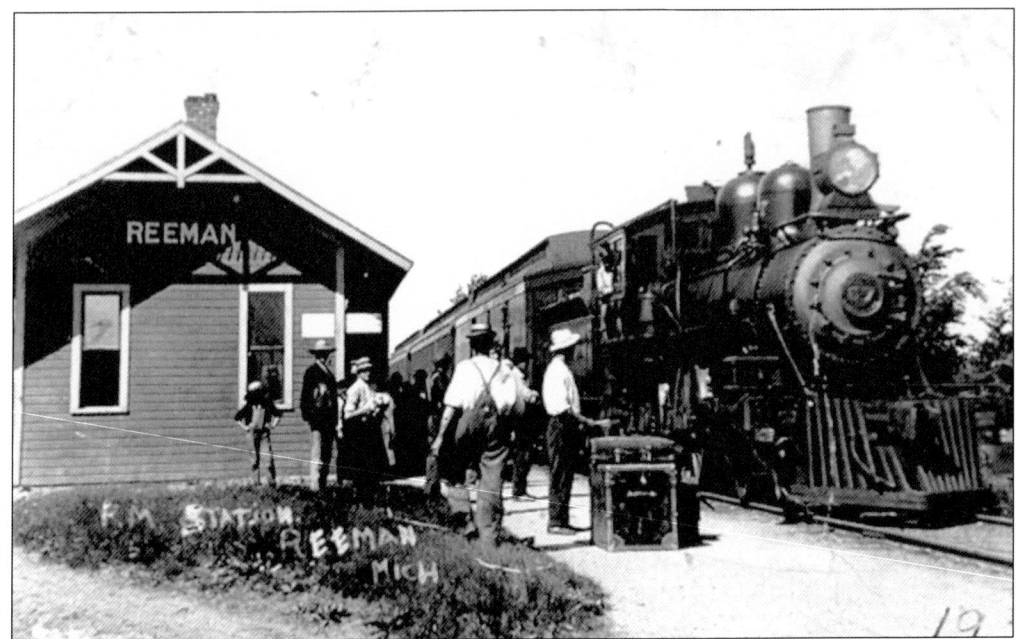

The area around Reeman was first called McQueen, after one of the first families to settle there. Later the name was changed to McQueen's Siding. When the railroad came to town in 1872, the farmers built the station and the railroad furnished an operator. In 1897, the name was changed from McQueen's Siding to Reeman.

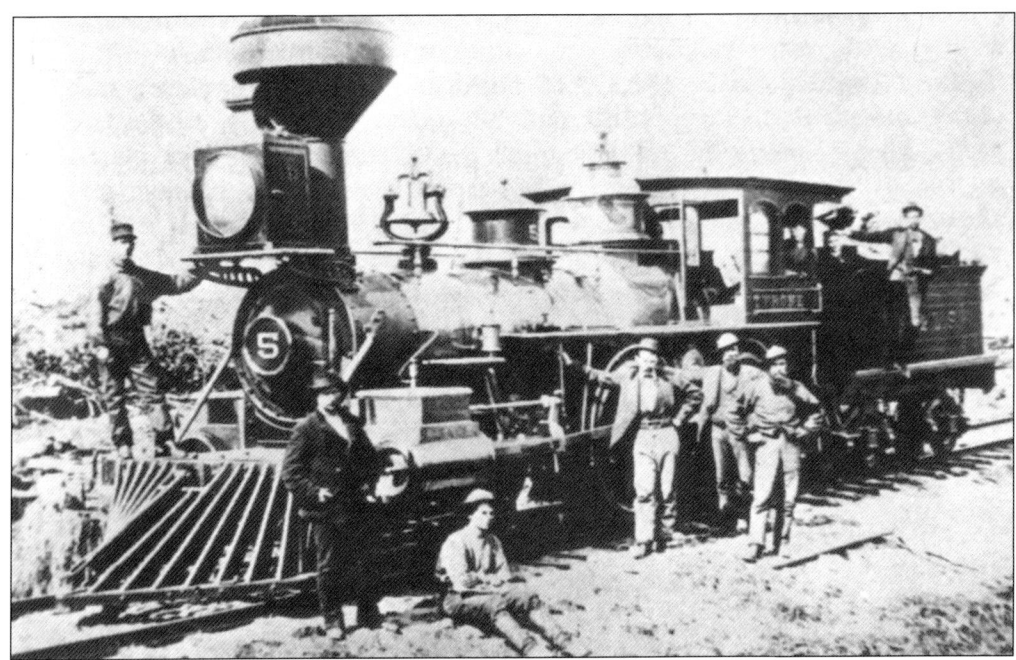

The railroad engine *Tyeane* was in service on the Grand Rapids, Newaygo, and Lake Shore. As logging increased along the Muskegon River, it was only natural that other waterways would be sought; in 1872, lumbering operations were started on the White River, which empties into White Lake at Lake Michigan.

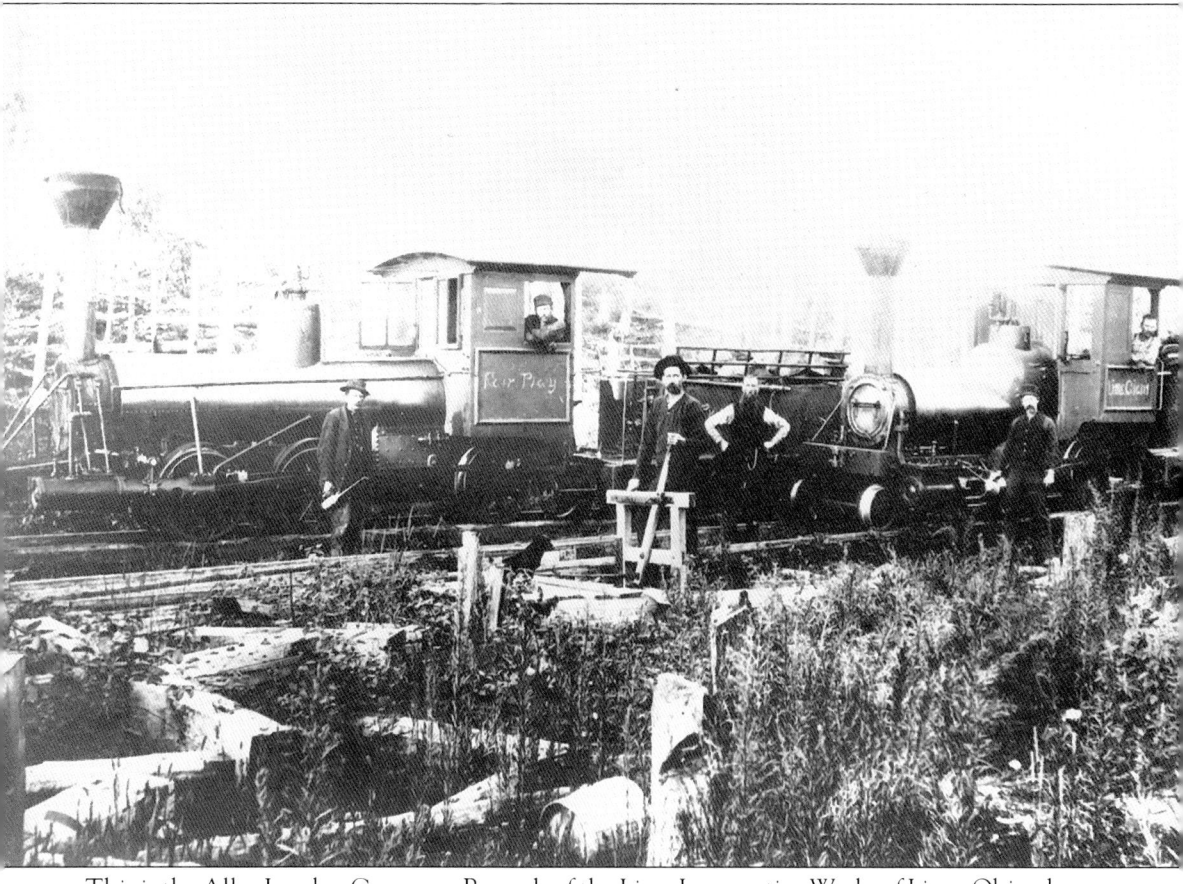

This is the Alley Lumber Company. Records of the Lima Locomotive Works of Lima, Ohio, show that the first three locomotives built by that firm for use in the woods were sold to James Alley of the Alley Lumber Company of Alleyton, Michigan. They were shipped by the maker on June 18, 1879.

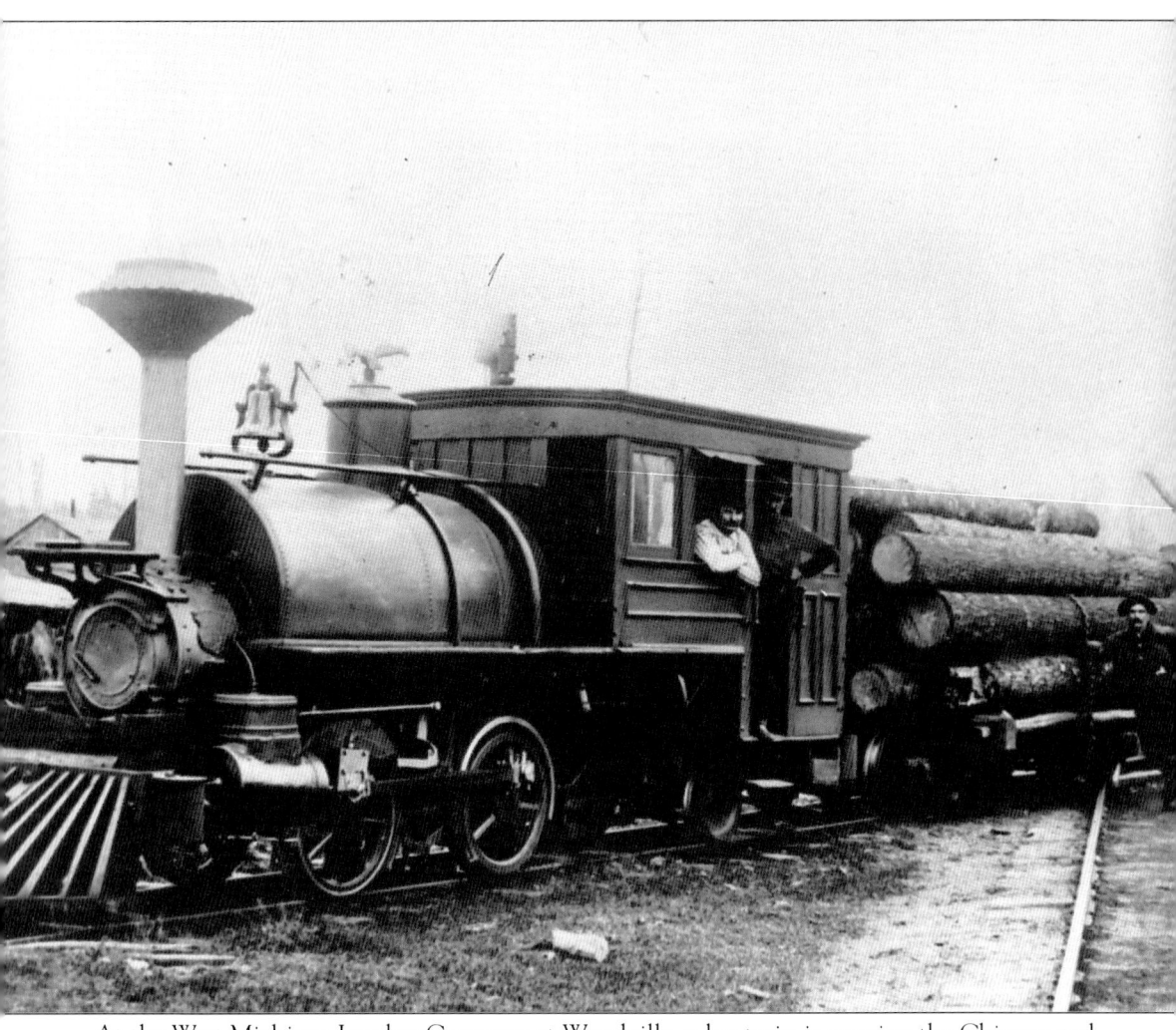
At the West Michigan Lumber Company at Woodville, a log train is crossing the Chicago and West Michigan track. The engine is a Porter 9-by-14-36 gauge.

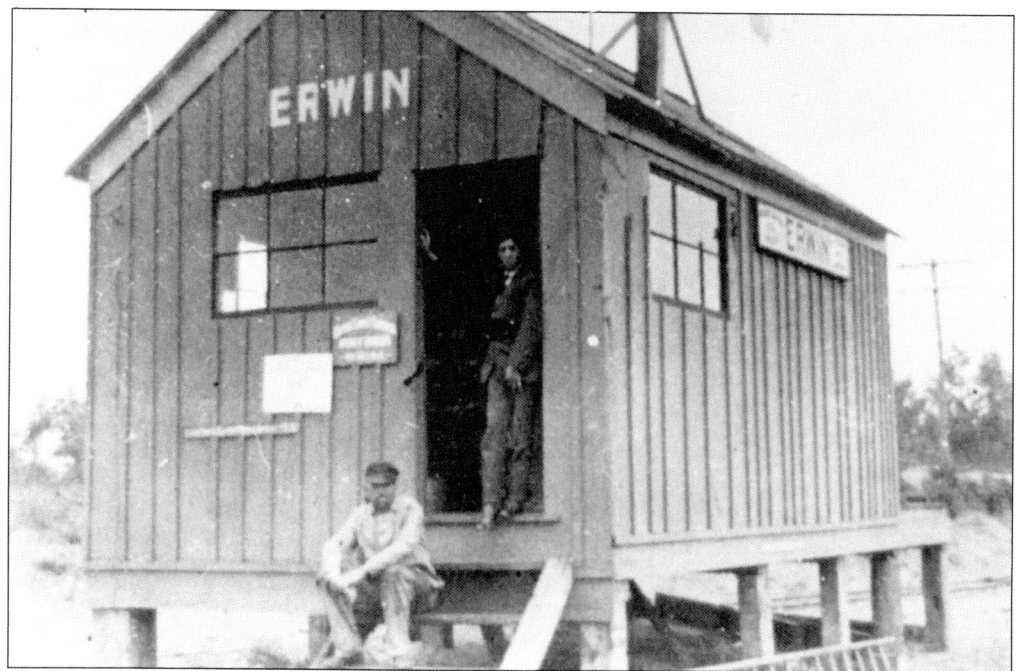

This is a railroad way station (named after George E. Erwin) at the Croton switch junction, between the main line of the Pere Marquette Railroad and the construction site of the dam. The track carried all the construction material to the dam site. Early trout fishermen also used the train on their way to Bigelow Creek.

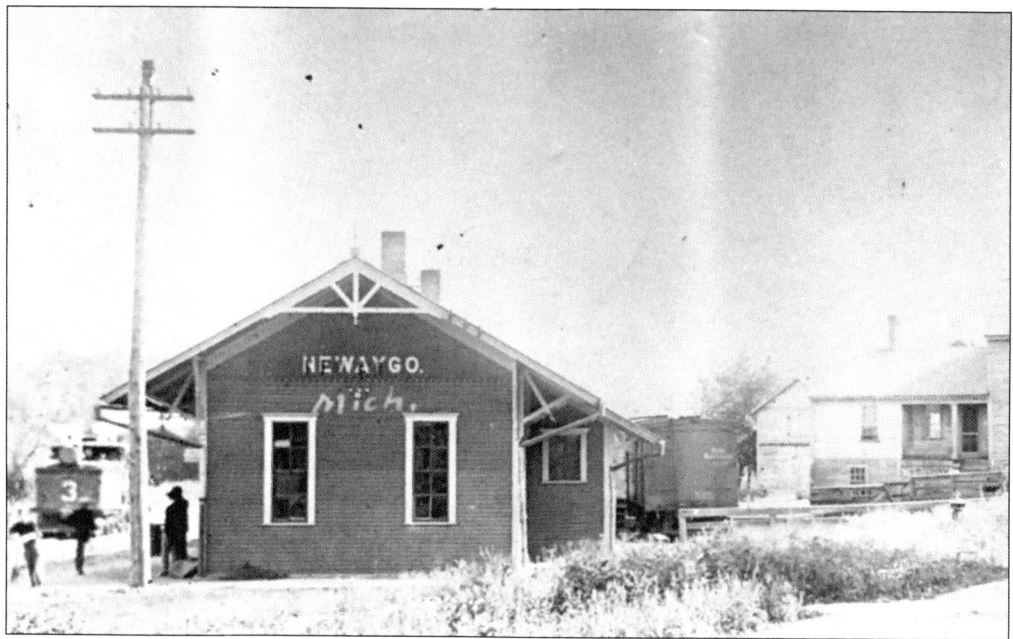

The Newaygo depot was built by the Chicago and West Michigan in 1891. The people in Newaygo complained about the appearance and condition of the first depot built by D. P. Clay. The railroad bought the old Kritzer property on the north side of State Road and built a small replica of the new station at Traverse City.

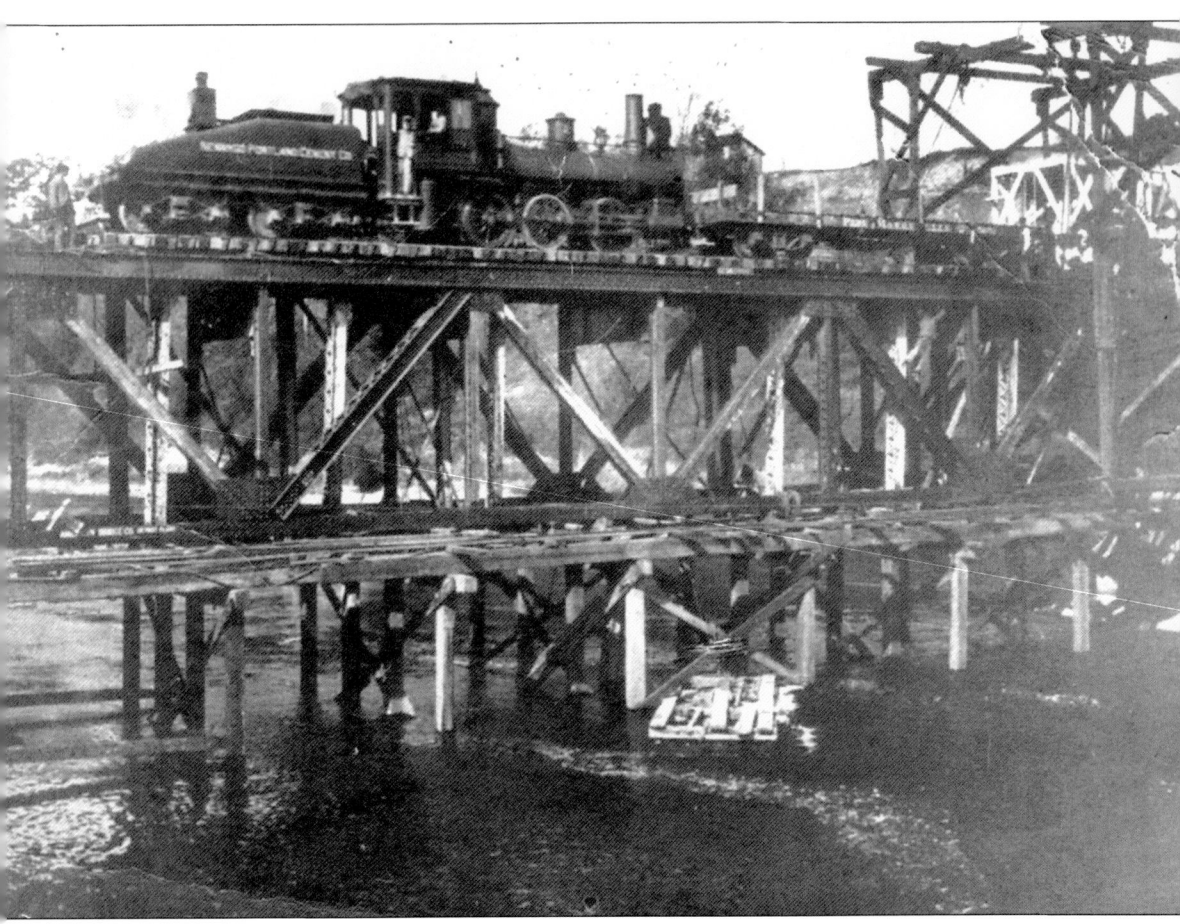

A train engine on the Pere Marquette Railroad is photographed on its way to the marl lakes with empty hopper cars to be loaded with marl. Marl was sludge that was dug from the bottom of many Newaygo County lakes. It was then taken to the Portland Cement Company, where it was made into cement.

# Three

# THE POWER OF THE RIVER

A fire had destroyed most of the buildings of Croton (Forks Sterns Mill) in 1899, and no attempt was made to rebuild them except for a short period of time. Rumor of a new dam became a reality, but it meant losing an old village. The old village is now underwater, leaving behind the Croton Dam and providing a recreational area. When logging declined, it was soon decided that the rivers could be used to develop waterpower and generate electricity for use in Grand Rapids and Muskegon. The Grand Rapids–Muskegon Power Company was organized in 1904. Croton Dam, which is one of the oldest and most scenic of the Consumers Power hydroelectric projects, was placed in operation in 1907.

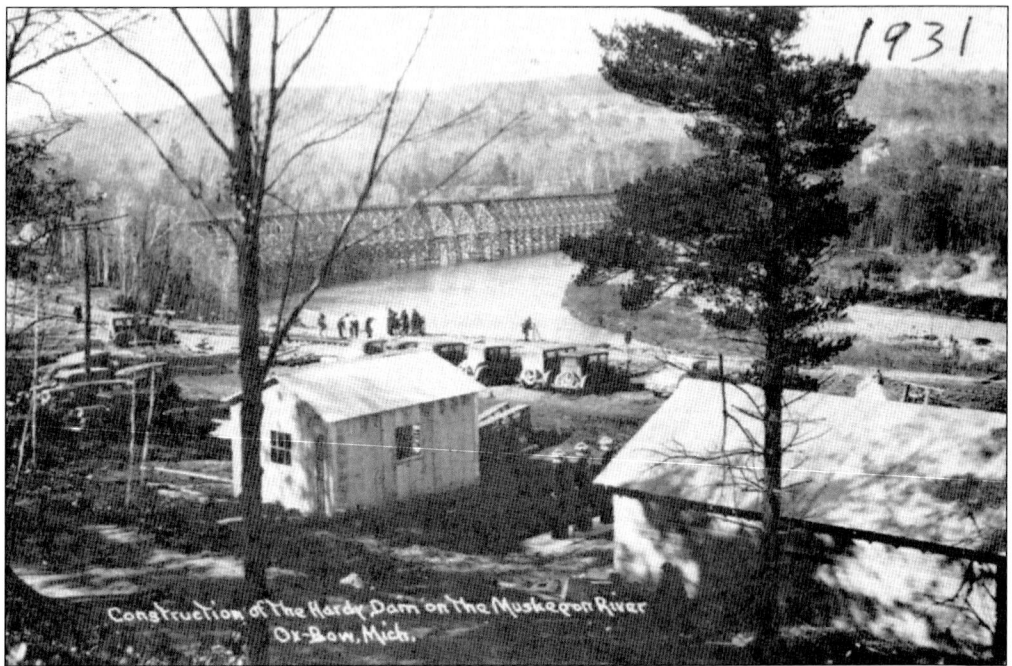

Hardy Hydroelectric Plant possesses statewide significance in the area of engineering as a symbol of Consumers Power Company's extensive, nearly statewide system of power generation and supply. By the 1920s, Consumers Power Company had established a string of hydroelectric and coal-burning steam plants tied together with high-voltage, long-distance transmission lines that distributed power throughout Michigan's Lower Peninsula. Hardy Hydroelectric Plant, the final link in that chain and the largest hydroelectric plant built by Consumers Power Company, was intended to be a showpiece of the system.

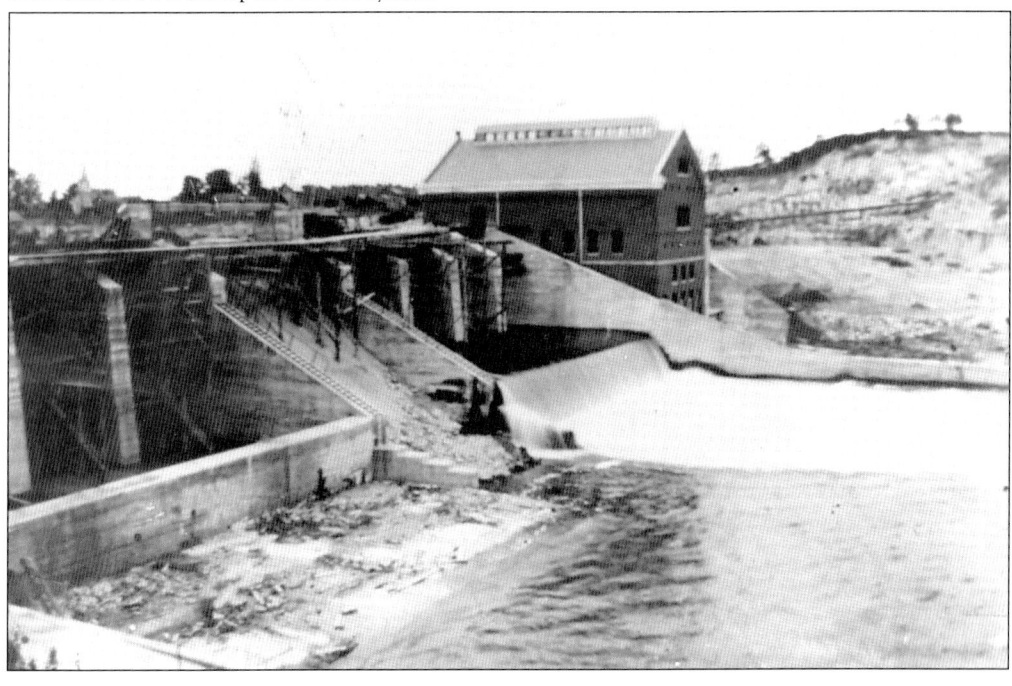

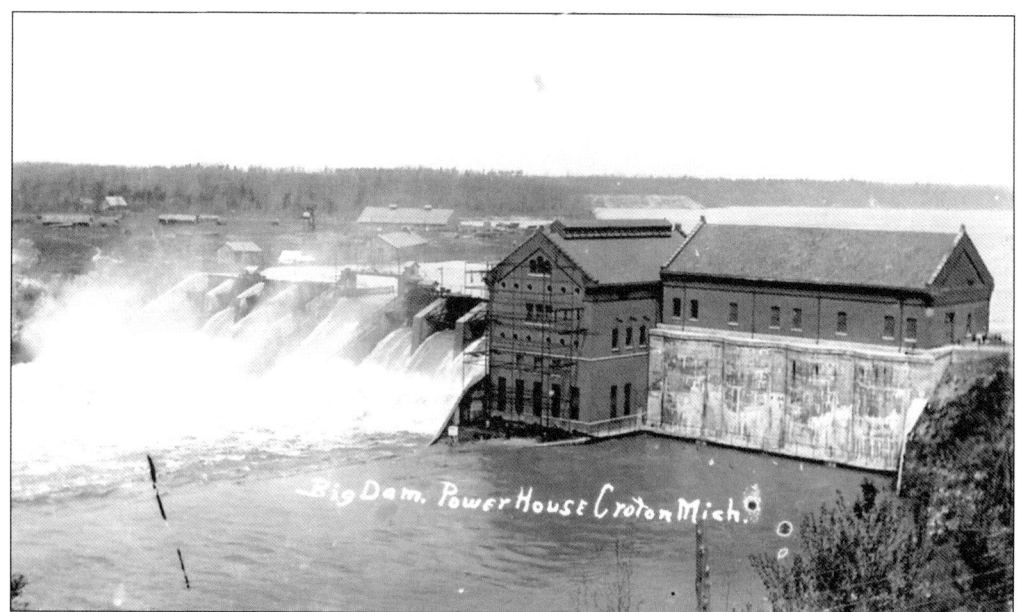

The Croton Hydroelectric Plant, completed in 1906, measures 670 feet long from the east bank to the west bank of the Muskegon River and is composed of an earth embankment measuring 200 feet long, 200 feet wide, and up to 60 feet high; an L-shaped powerhouse standing 60 feet high on a reinforced concrete foundation, topped by gable roofs that contain the turbine and generator rooms, connected on its side to the spillway that reaches to the river's bank.

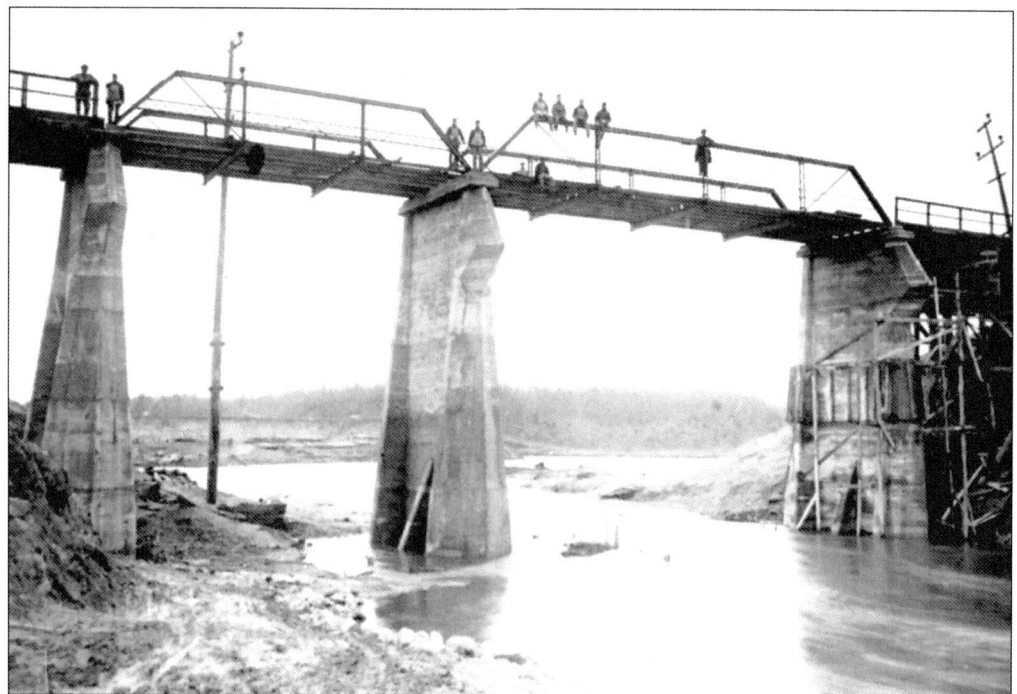

The causeway bridge over the Little Muskegon Channel had to have tall foundations in order to reach the present road.

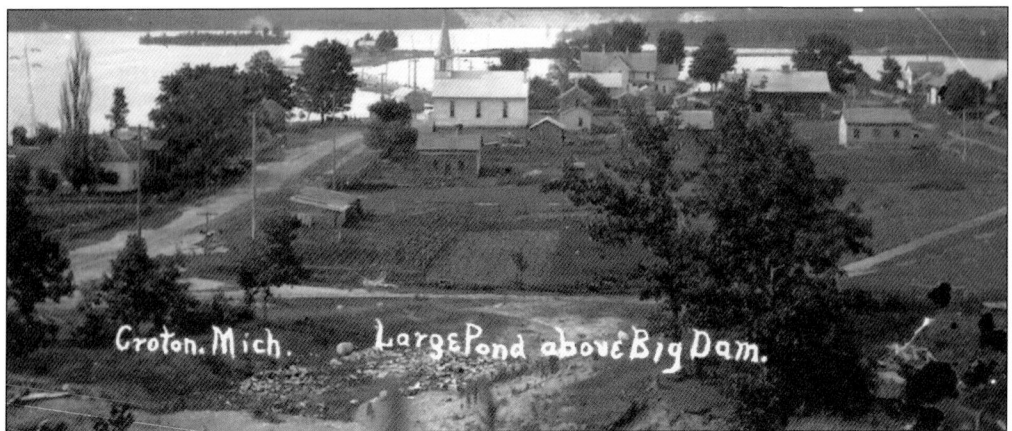

A new Croton replaced the quaint lumber village that was settled in 1837 and later was covered by water. The large pond behind the dam has become famous for a summer resort and the fall run of salmon on the Muskegon River.

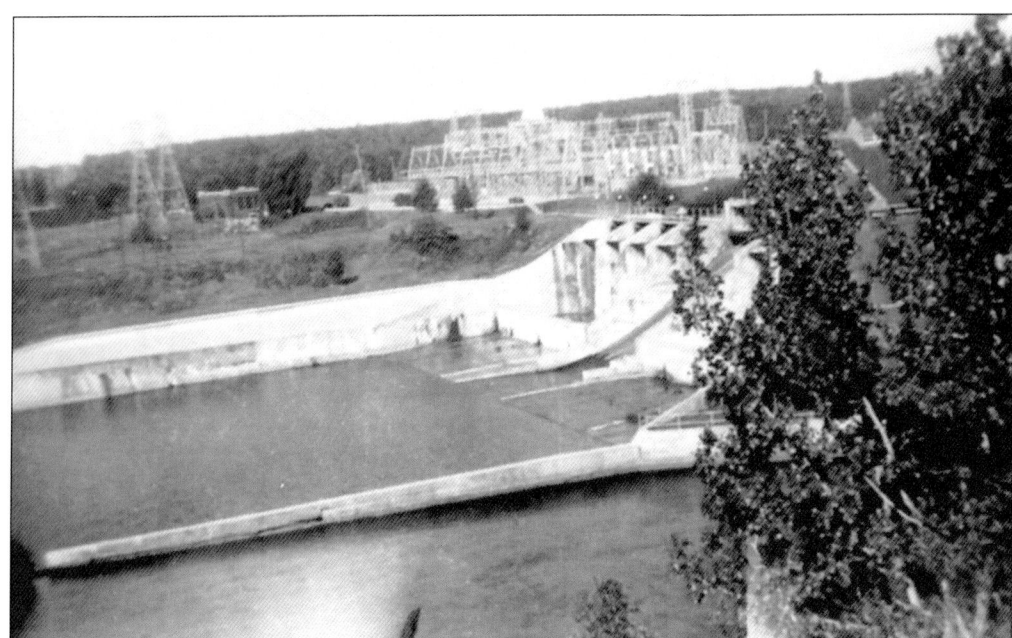

The Croton Dam and Consumers Power Company have played a major role in the development of electric service for the state of Michigan. Even in 1883, when Augustus Pennoyer came to the Newaygo County area, he saw the beauty and usefulness of the Muskegon River.

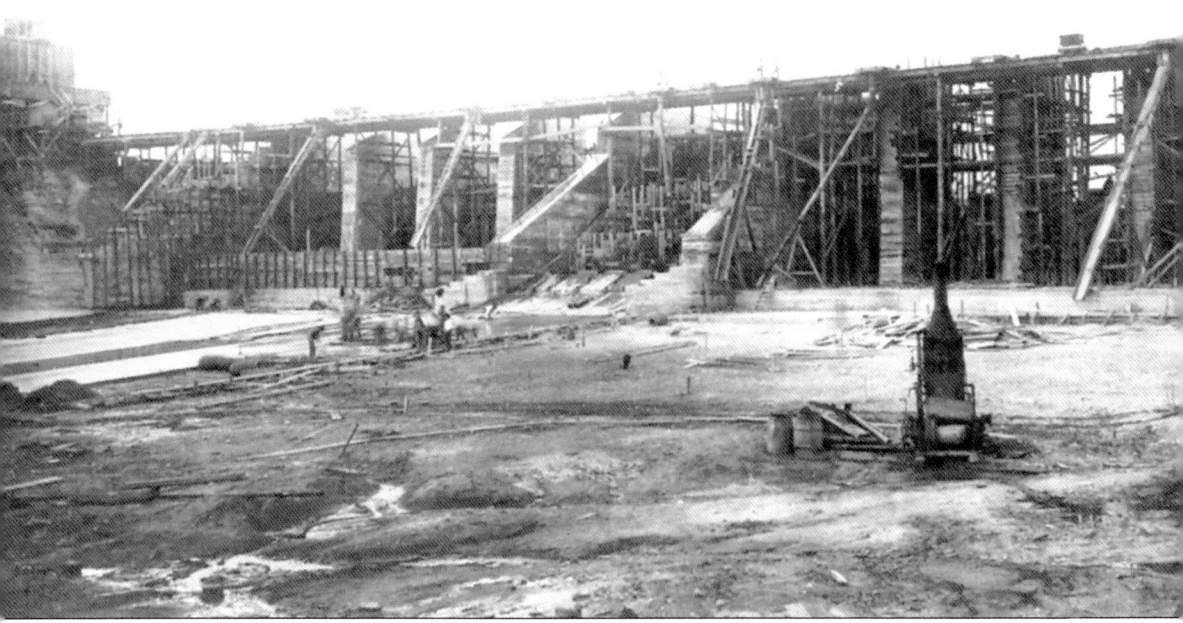

The Muskegon River, Michigan's largest river, became the lifeblood of the area, first for transporting lumber and later for hydroelectric power. Three huge dams were built after 1900: Croton, Hardy, and Newaygo. The Croton and Hardy Dams remain today, Hardy Dam being the largest earthen dam east of the Mississippi. The building of the Croton Dam, pictured under construction above, was a major undertaking.

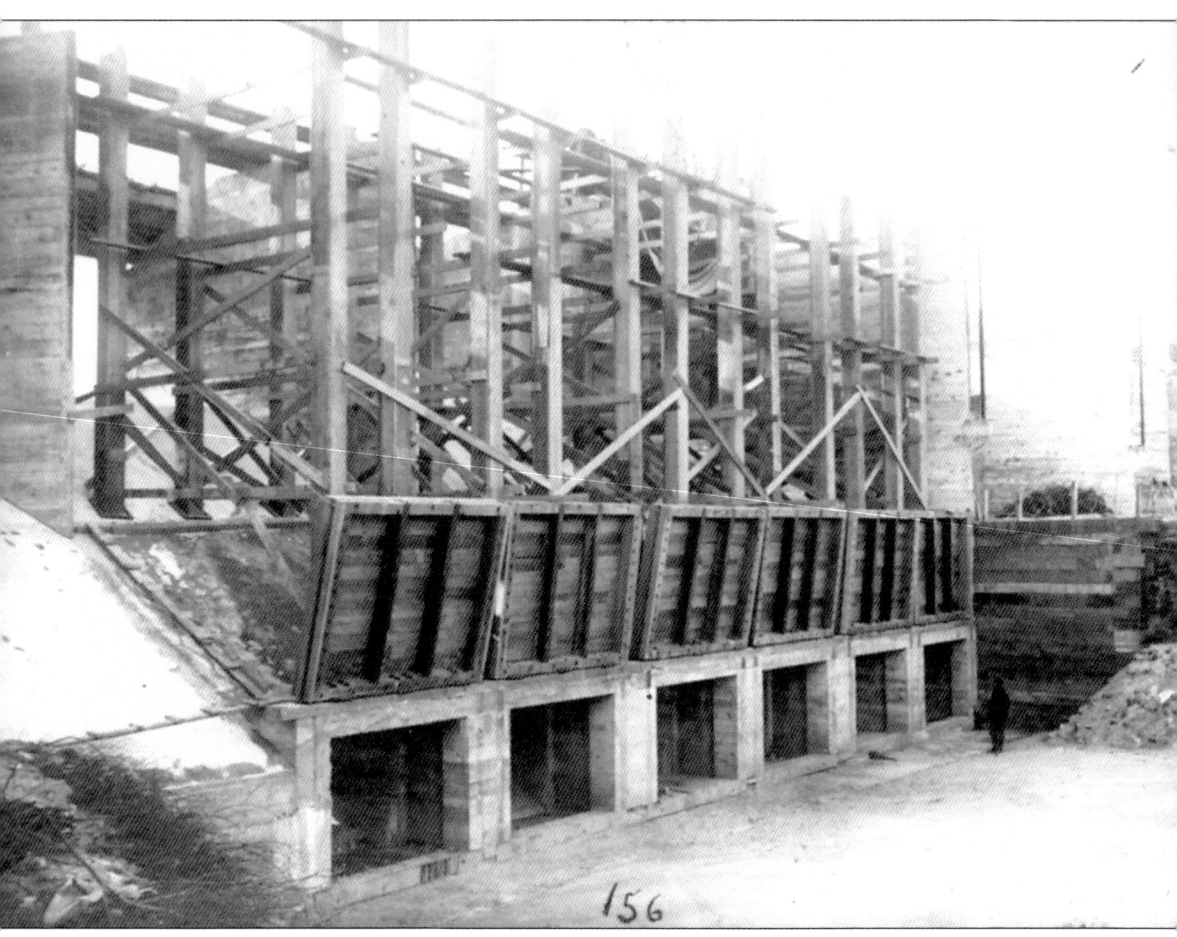

Pictured above, during construction, the old redbrick dam across the Muskegon River has become a well-known landmark. Croton Dam was placed into operation in 1907 and has been in continuous operation since. The Hardy Dam upriver is the largest hydroelectric plant in Michigan and has been in service since 1931. The 3,000-acre Hardy Pond is well known and loved for its beautiful shorelines and great year-round fishing.

## Four
# EARLY SETTLEMENTS

Until 1936, Newaygo County was wild country inhabited by Native Americans, wild animals, and a few white trappers. White man started to come to Newaygo County for many reasons as they recognized the many advantages that the new area offered. The lumbering trade had become a mainstay in the area, and Newaygo became a county in 1851.

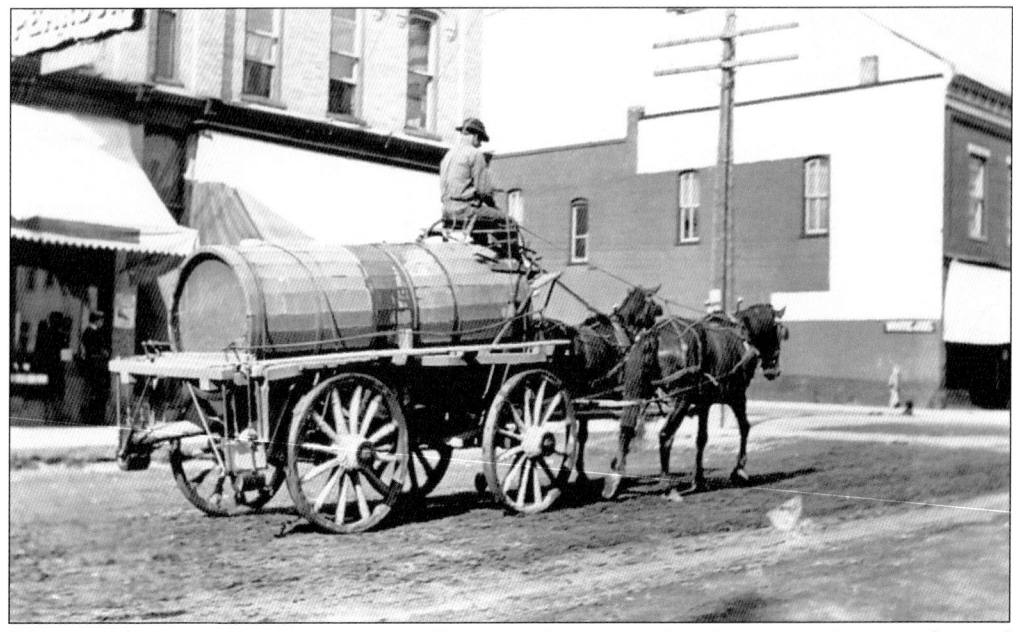

Watering the streets was necessary in Fremont Center, as the dirt streets became dry and dusty with the traffic of carts and horses. Watering down the streets helped to keep the dust to a tolerable level.

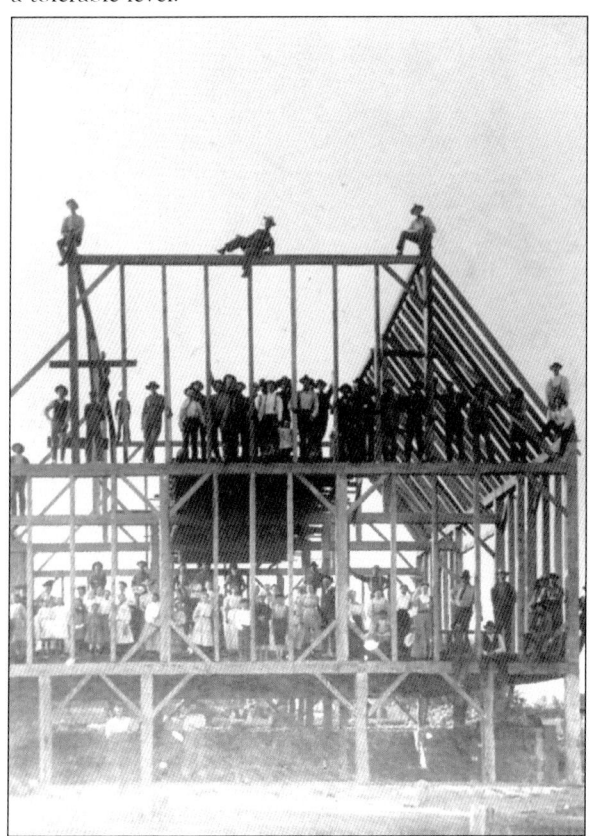

This is Albert Dodge's barn raising in 1927. The Dodge family was an early family in Fremont Center. Neighbors, friends, and family would gather together to help when someone needed a barn. While the men raised the barn, the women prepared the meals.

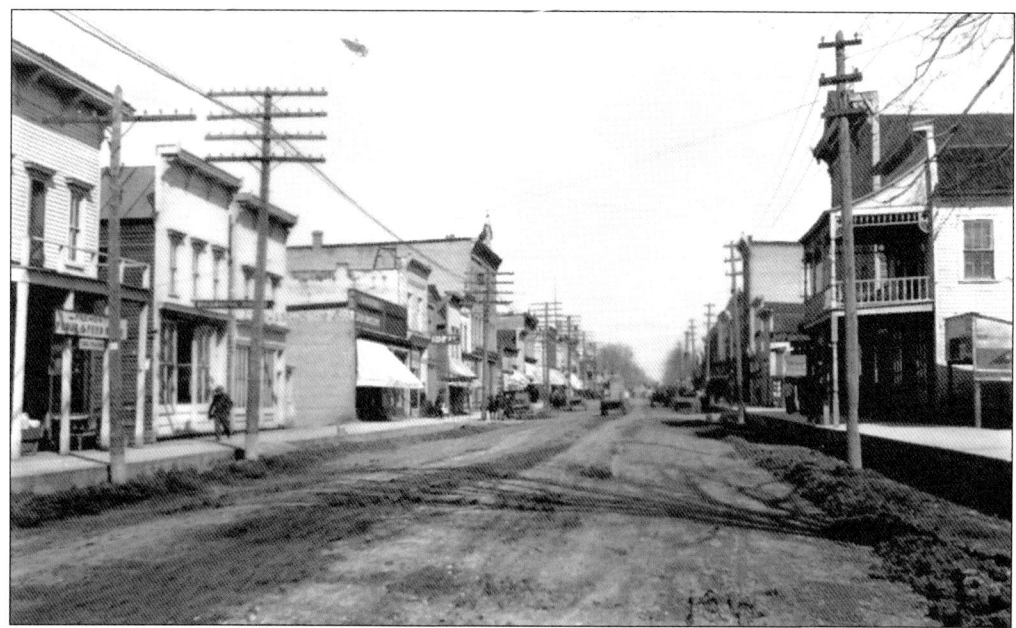
The view shown here is looking east on West Main Street in Fremont Center. Notice the wooden buildings and dirt streets. After the big fire, an ordinance was adopted to allow only brick buildings to be built downtown.

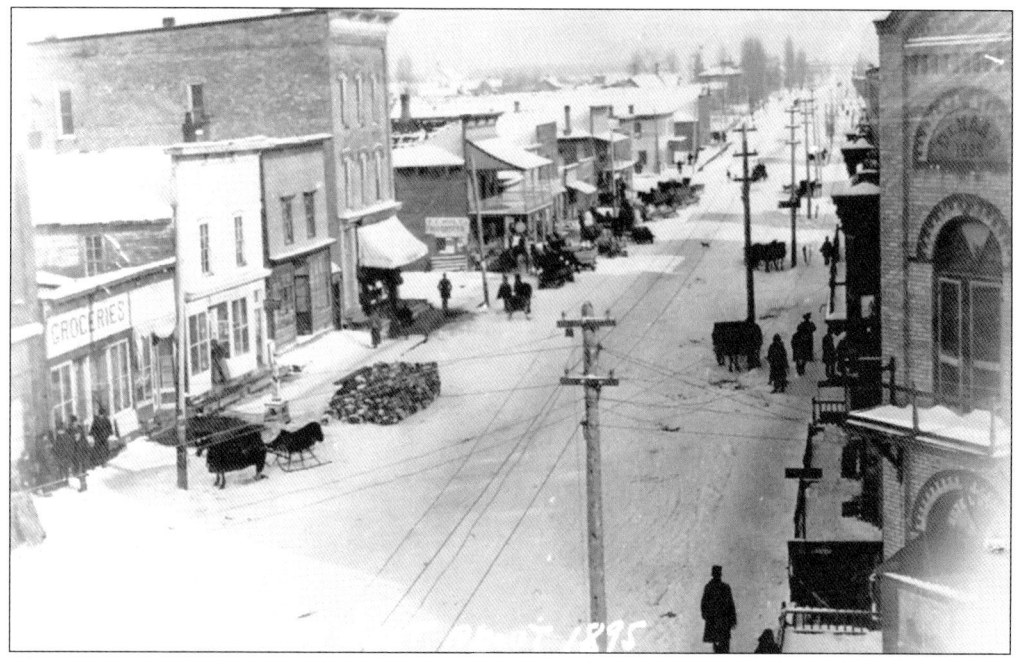
This view is looking east on Main Street in Fremont Center, shown in about 1895. Notice the horse-drawn sleighs.

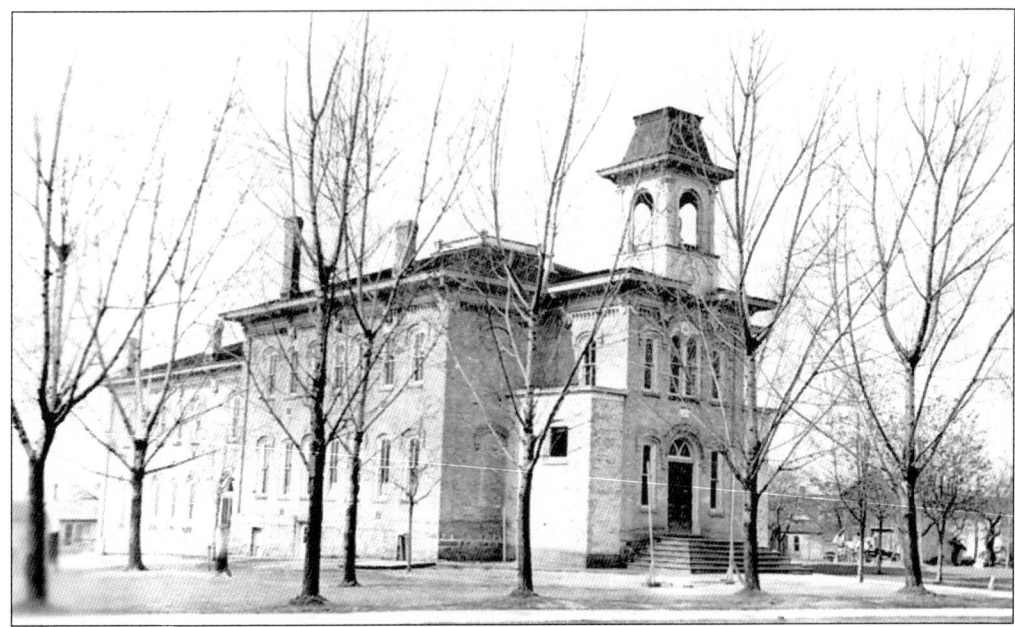

By 1888, it was apparent that the Fremont School facility needed an addition to accommodate the increase in the number of students attending. The addition of a second unit of four rooms was built in 1889.

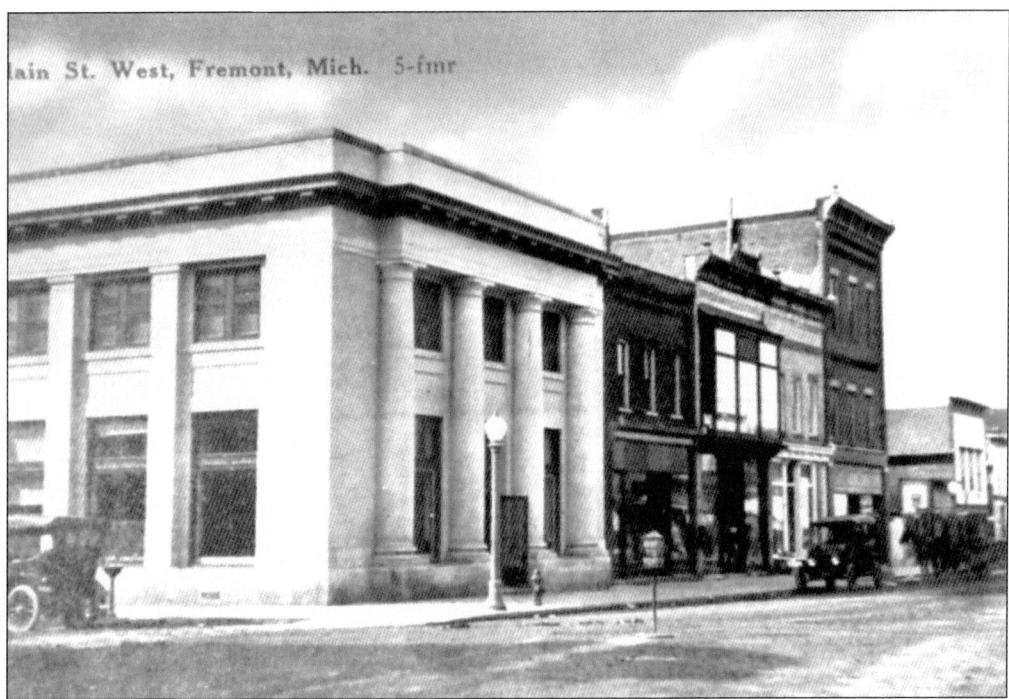

In 1882, William Webber came to the village of Fremont Center with the intention of opening a bank. The official year of establishment of the First State Bank was 1883; however, the first business conducted was on November 1, 1882.

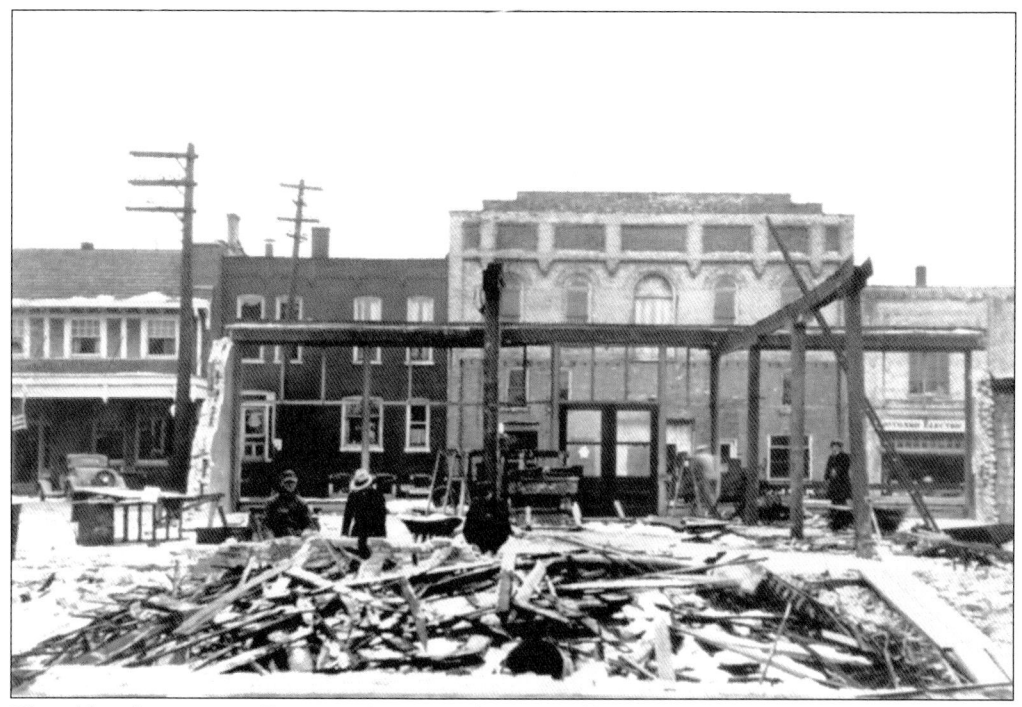

The oldest business in Fremont Center is the post office. Daniel Weaver established the first post office in his house, which was located on the northwest corner of Main Street and Stewart Street, on August 23, 1856. It was first called the Weaverville Post Office. In the 1930s, a new brick post office was built on South Division Street.

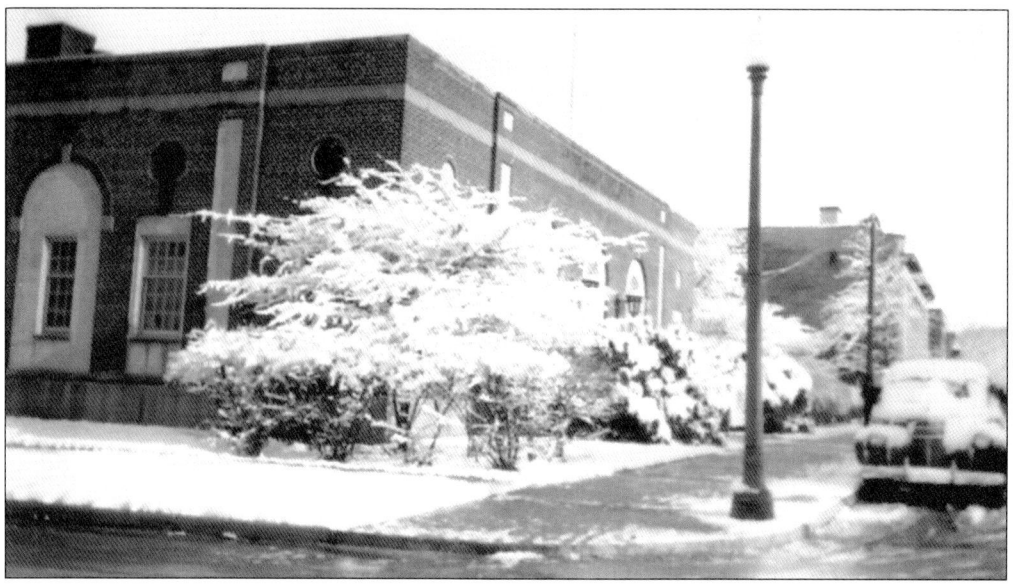

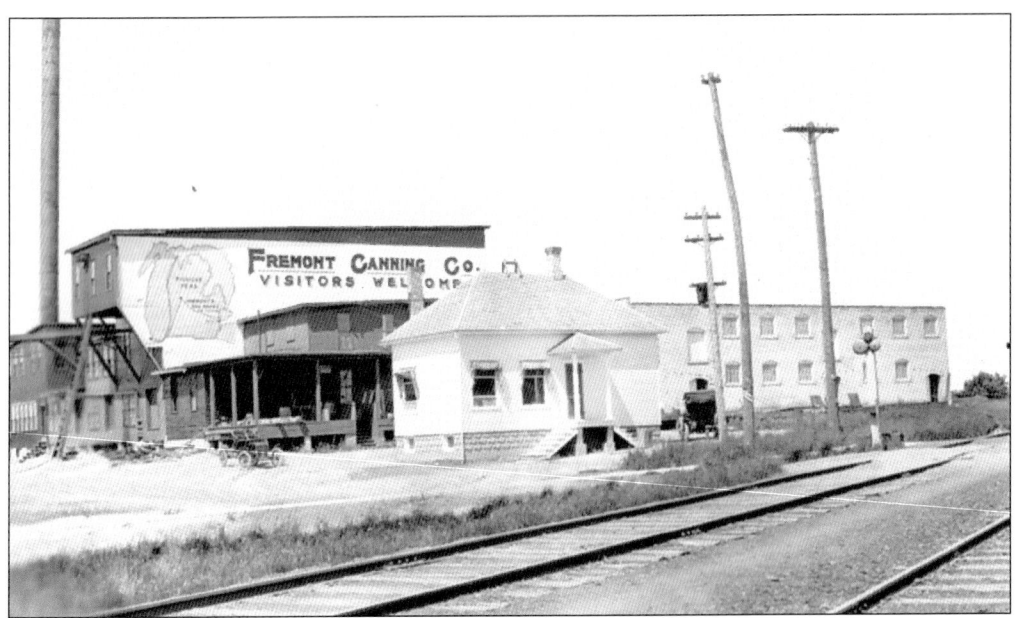

By 1923, the Fremont Canning Company was a modern brick plant, which stood out as a leader among Michigan canning concerns, having shipped out approximately 500,000 cases of goods in 1922. The total business amounted to $1.25 million, according to Frank Gerber, who was president of the company. The plant, which had 65,000 feet of floor space, was in operation year-round, employing 175 to 250 people, depending on the season and yields of fruits and vegetables. In 1923, it was pushing pork and beans and red kidney beans. Some of the labels that the Fremont Canning Company used were Miss Michigan, Fremont, 999, Newaygo, and All-Time brands.

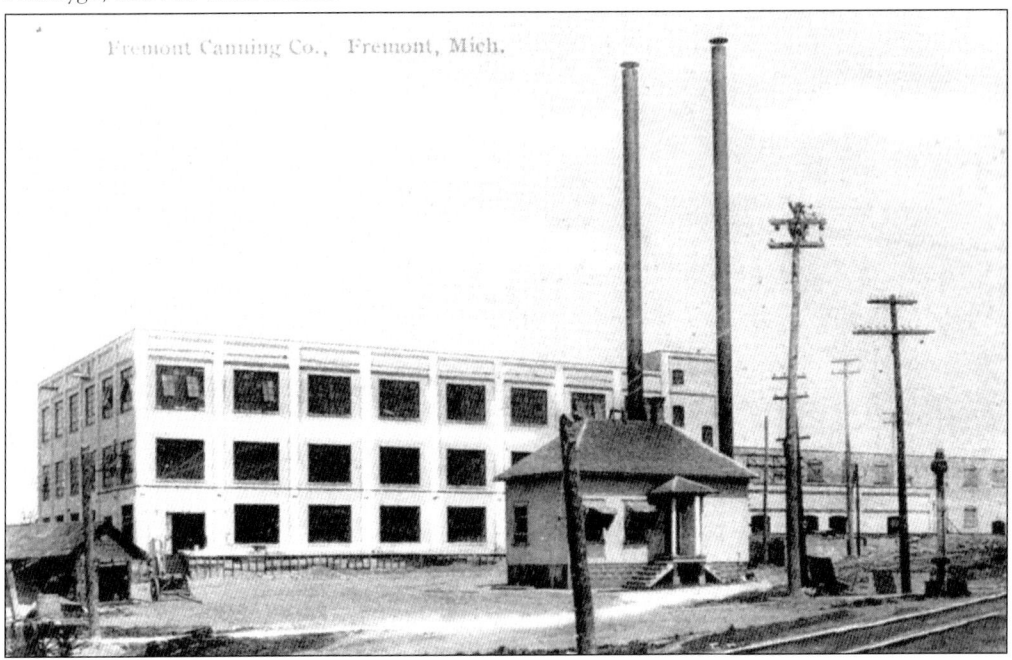

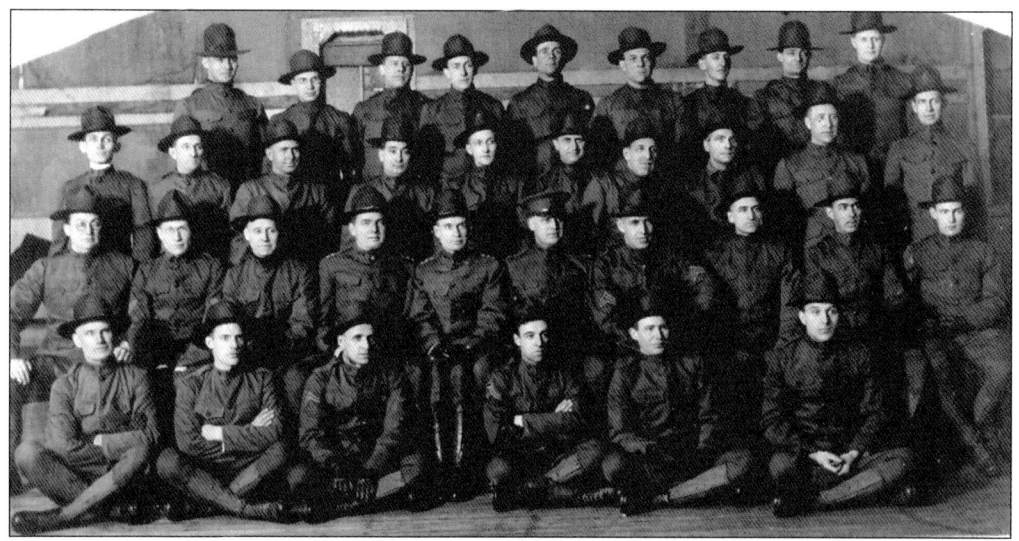

In the fall of 1917, a unit was formed in Fremont Center with Louis Webber as commanding officer. Around 50 young men went into training, concerned about the threat of German world domination. Under the leadership of Louis Webber were 1st Lt. Erwin Tinney and 2nd Lt. Earl Johnson. These men took the initiative of forming the Fremont Center unit and training the men.

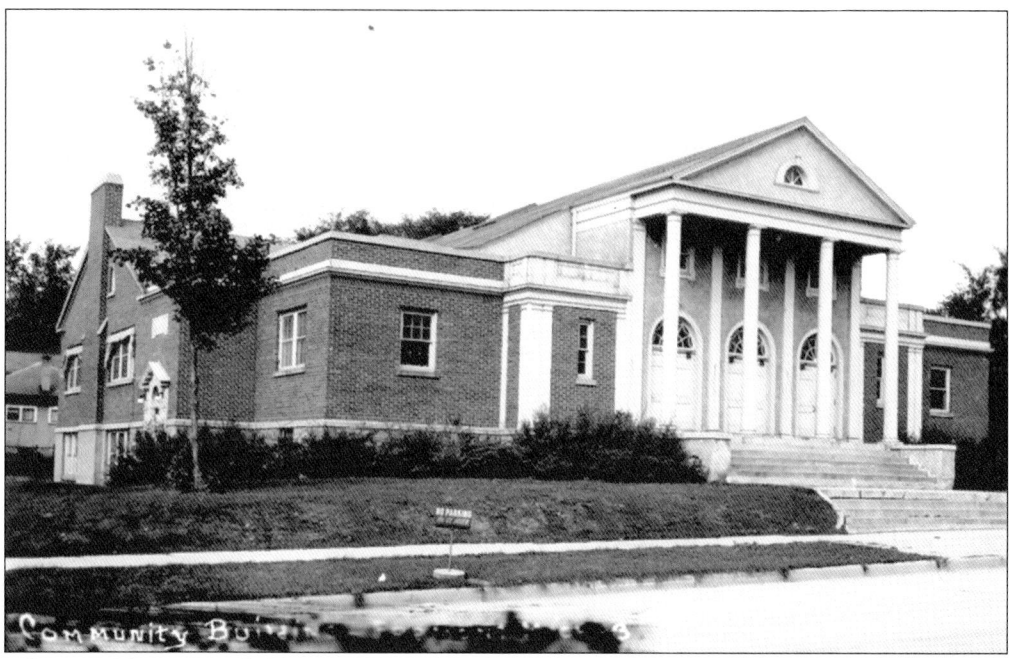

After World War I ended, the residents of Fremont Center wanted to construct a memorial to remember the 225 men from Fremont Center who served their country and the 9 residents who died in the war. The custom of erecting a bronze and stone monument did not seem sufficient, so the residents came up with the idea of erecting a memorial building. This idea led to the planning and construction of a community building as a memorial.

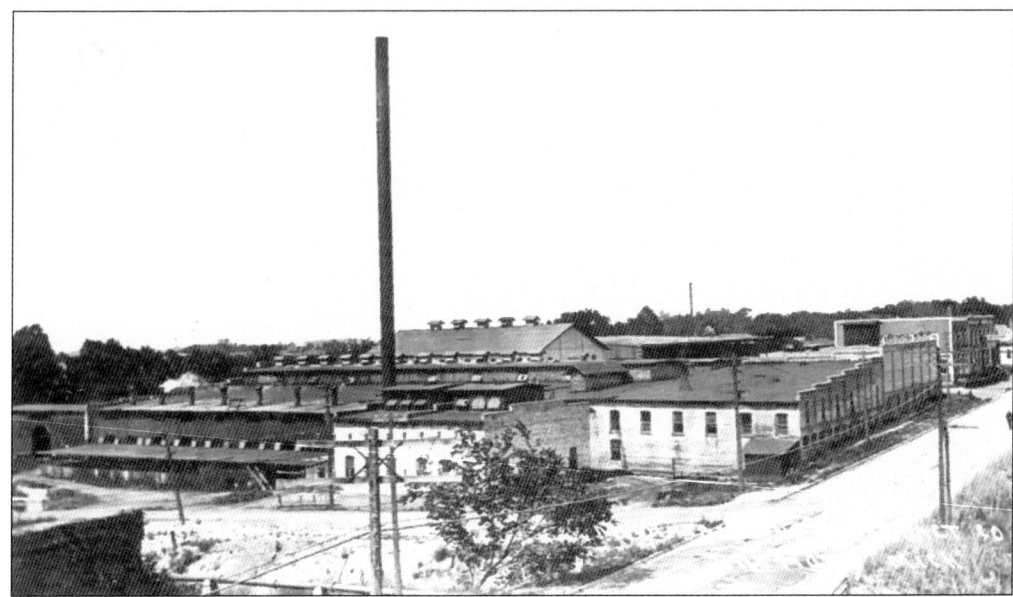

Fremont Center became home to a company that utilized the forests. The tannery of D. Gerber and Sons was operated by Daniel Gerber and his sons Joseph and Cornelius. In 1876, J. Andrew Gerber, another son, became a member of the firm. From its opening until its sale to the Michigan Tanning and Extract Company in 1907, it was in constant operation in good times and bad.

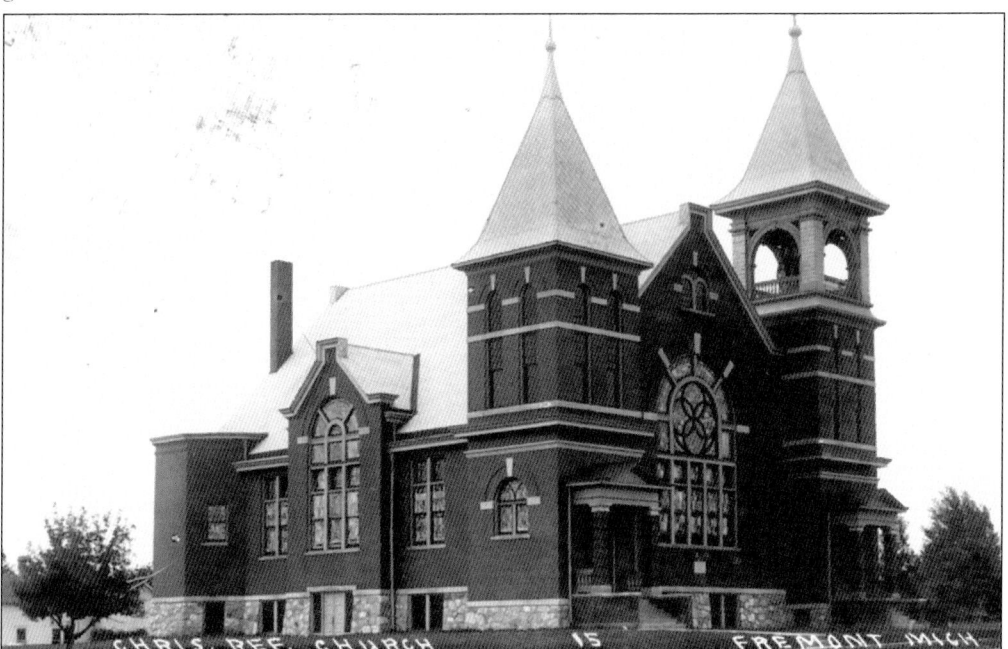

In 1870, the Dutch community in Fremont Center established a congregation of the Reformed Church in America. The First Christian Reformed Church of Fremont was established in 1882 by members who had withdrawn from the Reformed Church the previous year. A small frame building, costing $295, was built in 1883. By 1908, the congregation had grown to 174 families, necessitating a larger church building. A cornerstone was laid in July 1909.

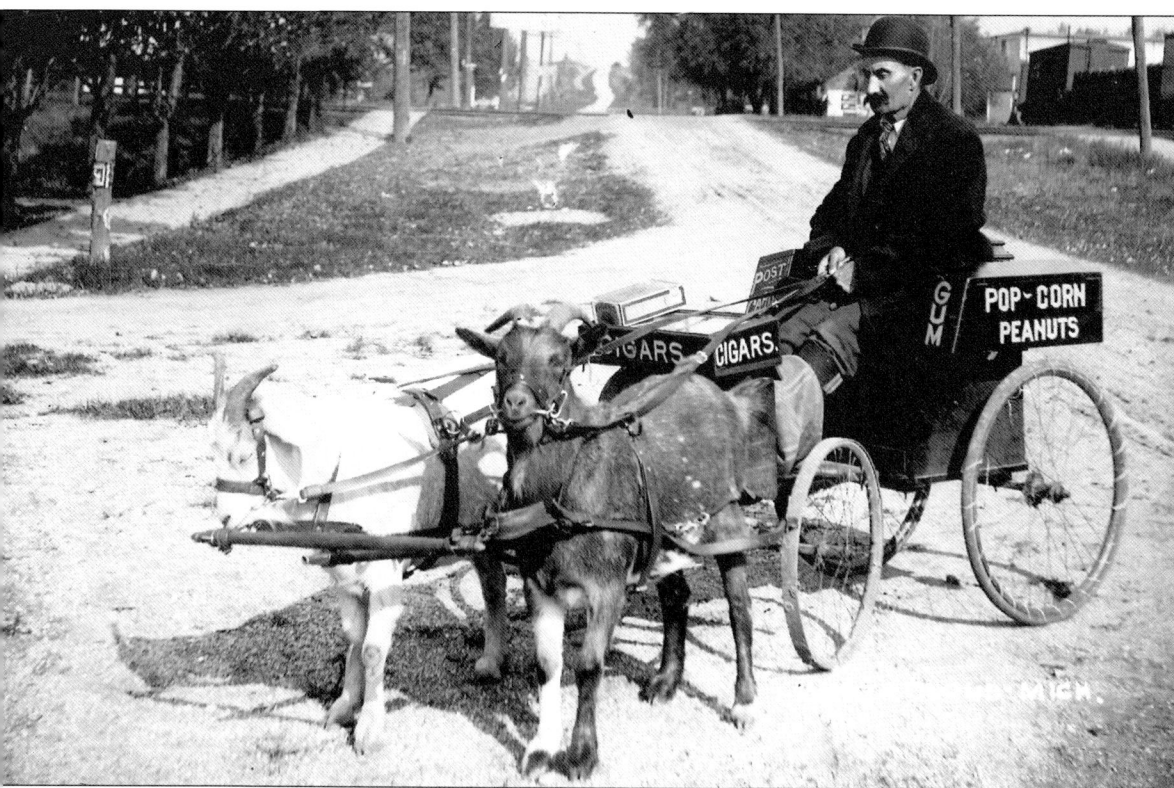

Billy McGogan and his goat Rufus greeted people getting off the train in White Cloud for many years, making McGogan a local celebrity. He would load his goat cart with candy, popcorn, peanuts, and cigars and offer the items for sale to the arriving train passengers. After the long train trip from Grand Rapids, the passengers were happy to have the opportunity to purchase a snack.

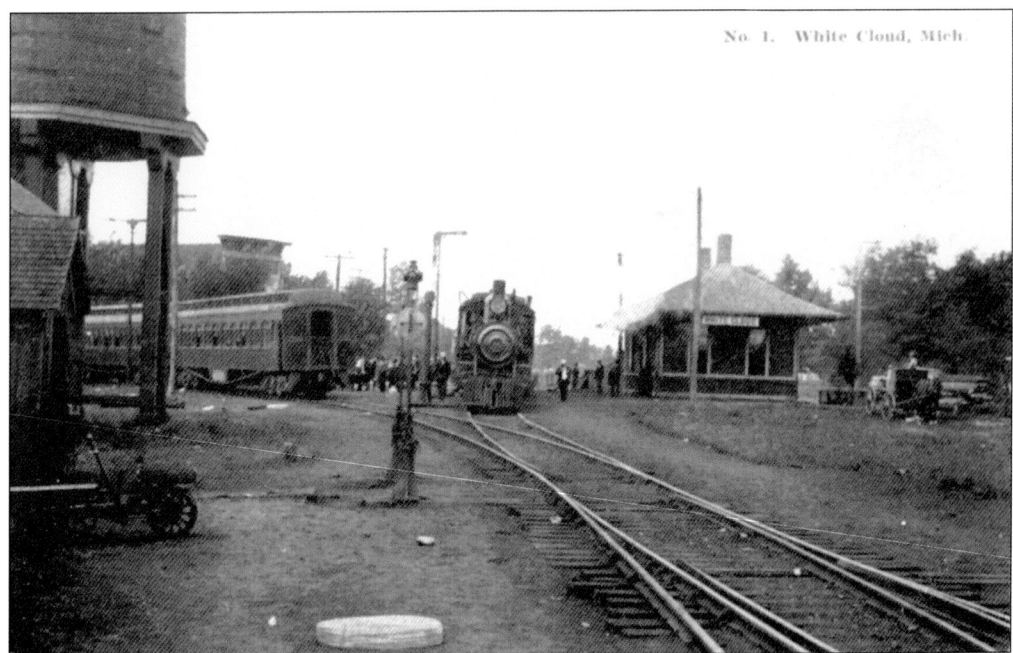

The Grand Rapids, Newaygo, and Lake Shore Railroad came to Newaygo County in 1872 and was connected to White Cloud in 1875. The Chicago, West Michigan, Muskegon Railroad went to Big Rapids through White Cloud in 1873, and then north to Nicholas Lake in 1875. Both railroads were sold to the Pere Marquette Railroad in 1899. At the time of this photograph in the second decade of the 20th century, White Cloud had 12 local passenger trains daily, plus two night flyers, a coal duct, and a water tank.

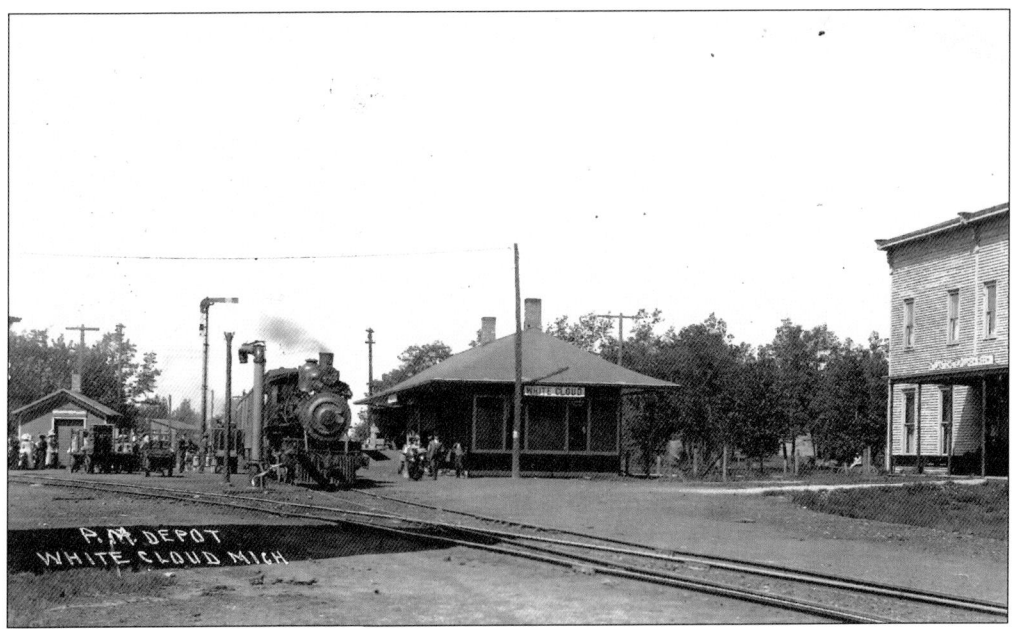

Engine No. 377 is waiting at the White Cloud train depot around 1900. White Cloud also had a coaling station and an engine house.

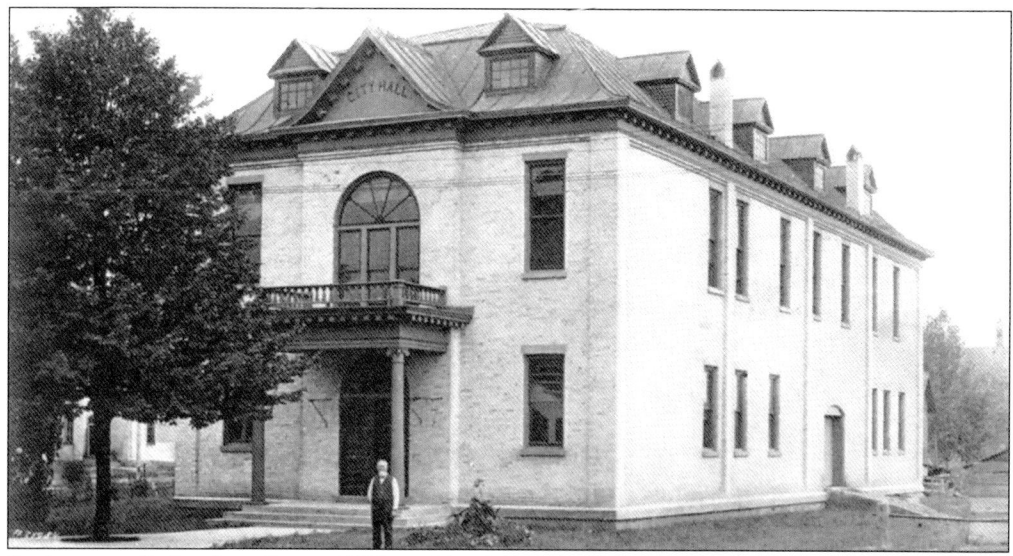

Built originally by the village of White Cloud as a city hall, this structure became the center of a county-wide struggle for possession of the county seat, which was first located in the village of Newaygo. The White Cloud village officials offered the county supervisors free use of the city hall for seven years, as well as free electric and water service, if they named White Cloud as the new county seat. As an added incentive, White Cloud businessmen signed a $10,000 bond to guarantee that the city would keep its pledge. On April 4, 1910, residents of the county voted to move their county seat from Newaygo to White Cloud.

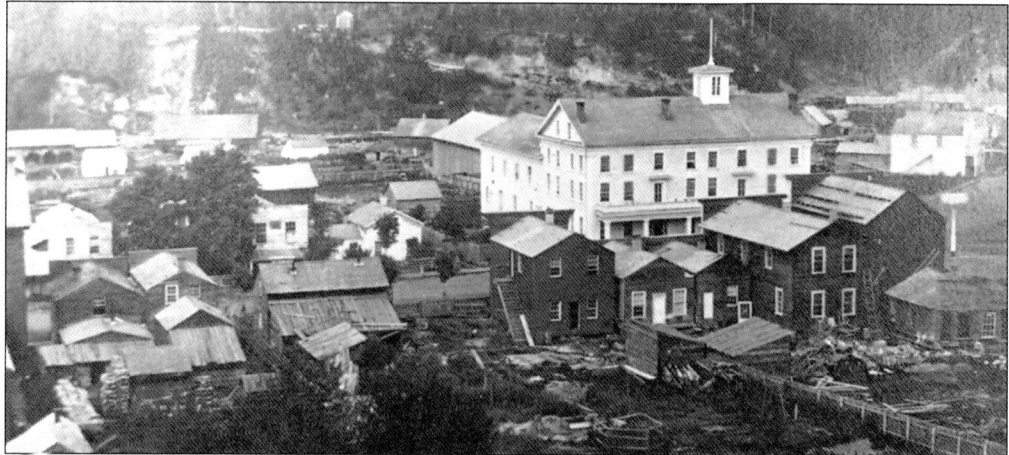

This picture, taken in the late 1860s, features Newaygo as a growing village in the wilderness, reached only by water or stage road. The *Newaygo Republican* newspaper reported that the first agricultural fair was organized and held in the rear of King's Harness Shop in 1873. It was a success, but it was agreed that the area was too small. The second year, the fair was held across the river, where the Department of Natural Resources now has a recreational area. This same year, a Driving Park organization created the racetrack on the fairgrounds, and it was considered the fair's main attraction. The fair was held for several years but was discontinued in 1881; it was a case of too early, too little. The Brooks House, with the cluster of small buildings around it, appears to dominate the scene in this photograph. Most of the buildings were later destroyed by fire. Across the river, a narrow gash appears in the bank, which indicates the road to Elm Center (Fremont Center). A roll way is in use upstream from the Big Red Mill.

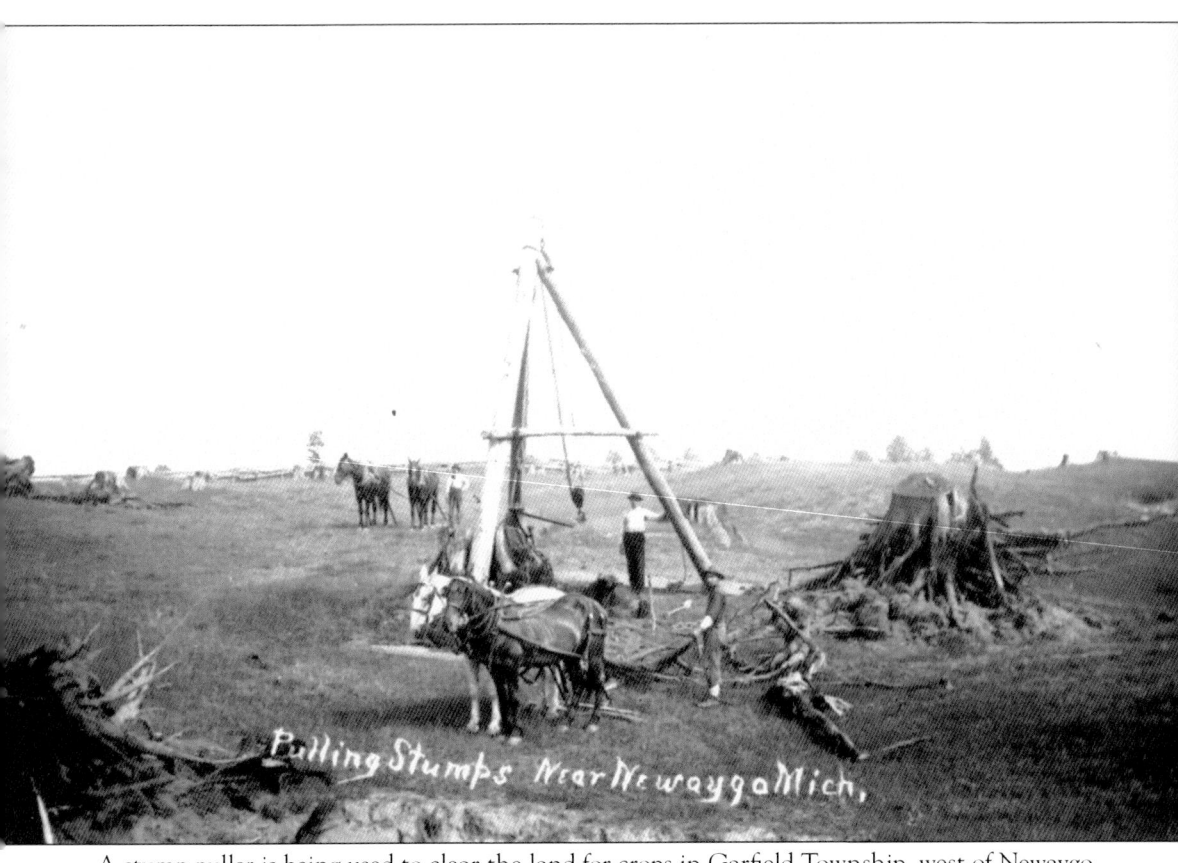

A stump puller is being used to clear the land for crops in Garfield Township, west of Newaygo. The large stumps indicate a better type of soil.

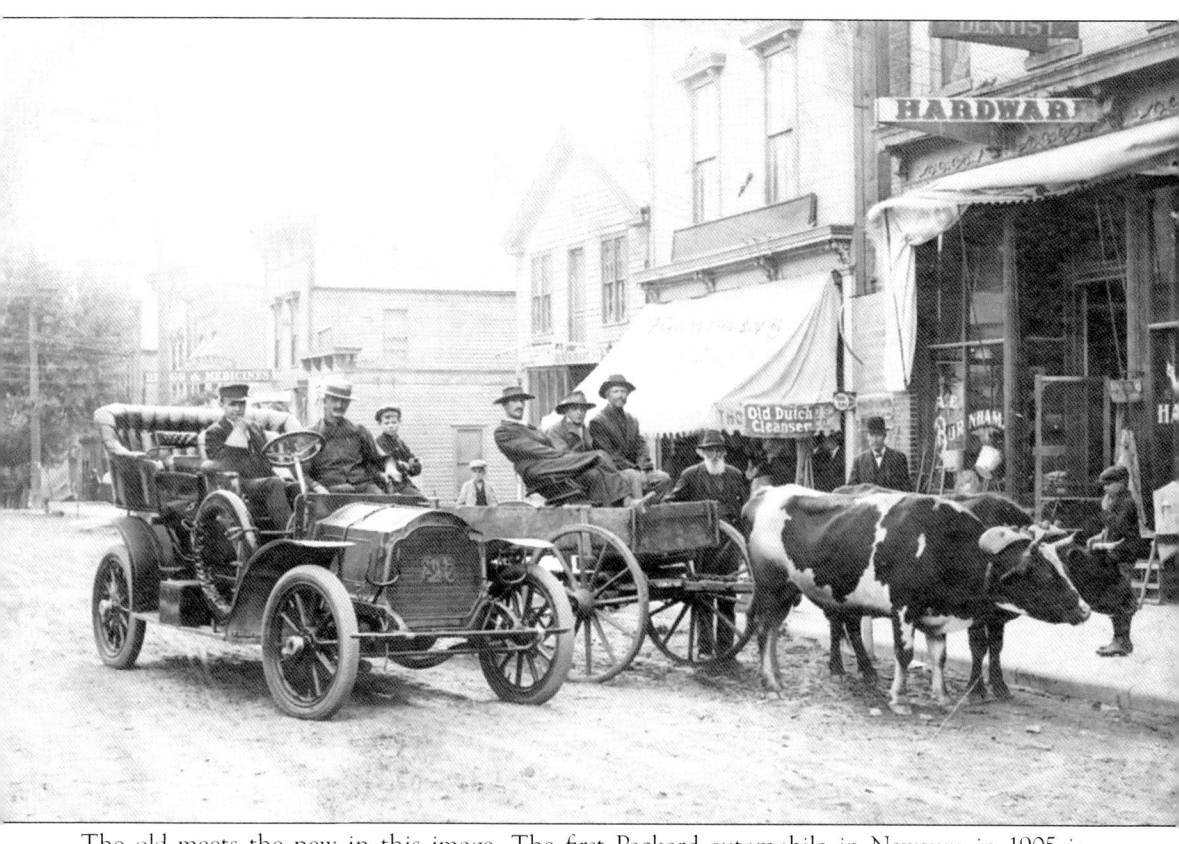

The old meets the new in this image. The first Packard automobile in Newaygo in 1905 is pictured alongside the horseless carriage with yoke and oxen, owned by the Siders family who resided downriver from Newaygo. This picture became a widely circulated postcard.

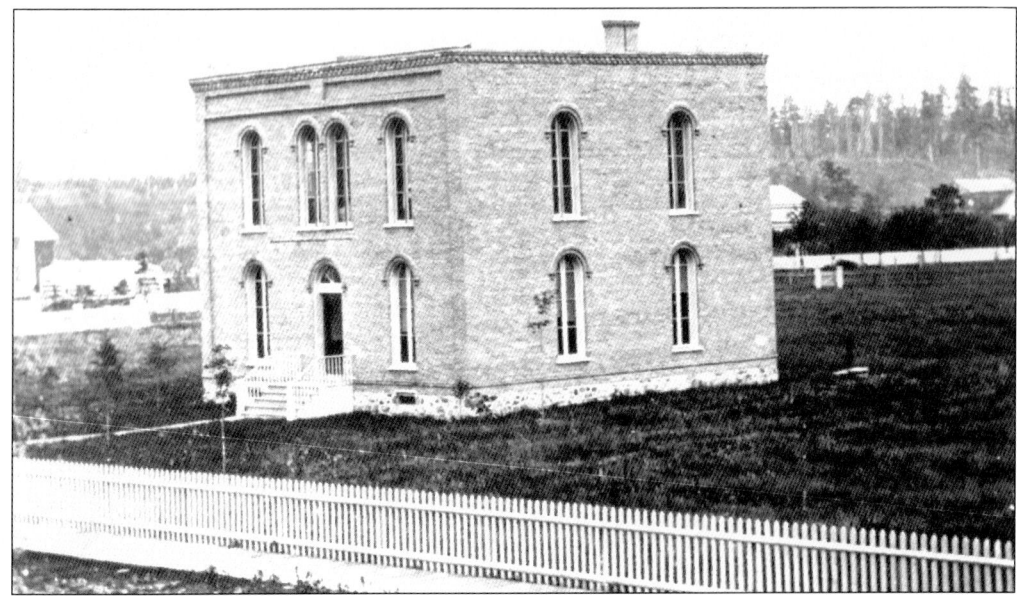

During the early years, the Brooks House rented a part of its hotel space to hold court proceedings. As the hotel business increased, the owners felt they could no longer rent space out for court, and a courthouse was needed. Newaygo County residents voted to build a courthouse at Newaygo in 1866. The deed was obtained from John J. Brooks the following year, and construction started on the building. The committee, however, soon ran out of money. Local merchants came to the rescue, and $1,000 was borrowed from the contingent fund. The plans mentioned adding a second story, having H. I. Brow from downriver furnish the brick and Thompson and Dickinson burn the lime at its kiln on Pennoyer Creek. In 1870, the ground was leveled, maple trees were planted, and the entire area was closed in with a white picket fence. In 1876, Gov. John J. Bagley requested that the supervisors plant 40 hard maples, some of which are still standing, on Arbor Day as a memorial for the centennial year celebration. The supervisors voted 11 years later to replace the original structure with a modern two-story building, at a cost of $4,750. Brick at that time was priced at $14 per thousand units.

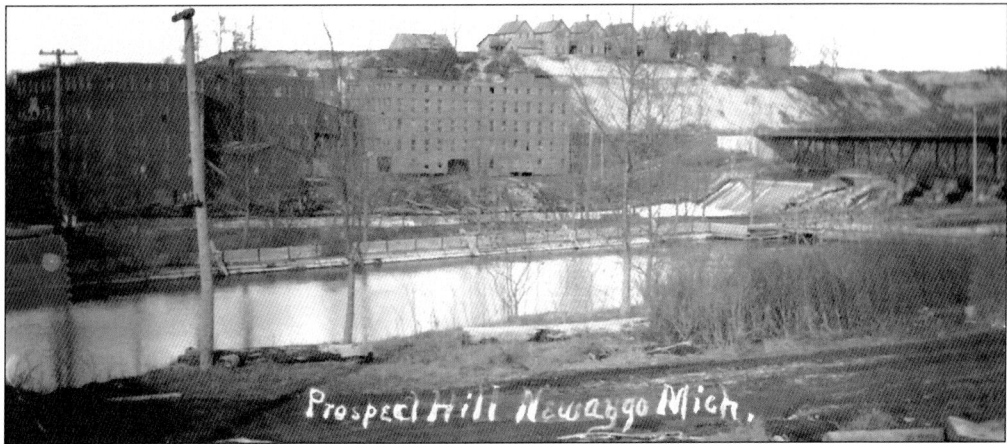

The nine row (also known as murder's row) was built by D. P. Clay around 1884 for his employees who worked in the furniture plant below the hill. In the foreground is the race (or channel) that delivered logs from the Muskegon River to the Big Red Mill. This picture was taken in the early 1900s.

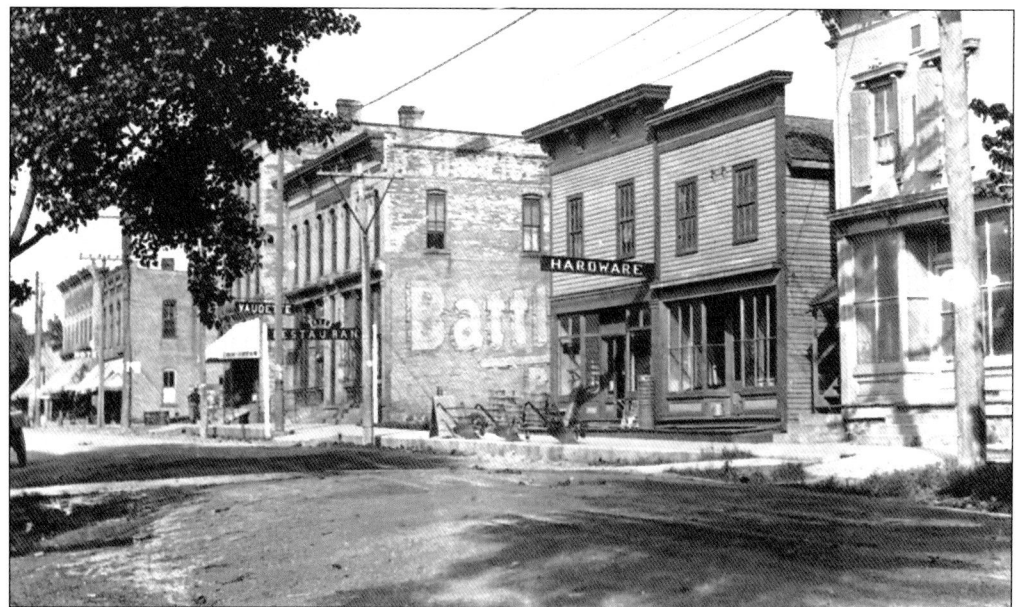

South State Street in the village of Newaygo shows (from left to right) the Day Block (Robinson), which was later the Shepherd's Art Gallery, Joe Butler's Hotel (later a doctor's clinic), the Surplice Building (later the State Hotel), Edwards Hardware (later Walker's Bait Shop), and the Macabee Building (Soper Drug Store), which later became a parking lot. Reinhardt's Vaudette is in the Surplice Building,

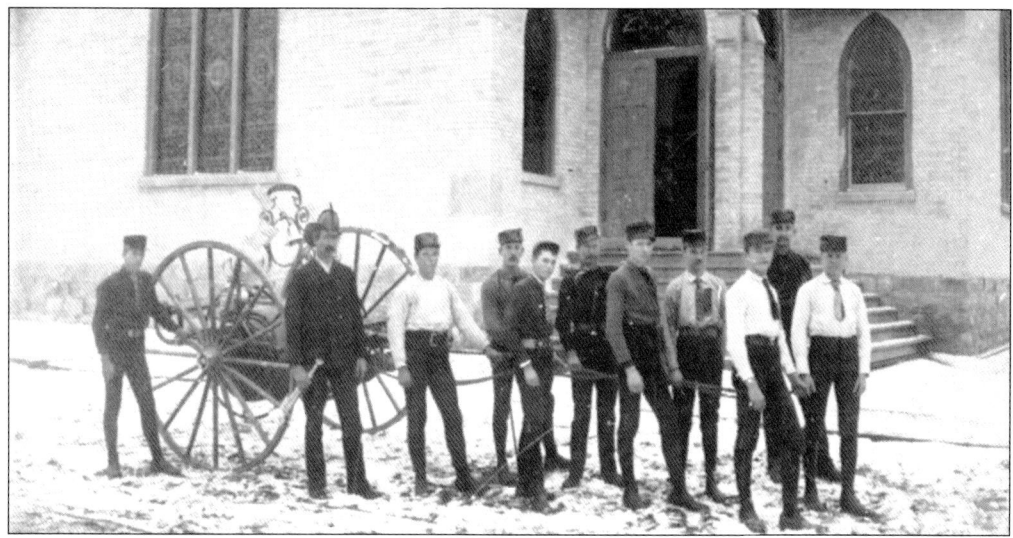

The Udine Hose Company was organized in Newaygo in May 1886. Pictured here are Capt. E. Burton, Capt. Harry Edwards, pipeman C. Boorman, leaders on the cart Fred Jacobi and E. S. Fuller, Albert Stillwell, R. Burton, W. H. Taylor, and C. W. Wilcox on the tongue.

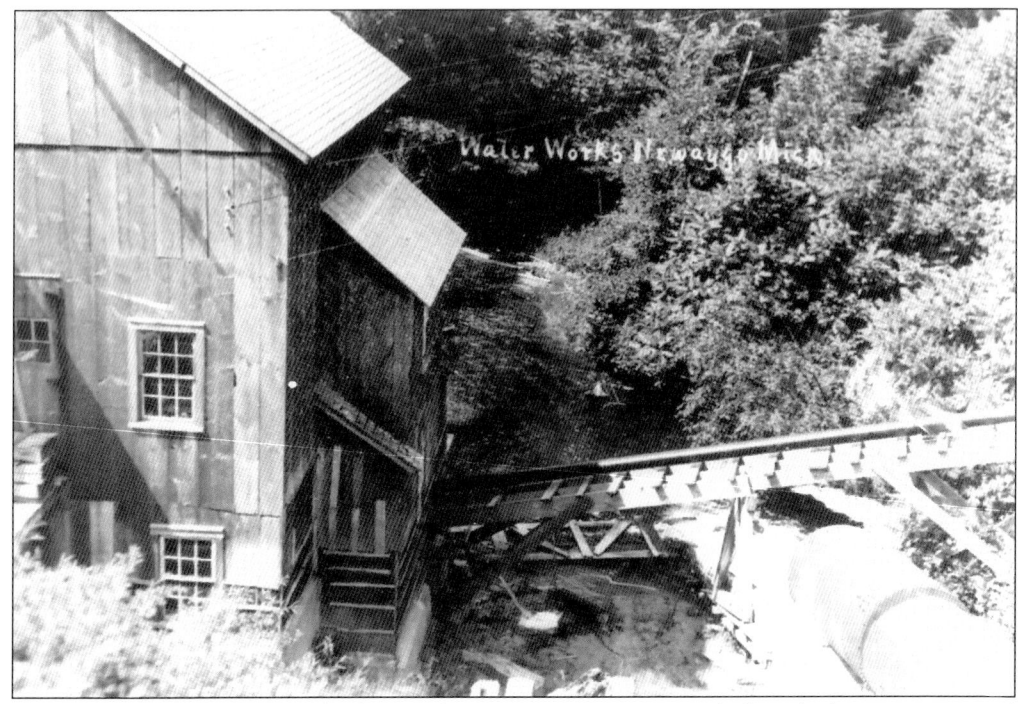

The original waterworks was built at Park Street Dam in 1888. It sheltered a large spring, used to provide drinking water for the village. The waterworks system was rebuilt from 1907 to 1912, and the wooden mains were replaced. On the right, a partial conduit supplies a new power plant about 500 feet below Park Street Dam. This picture was taken in 1913.

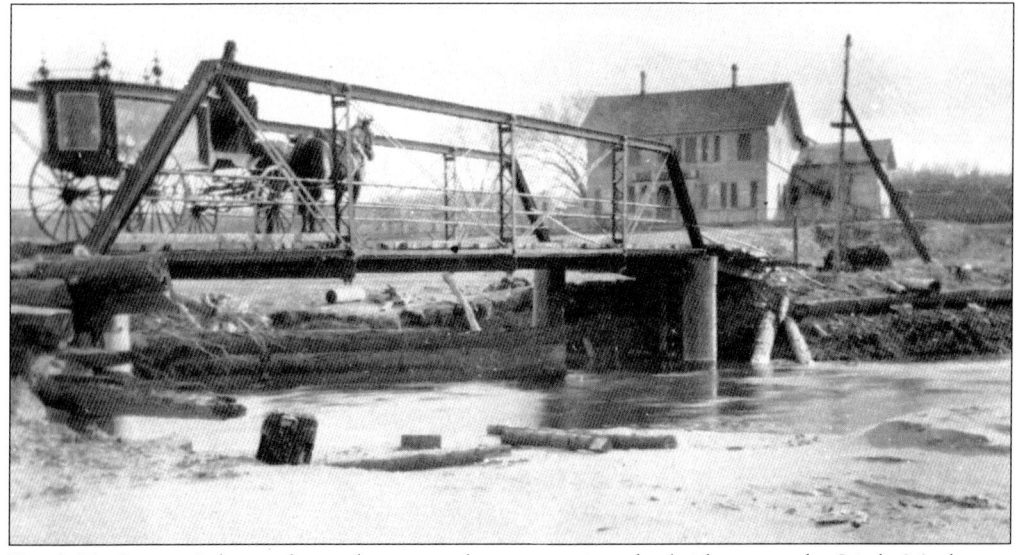

Frank VanLeuven's horse-drawn hearse is shown crossing the bridge over the Little Muskegon River at Croton, on its return to Newaygo around 1900.

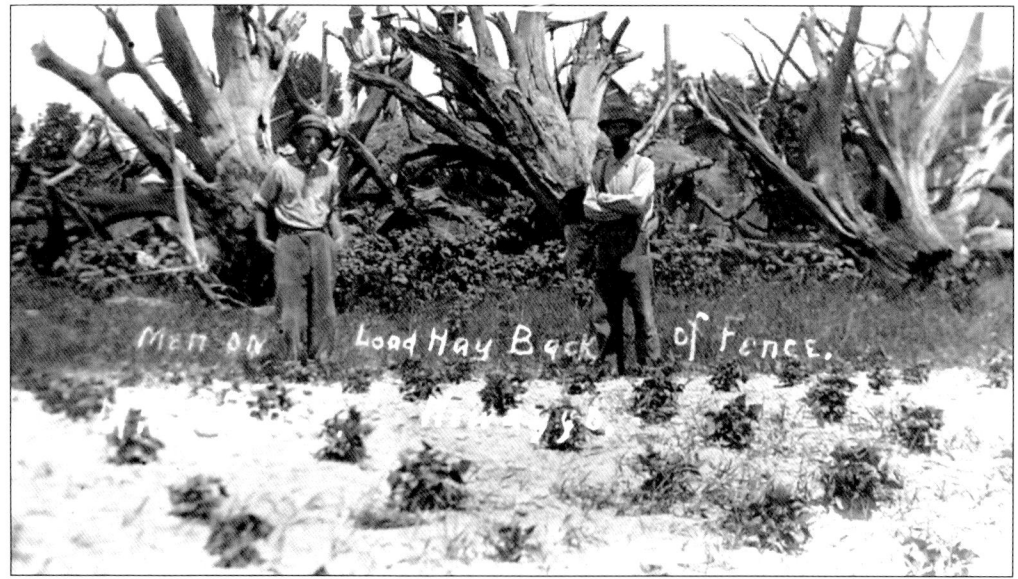

These pine stumps were removed by Art Crofoot and then used to enclose his truck garden, which was located in section 34 of Everett Township in Newaygo County. The stumps were placed in a position to form a rather attractive fence that gave added protection from the deer and offered a pleasant environment for the birds and wild game. In back of the fence, men are loading cut hay.

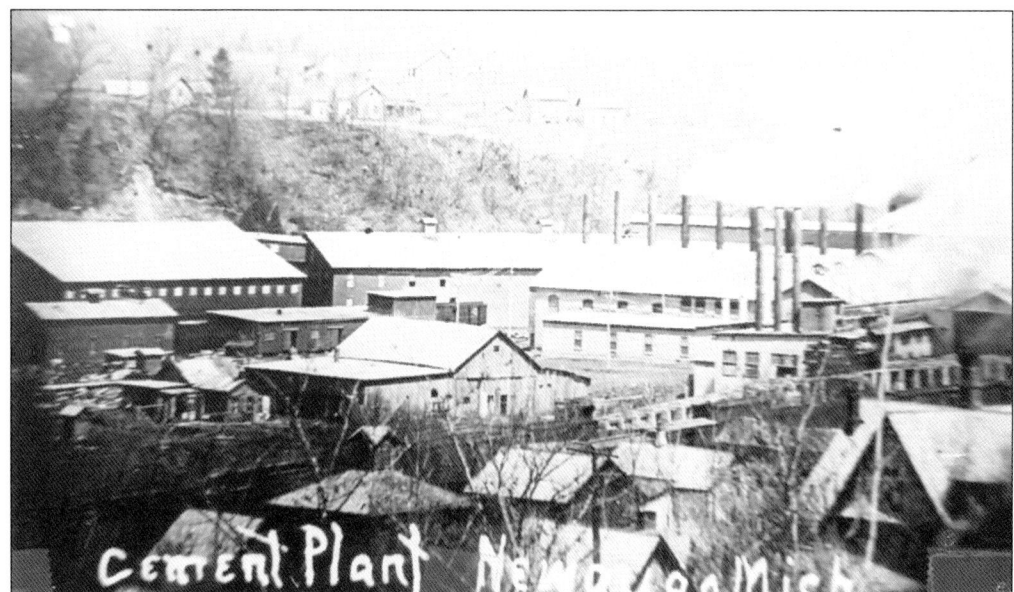

The factory of the Newaygo Portland Cement Company was spread out along the bank of the Muskegon River. The big horse barn in the center was the only building that remained from the Big Red Mill lumbering era.

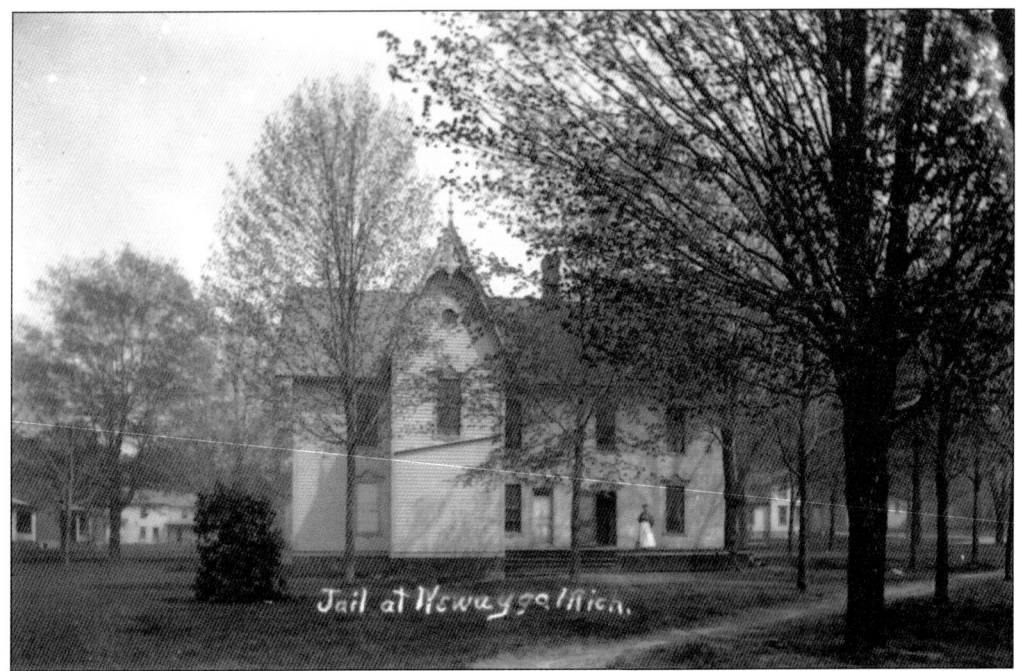

The Newaygo jail was located on the east side of the shuffleboard court of Brooks Park in Newaygo. Brooks Park replaced the old log jail. The photograph was taken in the early 1900s.

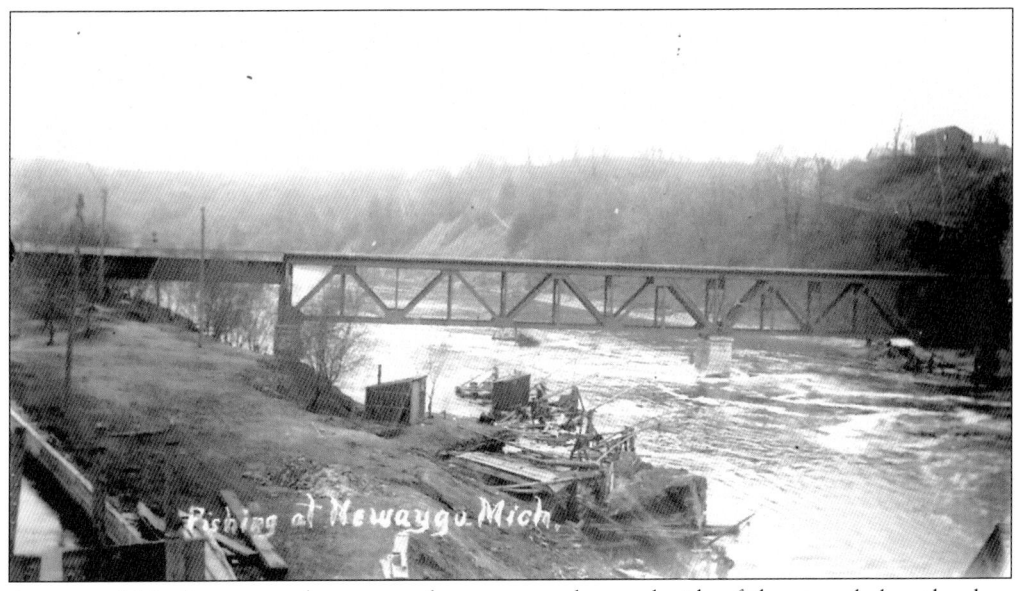

A group of fish dip nets are hung over the water on the south side of the river, below the dam at Newaygo, in preparation for the early spring run. Note the shack that kept the netters warm and dry. Part of the catch, black suckers, were sold legally. For a short season, a 24-hour day, it was a rough and venturesome time. For some, it was a hide-and-seek game played with the game warden, with the prize being the profitable sale of steelhead to waiting customers, which was, of course, still illegal.

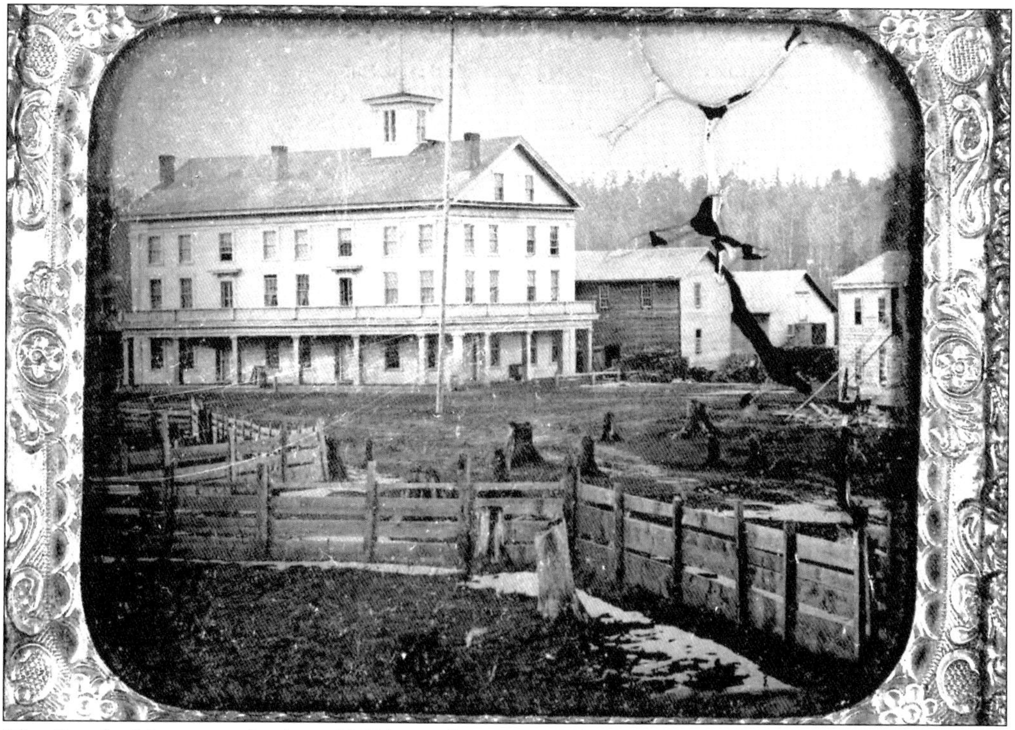

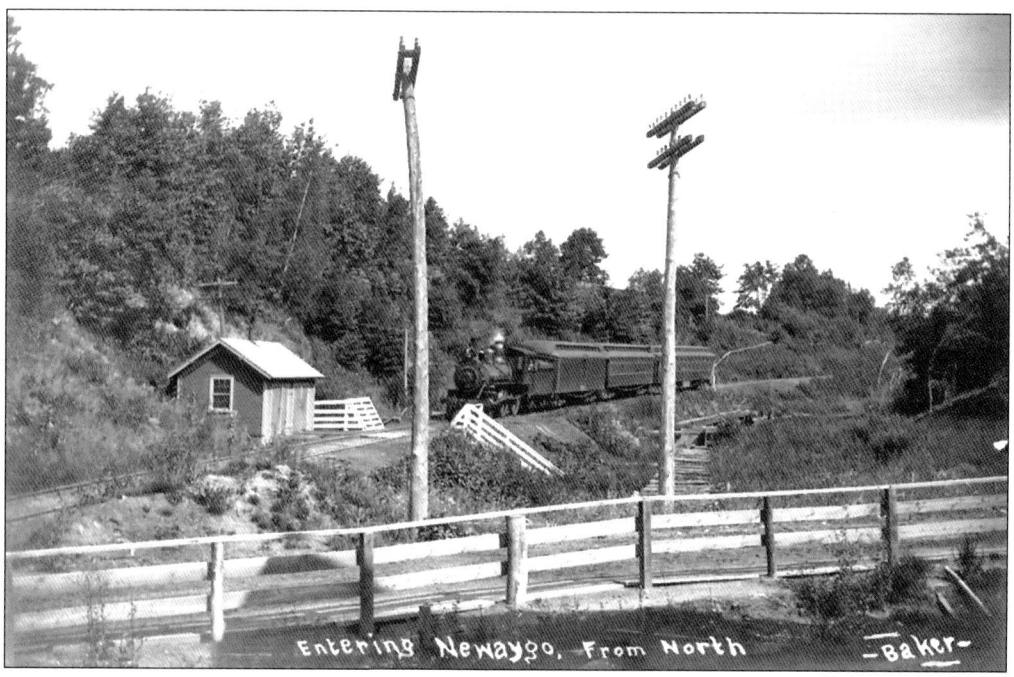

The Brooks House was built in 1857 by early pioneer John A. Brooks. It was a focal point for the area during the Civil War and for early state and county politics.

A passenger train is shown quietly slipping into Newaygo from the north. The handcar house and cow guards were located just north of Rowe's factory along the railroad.

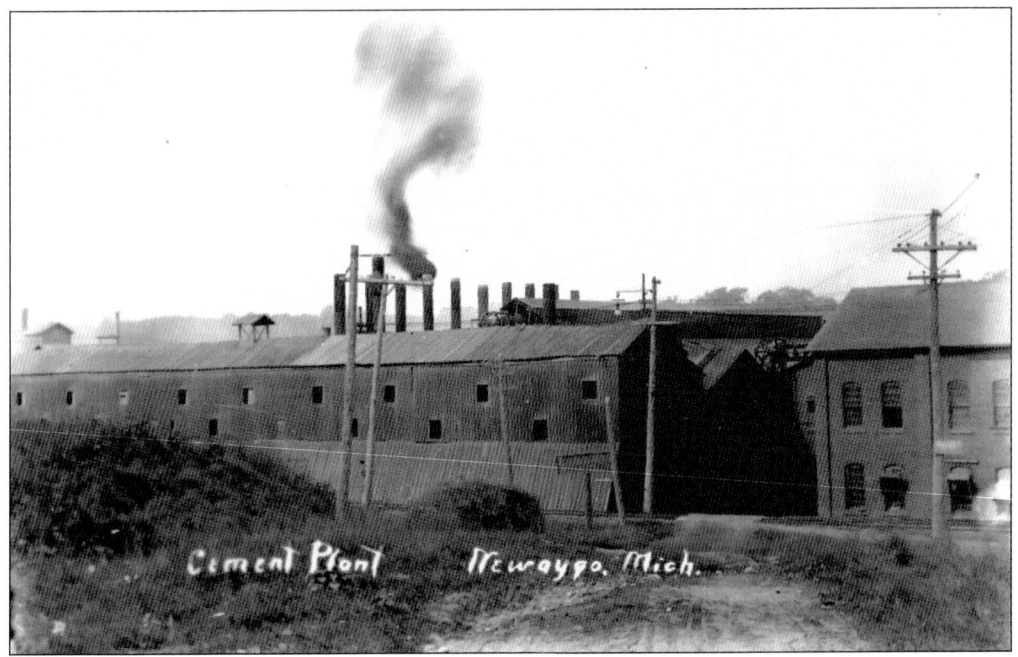

The south boundary of the Newaygo Cement plant was built along the main line of the Pere Marquette Railroad. The long building covers the elevated switch tracks and the storage bins. The stone train would climb the incline daily and dump the hopper cars, which were loaded with crushed limestone.

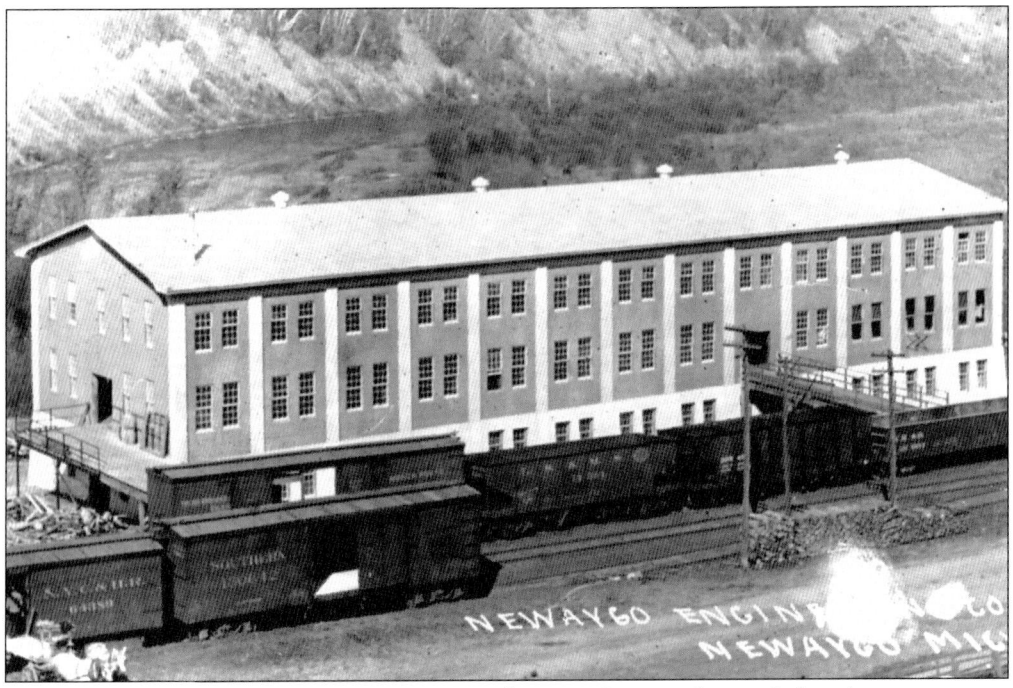

The Newaygo Engineering Company, erected in 1913, manufactured foundry equipment. W. J. Bell was president of the company. Henry Rowe had a similar plant located on Bridge Street, but it was totally destroyed by fire, before it turned a single wheel.

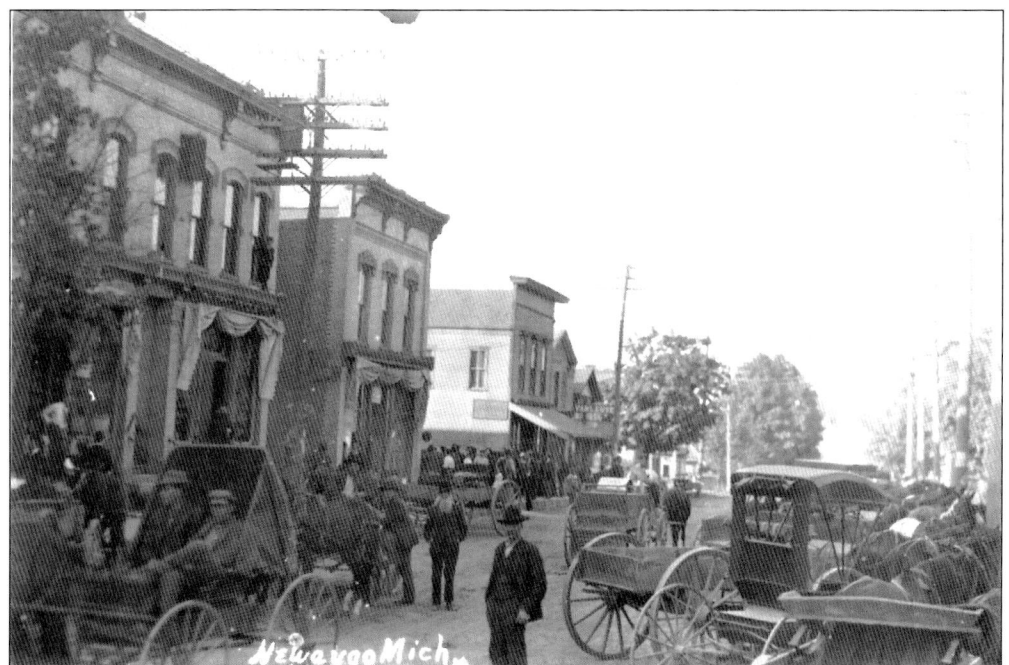

Interest ran high when court was in session in Newaygo. Farmers and others gathered in town to attend the court meeting at the courthouse across the street. All kinds of horse-drawn vehicles can be seen in this photograph from the early 1900s.

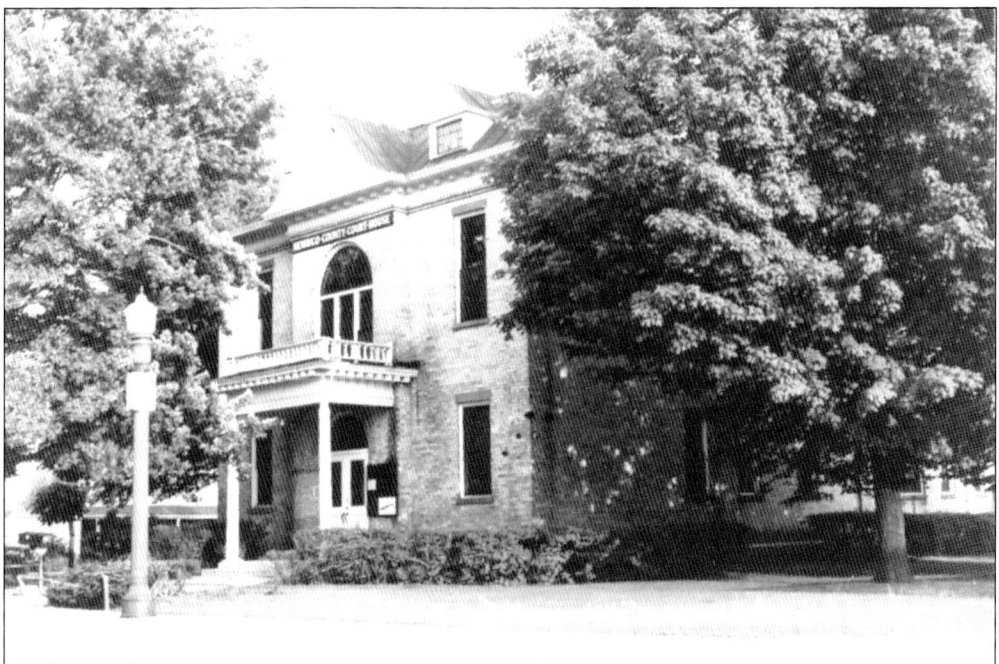

Pictured is the Newaygo County Courthouse as it appeared in later years. The trees are strong and healthy, and the grounds appear to be well kept and green. The supervisors did not like the appearance of the flat roof of the original building and voted in 1878 to change the design to a hip roof and to add an observatory.

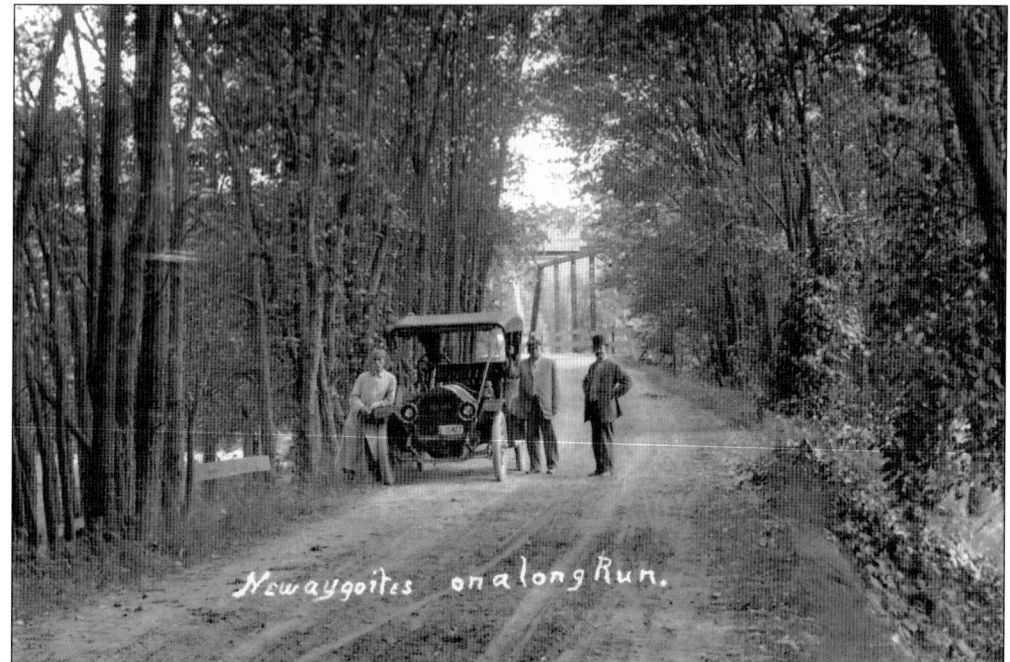

The Newaygo residents seen here, from left to right, Walter Pike, E. O. Shaw, and Alex McKinley, participated in the Hudson Auto Owners Endurance Run in 1909. The trio stopped for this photograph at the halfway point at the Grand River Bridge at Lowell. Notice the full-length driving coat.

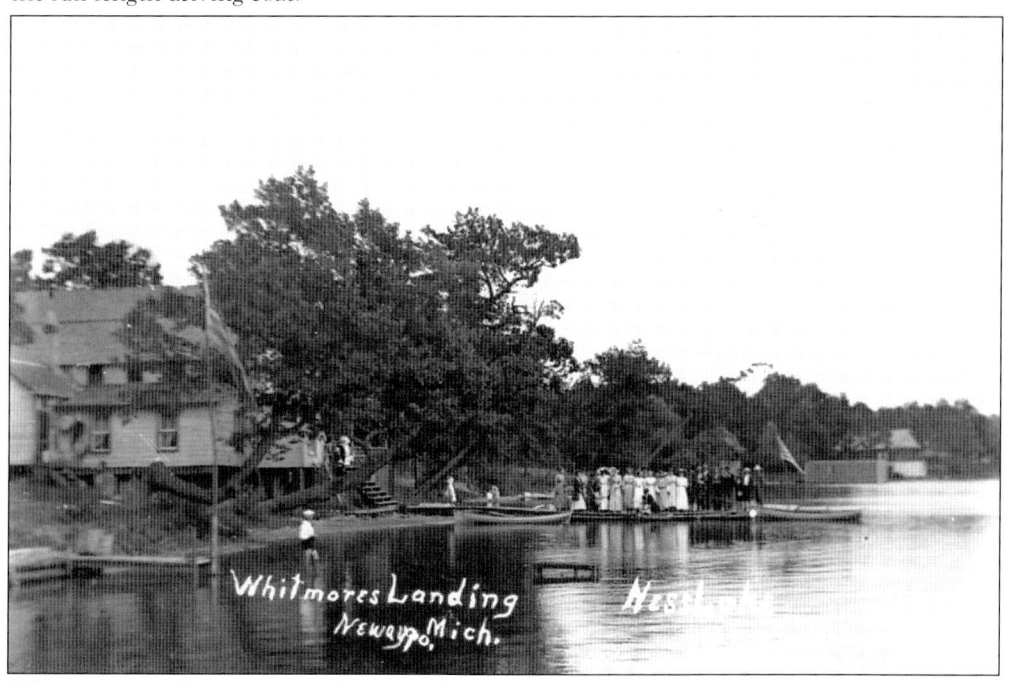

Whitmore's Pavilion at Hess Lake was a do-it-yourself amusement center that featured an early type of slot machine (one-armed bandit) that played nickels, dimes, and quarters. Resort visitors could purchase ice cream, sodas, boat rentals, and room and board.

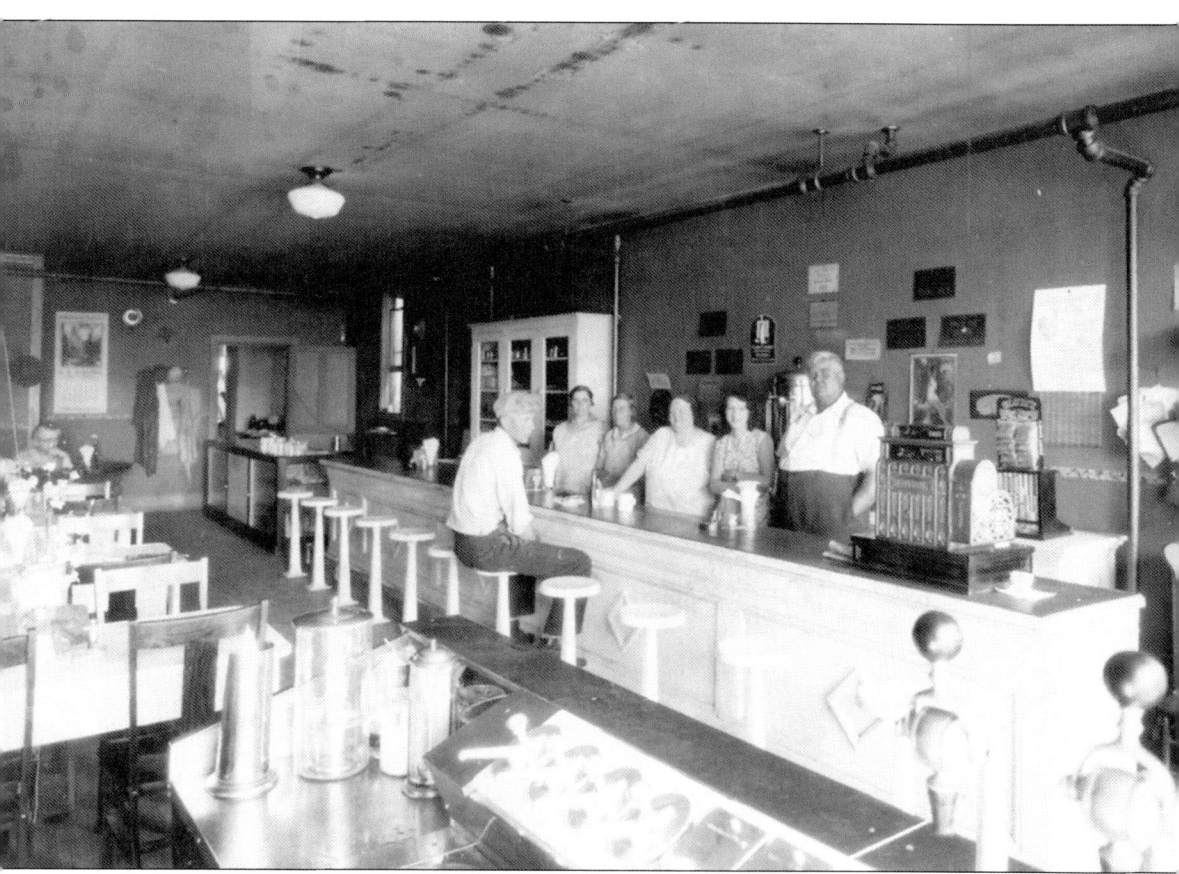

Here is the Old Switzerland Inn at Newaygo as it looked in 1930. Edna Stimson and her husband, Charles, owned and managed the inn. The Stimsons were originally from the village of Grant.

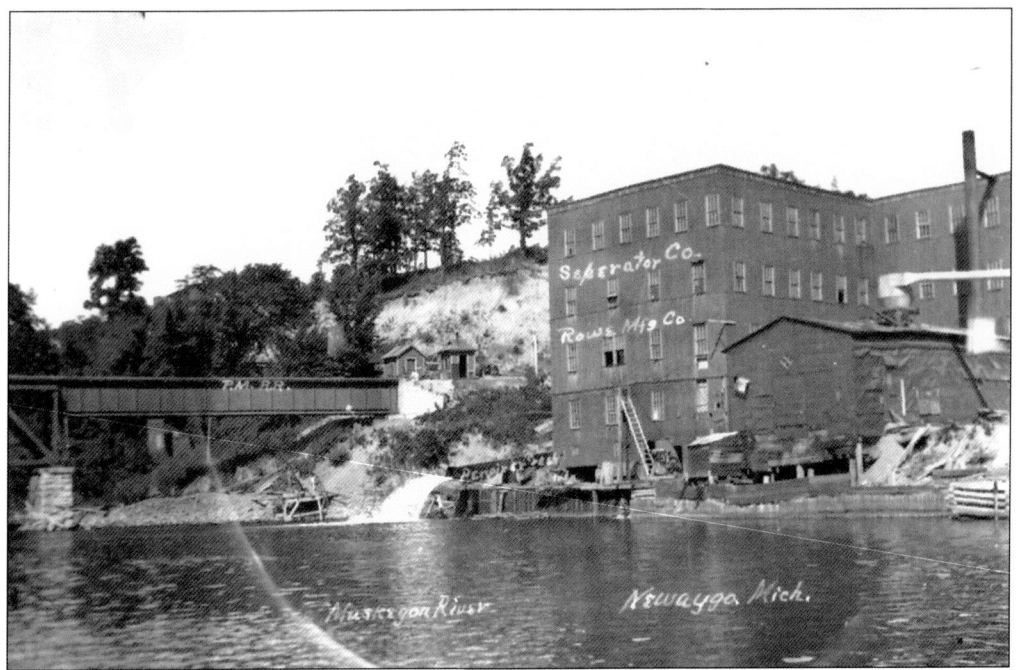

The Newaygo Furniture Company plant was built in 1884 by D. P. Clay, who was the company's president. The bridge connects the fourth floor with homes of employees living on the bluff along the north side of the Muskegon River. Clay later organized the Michigan Dairy Company and the Newaygo Brick Company.

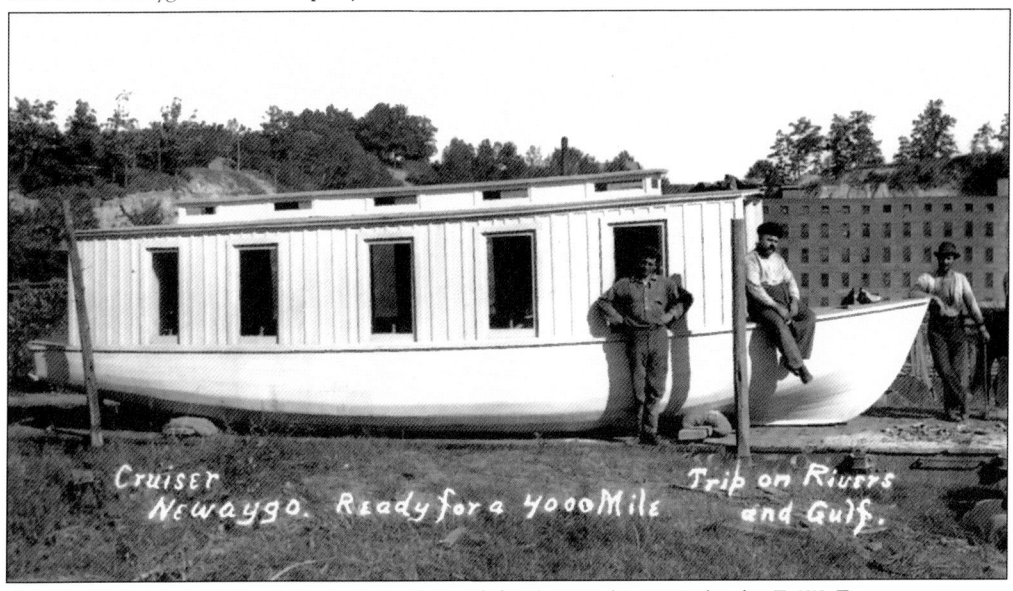

The cruiser *Newaygo* was built in 1911 by Ralph Sharp of Hess Lake for F. W. Foster, a pioneer hardware dealer at Newaygo, and his wife. The Fosters planned a trip to Florida via lake and river, including the Mississippi. The cabin was equipped with all the comforts of home for the 4,000-mile cruise. The cruiser launched in the Muskegon River in 1912. The boat, however, proved to be unseaworthy, and the 12-horsepower engine was inadequate. After many hardships, they did reach Florida. The boat was returned to Newaygo on a flatcar in 1913.

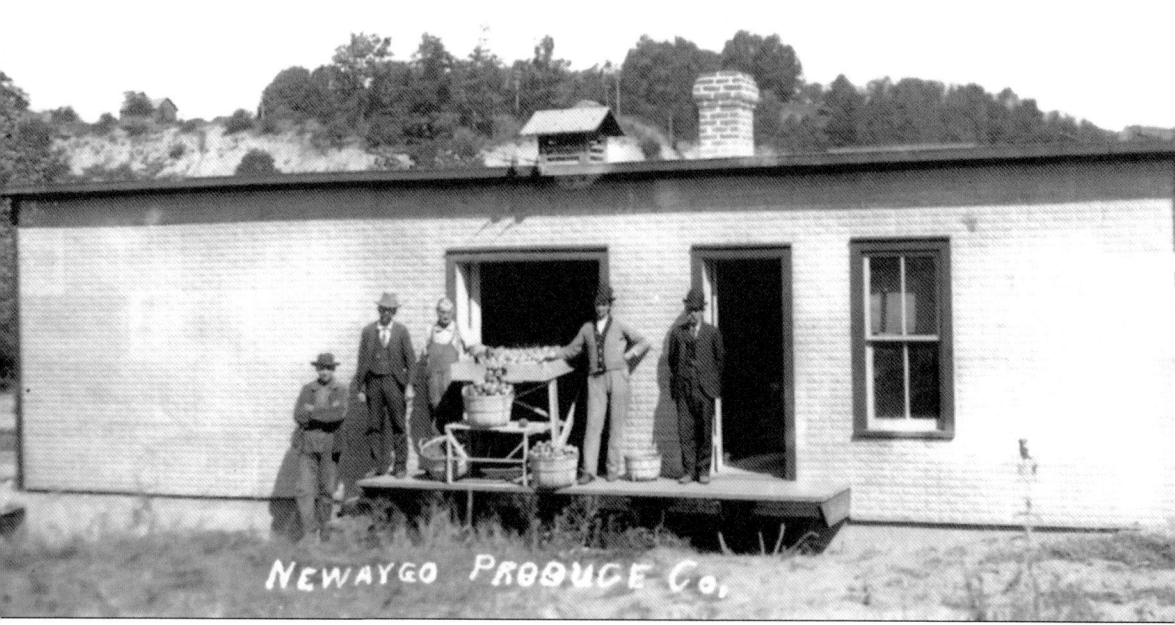

Dan and Harrison Edwards, sons of the pioneer hardware dealer in Newaygo, kept expanding their produce business, and the Newaygo Produce Company became a part of it. The company was located in the old remodeled salting station near the river (where the canoe livery is). Farmers had a market for potatoes, sending them by rail to the cities. A large produce warehouse was later built on West Wood Street in back of the lumberyard.

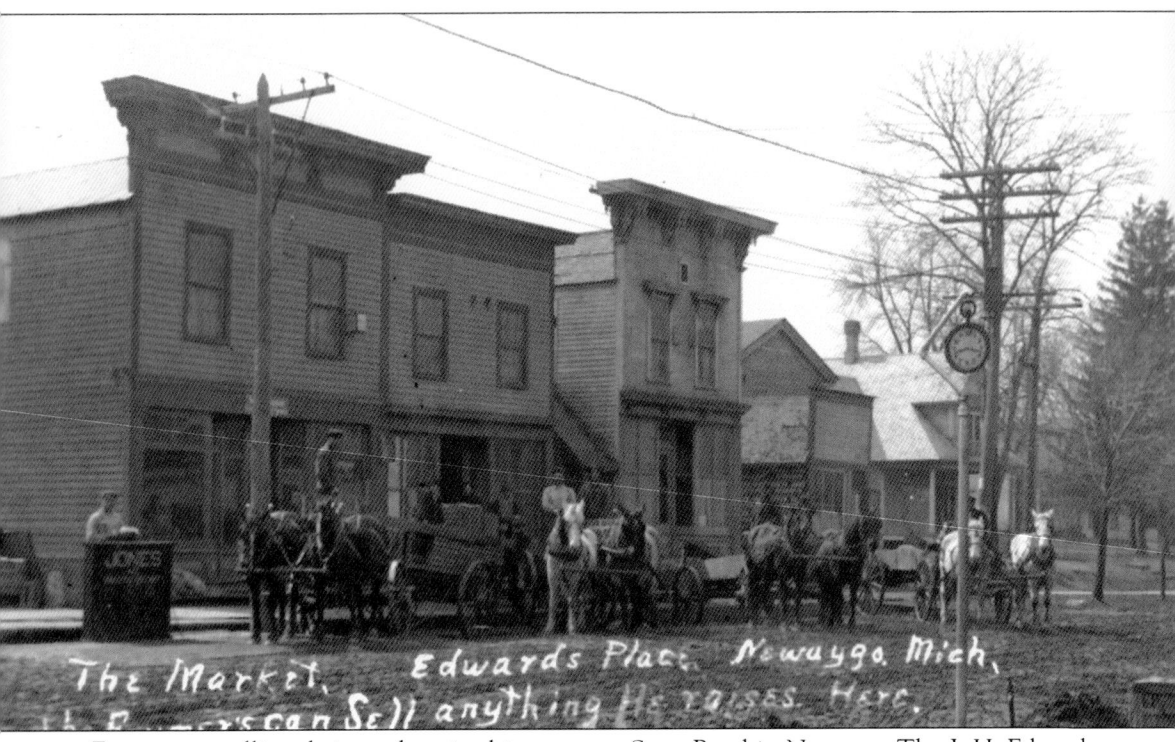

Farmers are selling their produce in this scene on State Road in Newaygo. The J. H. Edwards Hardware store (1865) is on the left. The hardware business was later closed, and the owner's sons took over and started a produce business. The building was later the Shumaker Bakery, which was destroyed by fire; after this, it became the Ferguson Quamset Hut-Fishing Tackle. The next structure is the Soper building (1860); it was later the Macabee Hall and then a parking lot. The third building is the Orton residence (1864), which was later John Brown's Shoe Repair Shop.

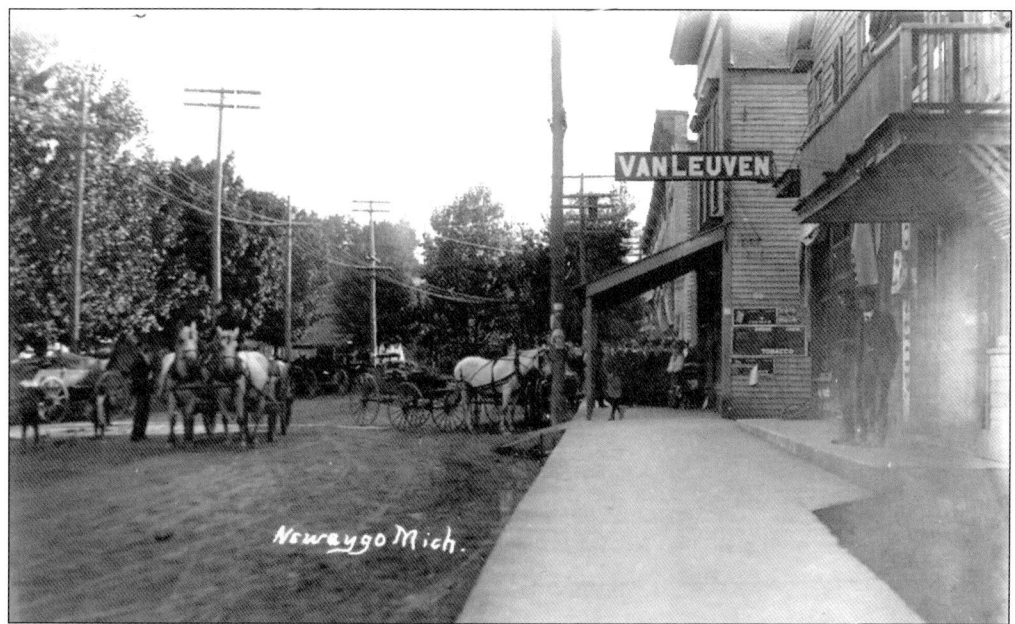

Cement sidewalks arrived in Newaygo on the north side of State Street in the horse-and-buggy days. The new cement sidewalks were the result of the 1901 plans of the Newaygo Portland Cement Company to replace the wooden sidewalks in downtown Newaygo. On the right is VanLeuven's undertaker building and photographer George Turner's meat market (Hummel's). People enjoyed looking for money and dropped treasures after the wooden sidewalks were removed.

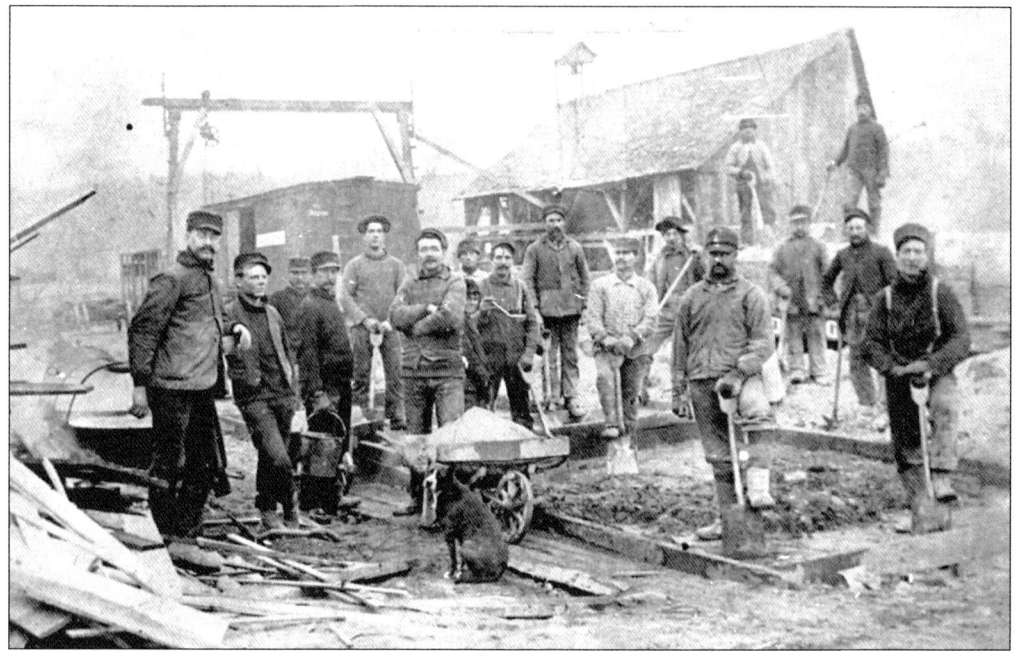

It was the start of a new business era for Newaygo after the great fire. Once again, men were called to work to tear down the old burned buildings and build new structures. The old bell from the cupola of the days of the Big Red Mill was used to call the men to work.

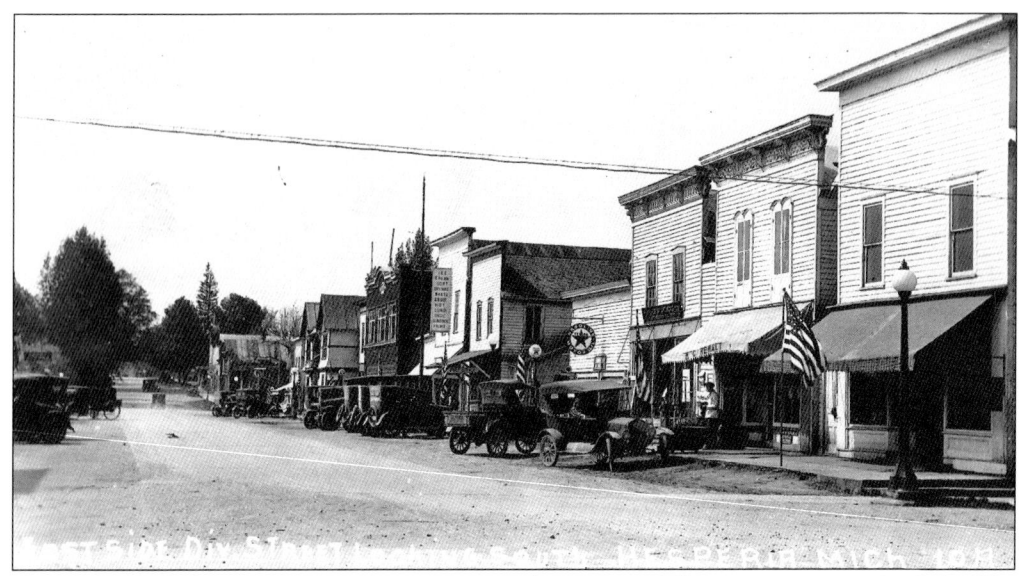

A north view of Division Street in Hesperia shows Ray Gillett's station on the left. The larger building to the north is Guy Knowles's cream station. Both of these businesses were active by 1931.

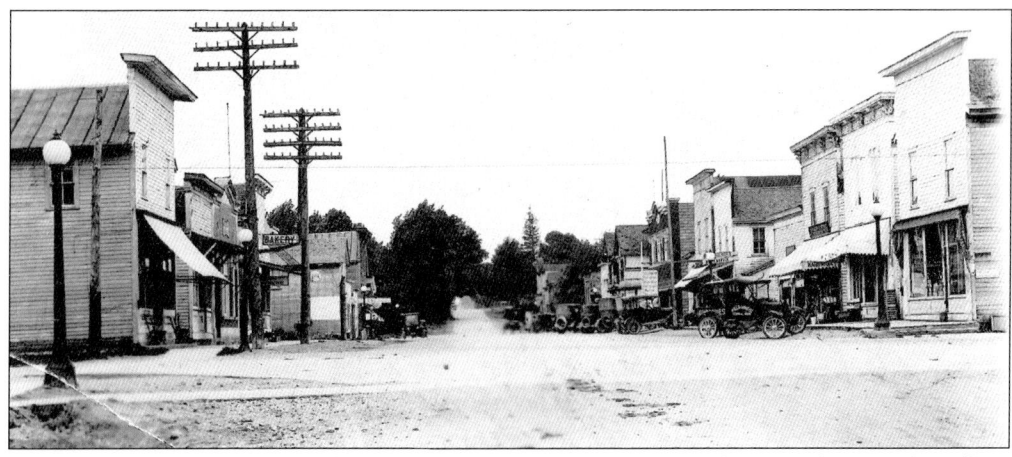

This photograph, taken around the dawn of the 20th century, is looking south upon the village of Hesperia. Steeples from the Methodist and Presbyterian churches can be seen.

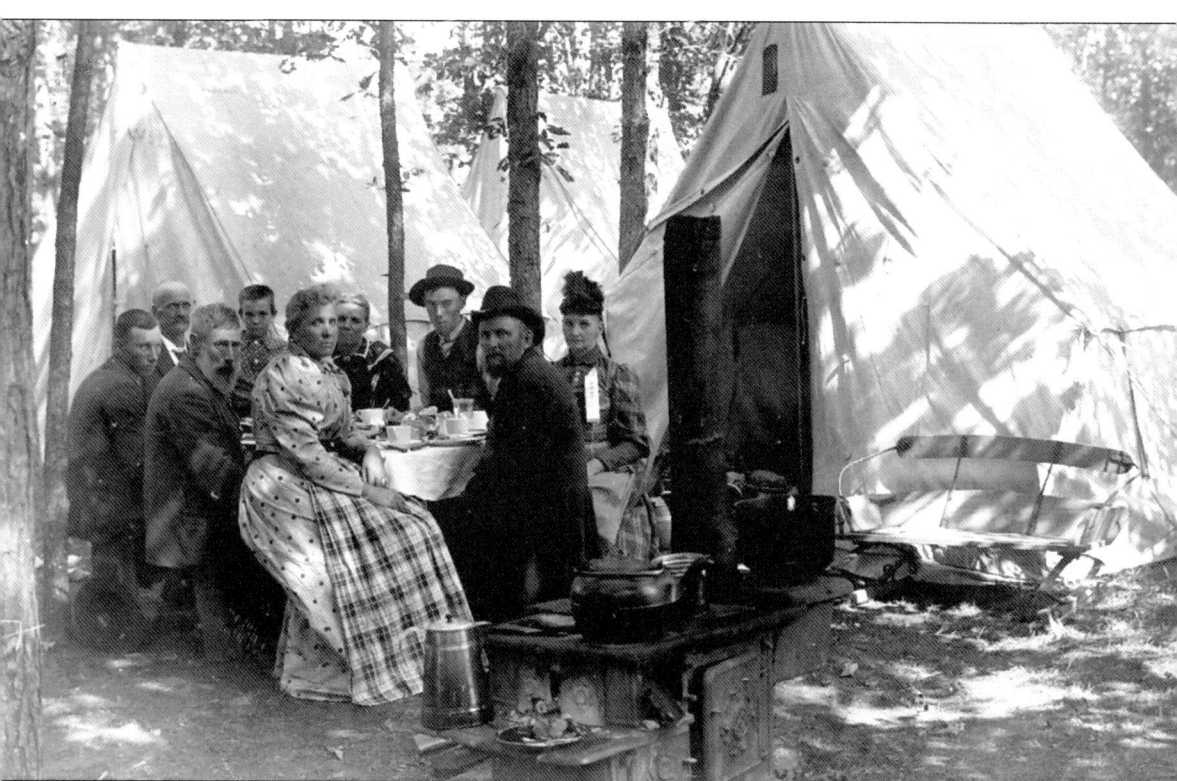

A Civil War veteran and his family are pictured at a Grand Army of the Republic encampment at Newaygo around 1900. There was also the Muskegon Valley Soldiers and Sailors Association, which started in 1888 at Newaygo and lasted several years. The association held the 14th annual reunion on September 8–12, 1902, at Shaw Park reunion ground. By 1890, the membership of the Grand Army of the Republic had grown to a total of 436,591. This appears to have been the high-water mark in its history. Along with the Grand Army of the Republic, there were several other veterans' organizations and auxiliaries. Some of these were the Ladies Aid Society, the Ladies of the Grand Army of the Republic, the Loyal Legion and Medal of Honor, the Sons of Veterans, the Union Soldiers Alliance, the Union Veterans Union, and the Woman's Relief Corps. Later there was the Daughters of Union Veterans. Most all of these organizations were for the aid of the veterans and their widows and orphans.

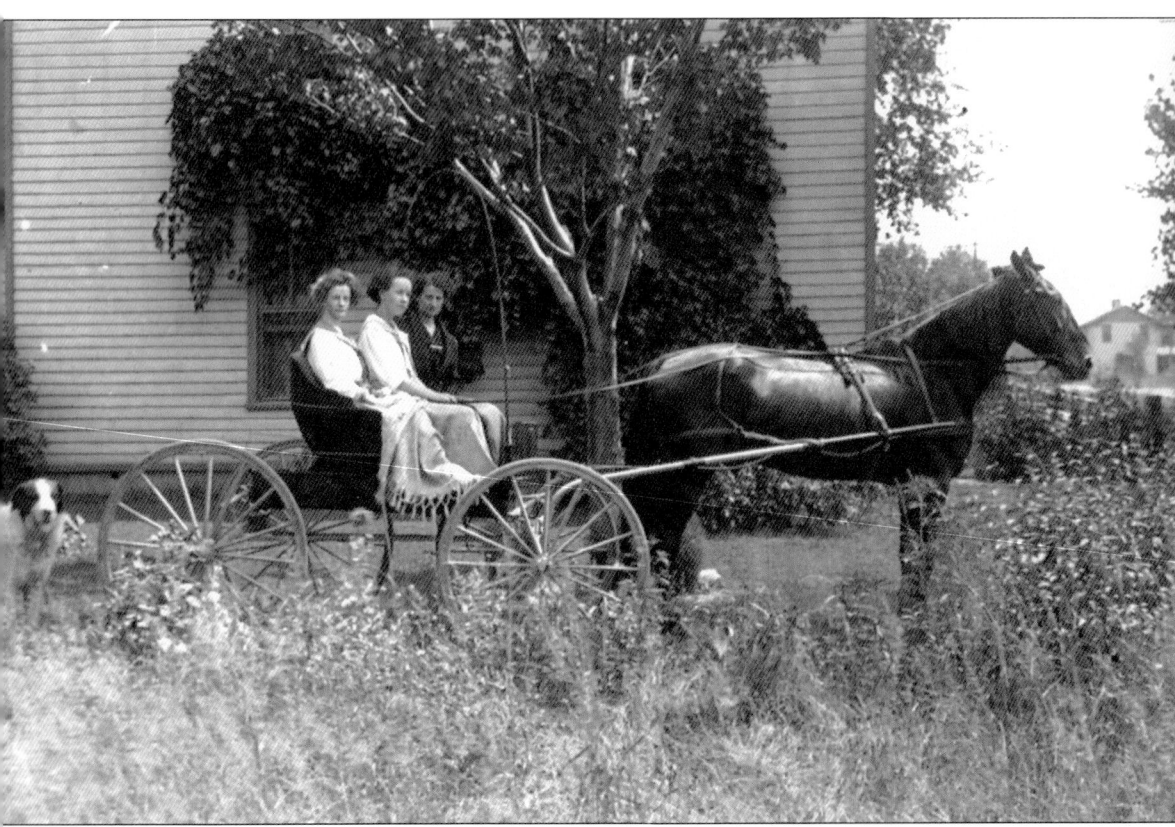

This is the home of Louis Larsen, located on River Street. Larsen was the postmaster of Newaygo and assistant superintendent of the Newaygo Portland Cement Company. His daughter, Laura, is seated in the center of the buggy with two friends as they get ready for an afternoon outing. Laura had a brother named Charles.

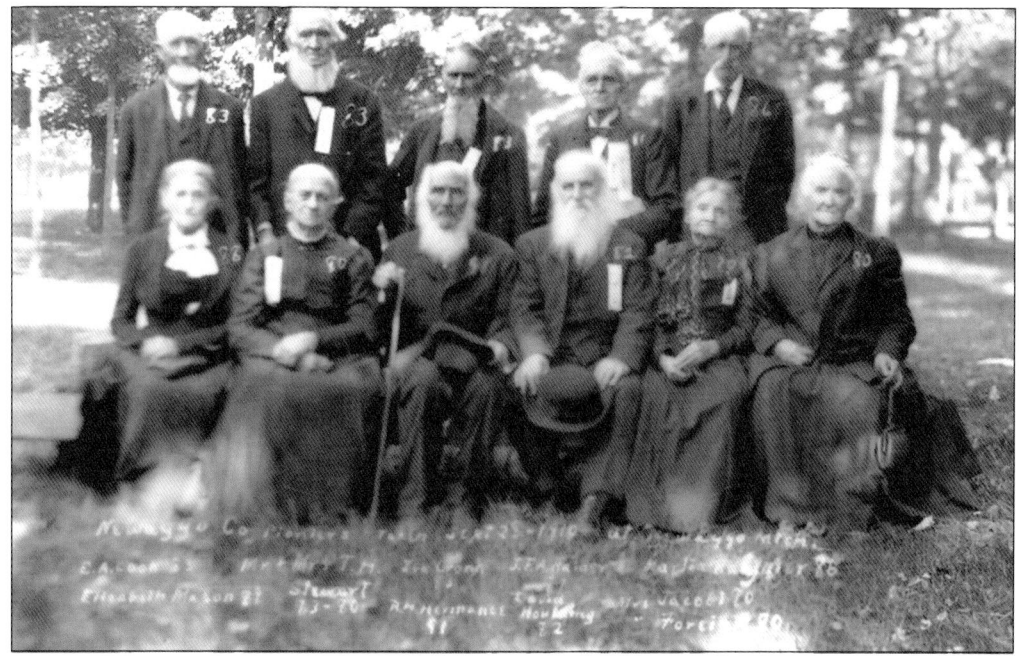

A group of Newaygo County pioneers poses for a picture on September 28, 1910, at Newaygo. Pictured from left to right are (first row) Elizabeth Mason, age 88; Mrs. T. H. Stuart, age 80; R. H. Hermance, age 91; David Houlding, age 82; Mrs. Jacobi, age 80; and Mrs. Foreign, age 80; (second row) E. A. Cook, age 83; T. H. Stuart, age 83; Ira Cronk, age 83; J. F. A. Raider, age 81; and Martin Ragnier, age 86.

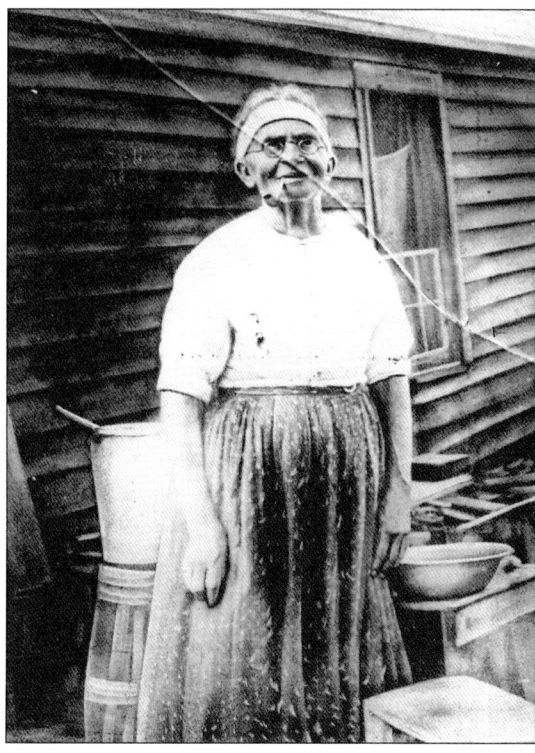

Florence Quick was born around 1830 in Canada. She lived in the village of Newaygo for about 50 years in a plain one-story dwelling. She had a crude, kindly way about her and took care of the distressed and hungry. On the subject of her marriage, she said, "The happiest moments of my life were the day I was married to Thomas Quick, and the day Thomas Quick died."

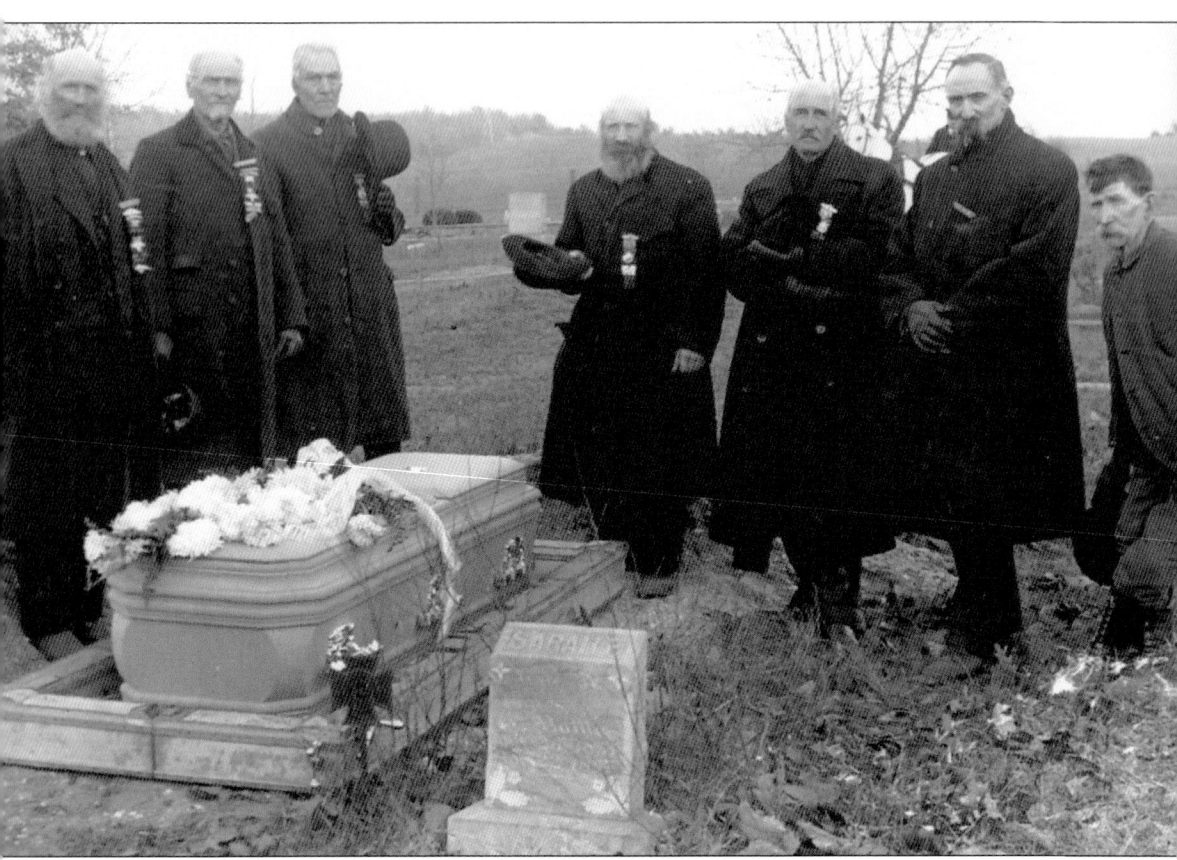

James T. Battles was born in Virginia on September 18, 1830, and died on December 19, 1913, at the age of 74. He enlisted in the 102nd United States Colored Infantry in 1863. He came to Newaygo in 1874 and purchased a lot in Garfield Township, where he resided and farmed for more than 40 years. He gained fame as a truck gardener and for serving hard lemonade at community festivals. This photograph was taken at the time of his burial in the Newaygo Cemetery.

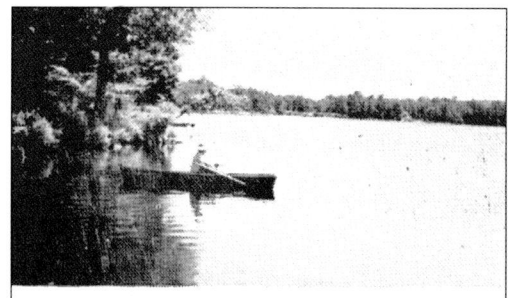

Ernest Jack Sharpsteen was born on July 8, 1888. He later became known as Ernest Jack Sharpe or his pen name of "Newaygo Newt." He bought and cleared land on Robinson Lake and built a summer retreat from show business. Sharpsteen thought it would be nice to write down some of the traditional stories of the backwoods that he had heard from the old-timers. He started sending postcard views of his resort to friends and an editor friend, with four-line verses pertaining to nature under the heading of "Newaygo Newt Sez." The postcards were also placed in newspapers. The verses connected with the public, and soon people were asking for longer verses, so the verses became longer, and the title was changed to "Tall Tales of Newaygo Newt." (Courtesy of the White Cloud Community Library.)

### WHERE? MICHIGAN

*Where the lakes, in emerald settings,*
*Reflect the skies of heaven's blue;*
*Where you're greeted with a handclasp,*
*So very firm you know it's true.*

*Where the bird songs seem much sweeter,*
*As they greet you in the morn',*
*Giving such a lovely feeling*
*You are glad that you were born.*

*Where the fishing is productive*
*And the hunting is the best;*
*Where people take vacations*
*And find joys and peaceful rest.*

*Where is this place like heaven,*
*That its wonders all relate?*
*Why, the place is dear, old Michigan,*
*America's greatest state.*

— Ernest Jack Sharpe

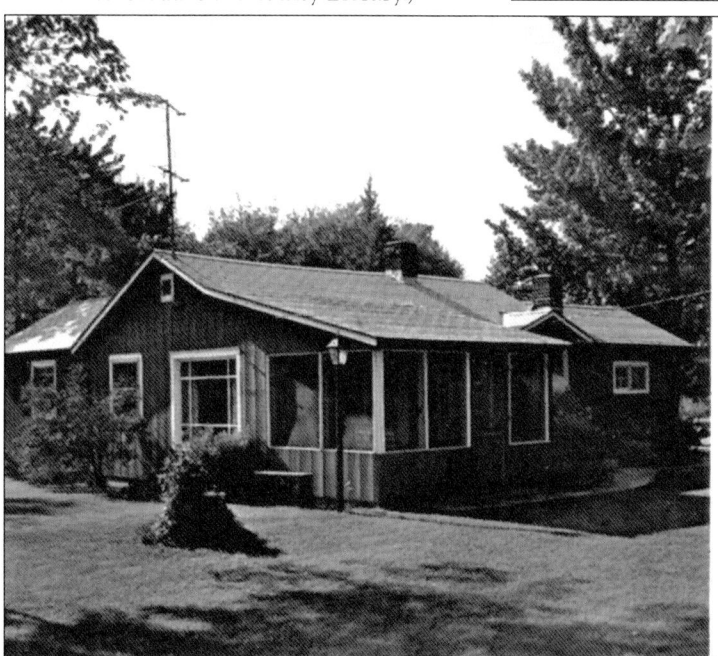

### NEWT'S NOOK

A low sprawling cabin
'Neath tall, spreading trees,
Where songs of the birds
Ride in on the breeze.
A yard full of shrubs
And sweet smelling flowers,
A bench 'neath a tree
Where I pass pleasant hours
A porch that looks out
On a lake full of fish;
What more in this life
Could an old fellow wish?
I rest and I dream
And contented am I,
While out on the highway
The world passes by.

— Ernest Jack Sharpe

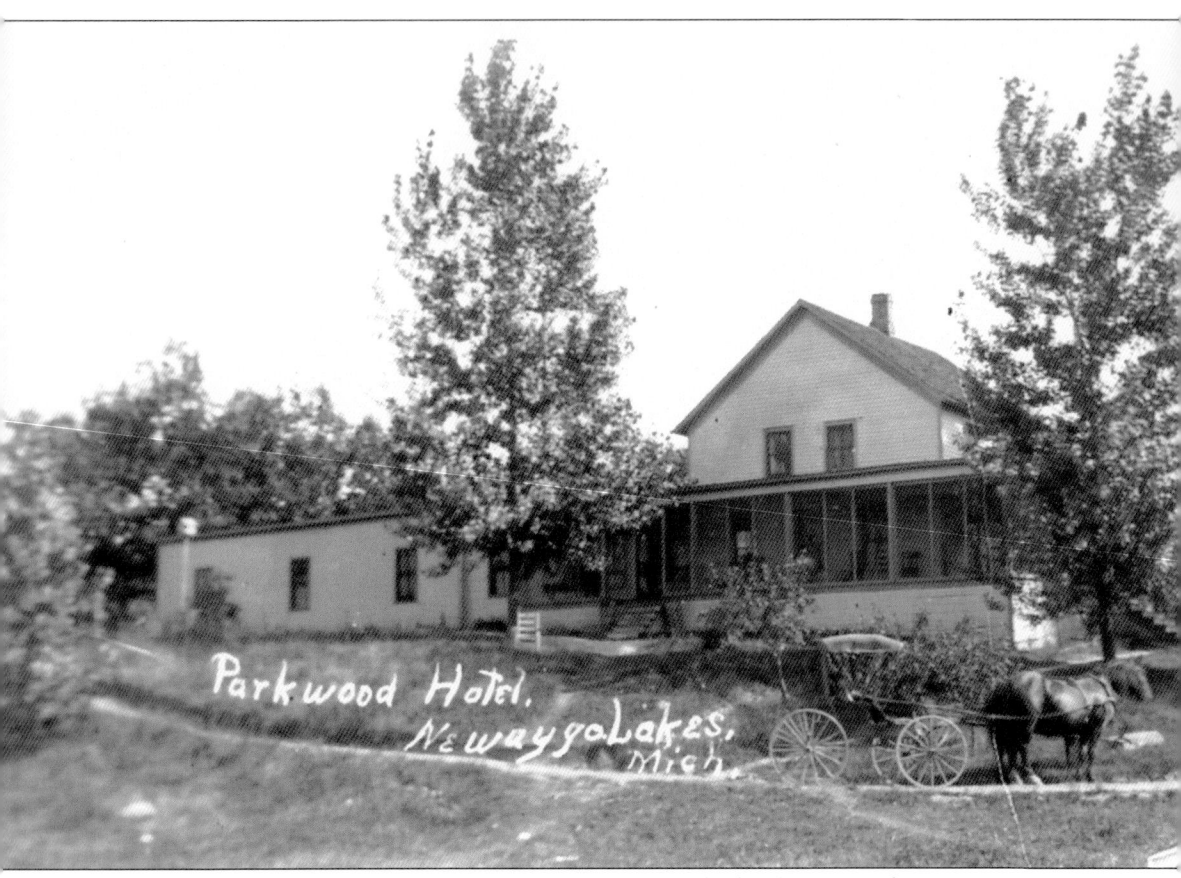
The Parkwood Hotel was a very popular hotel in the early development of Sawyers Resort on Emerald and Sylvan Lakes. The hotel was located near the channel to Pennoyer Creek and Pickeral Lake. Originally it was the site of the boardinghouse for the Newaygo Portland Cement Company employees who worked on the marl dredge.

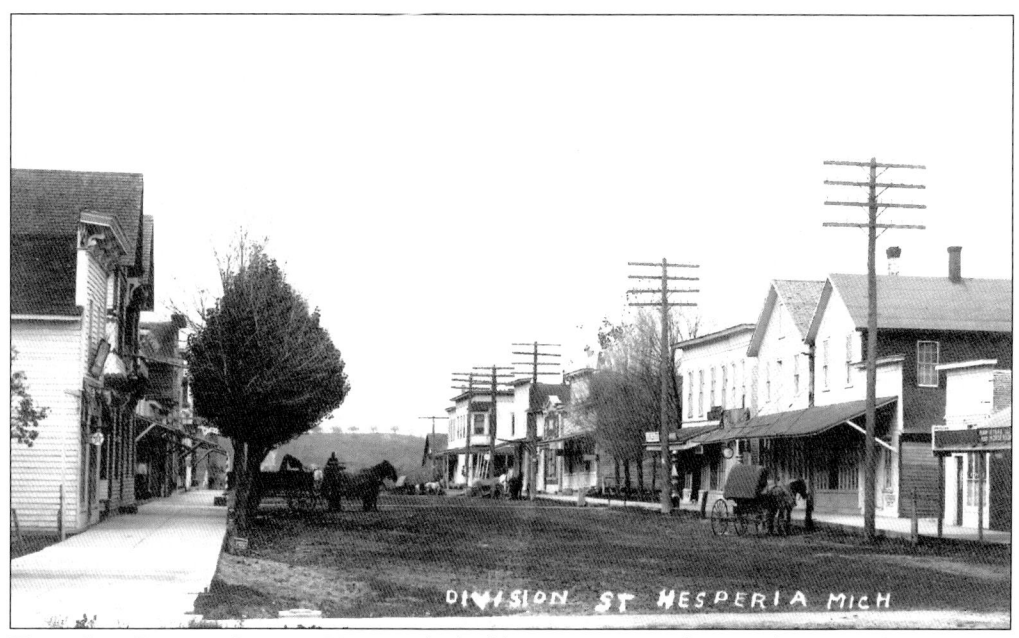

This is how Division Street in Hesperia looked between 1905 and 1916. The view is from Weaver Street corner looking northeast on Division Street. The St. Cloud, or Leland, Hotel is to the immediate left. The east side of the street from the farthest point north shows a portion of the McCallum Brothers Store, Mansfield Store, the bank, and a barbershop. The James Building, or Central Hotel, which burned, is by the buggy. A flour and feed store of Myers and Henderson is in the lower left. Telephone lines were placed on the east side of the street in 1905.

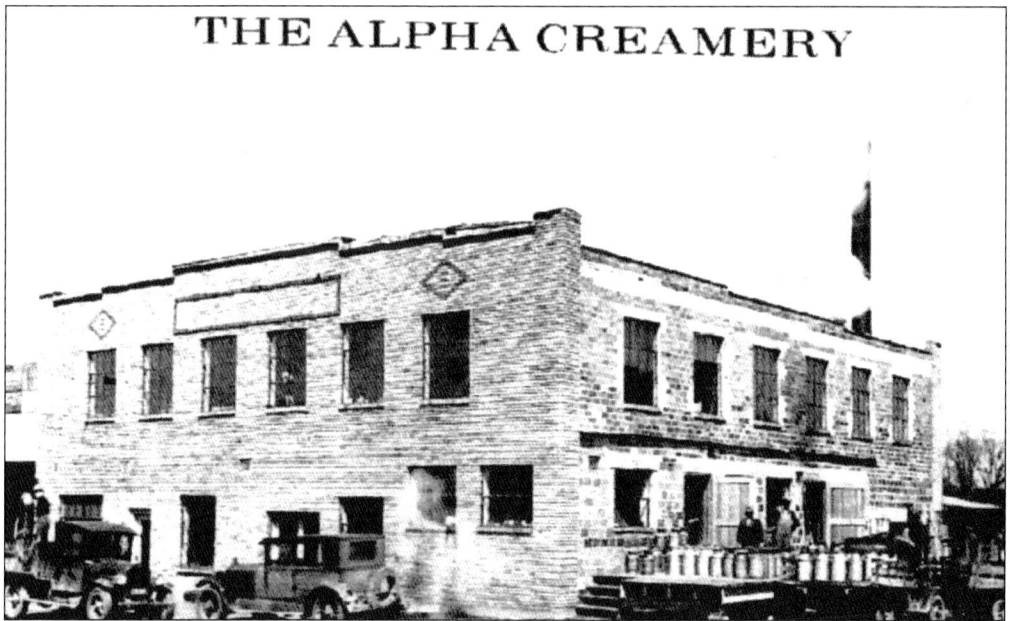

The Alpha Creamery started in Hesperia in 1919 and began with an output of 700 pounds of butter during the first week. In the last three months of 1919, it produced 28,156 pounds of butter. When operations first began, the office, boiler, and cooler occupied three corners of a small building, and one pasteurizer and one churn consumed the remaining space.

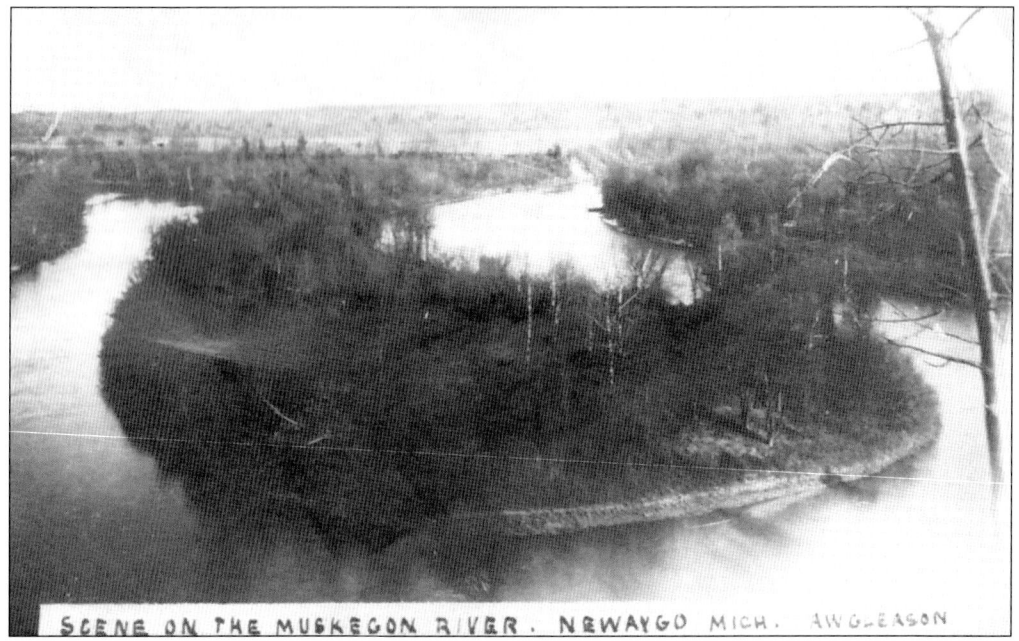

The Muskegon River begins its 300-mile journey from an outlet of Higgins Lake; it flows through Houghton Lake, trickles through leaves as a dead stream for a short distance, and then meanders in a southwesterly direction between low banks through Missaukee, Clare, Osceola, and Mecosta Counties. As it passes Big Rapids, it cuts through high banks and runs a torturous course through Newaygo County. In many places it doubles back, forming oxbows. Leaving Bridgeton, it passes through swampy Muskegon County, flowing between low banks and swampy areas with numerous channels that make navigation difficult. It then reaches the mouth of the river at Muskegon Lake.

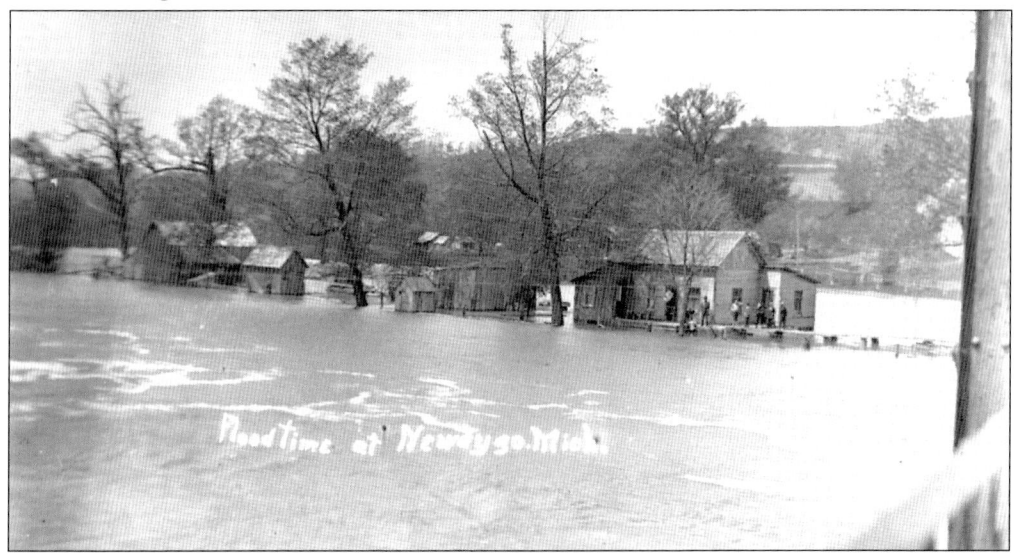

Flood time along the Muskegon River below the lower bridge in Newaygo had at least six people at Harve Barker's home on Sarell Street pondering the question "Shall we move to the second floor?" In the early times, these situations occurred every spring and more often during the big drives when logs jammed and formed a natural dam.

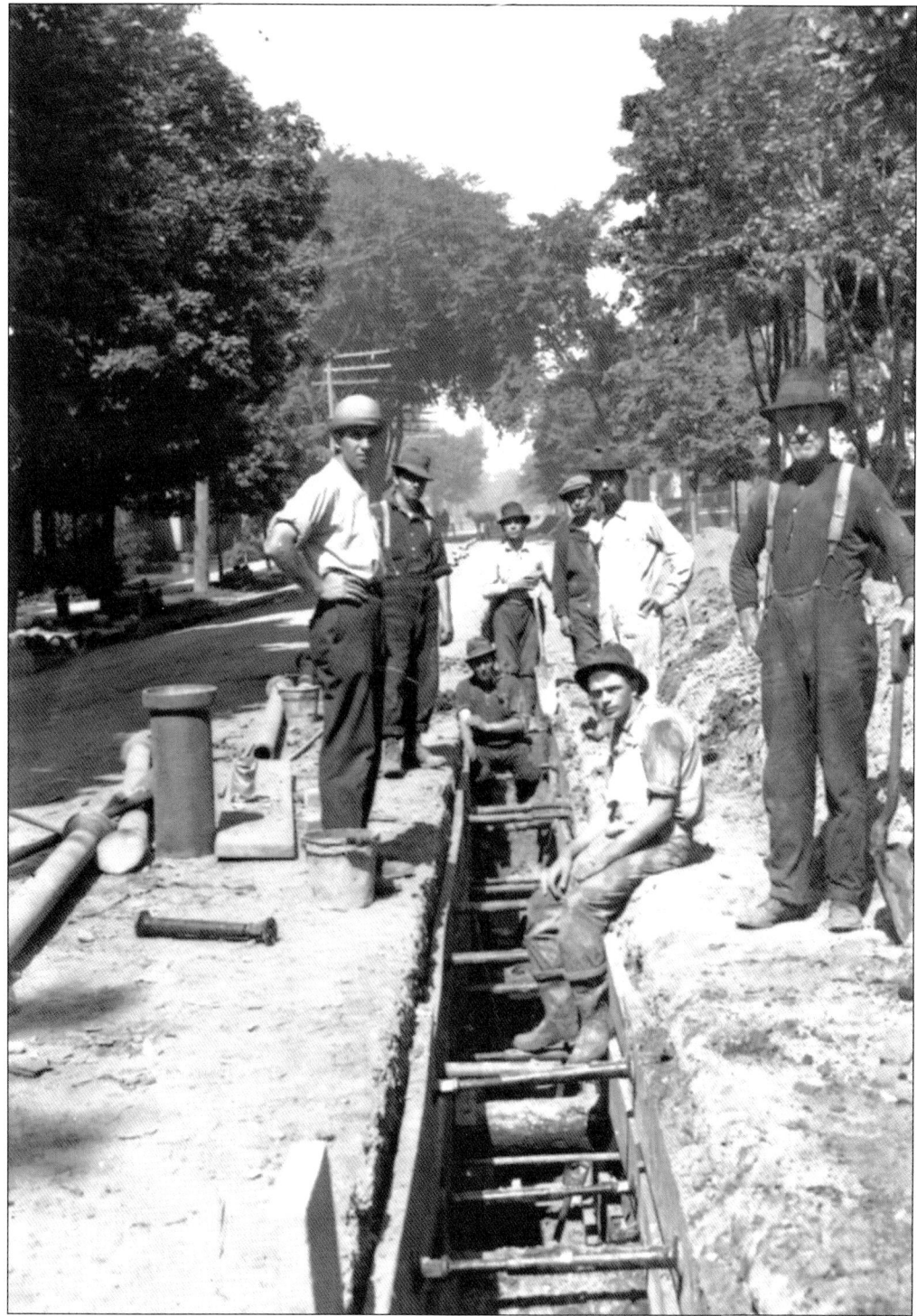
Workers constructed new water and sewer mains in lower State Road in Newaygo around 1912–1913. The loose soil required shoring up to prevent cave-ins. The work was slowed down due to the sunken logs, which were part of the corduroy road. Large elm trees can be seen in the background.

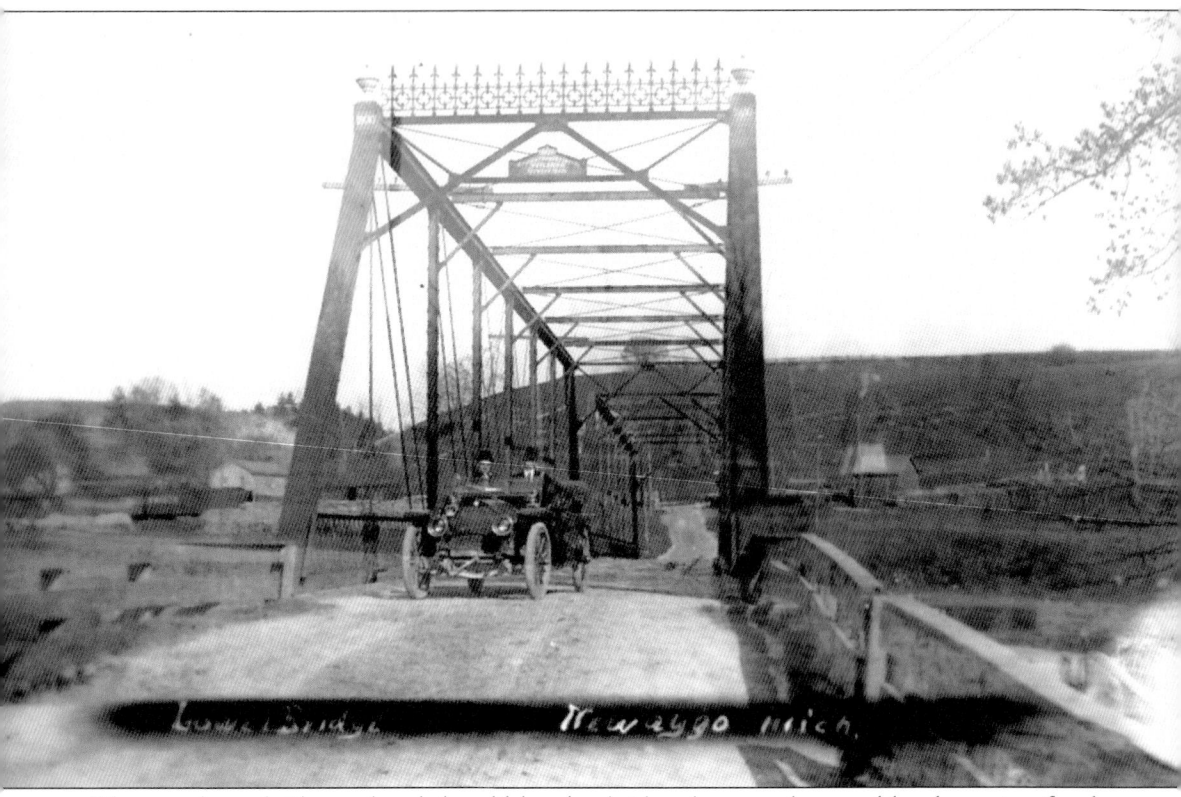

The new lower bridge replaced the old low log bridge that was destroyed by the spring flood of 1900. Banker Hatch is seen out for a spin in his new Hudson, with Louis Eckart the driver. Whiskey Wood was a challenge for any car.

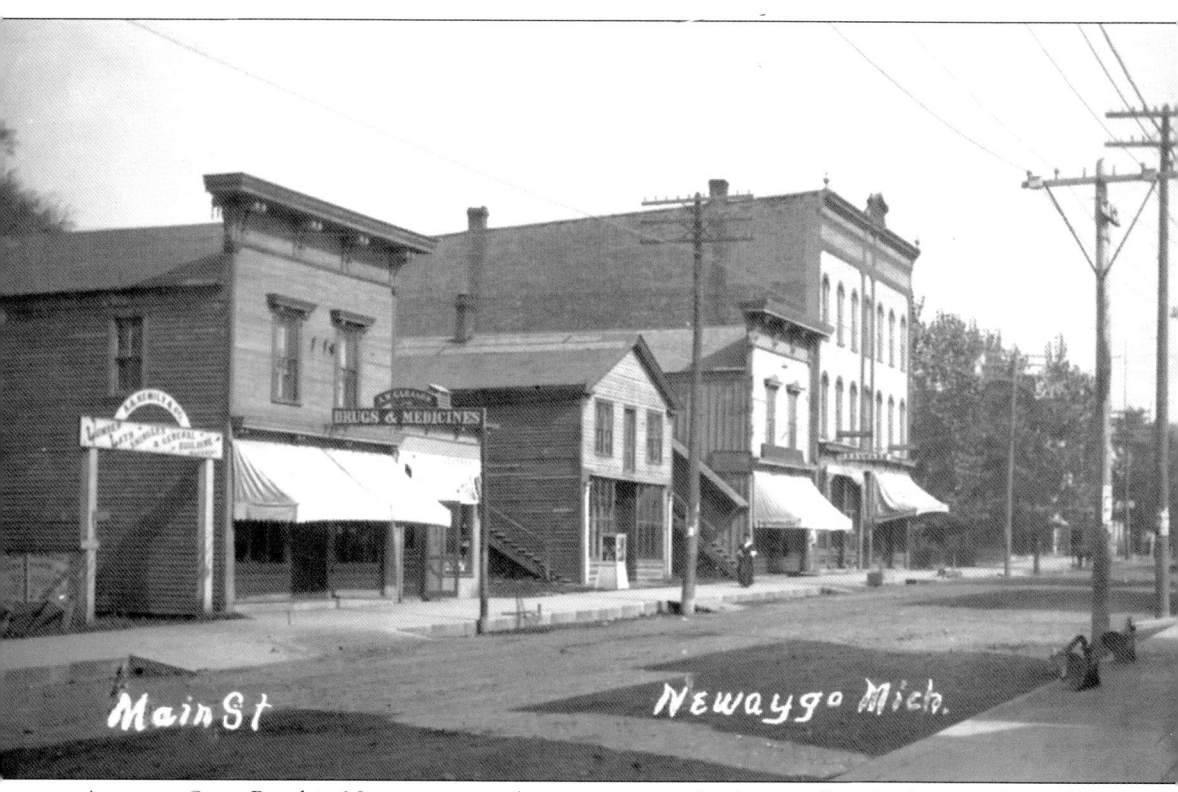

A vacant State Road in Newaygo gives the appearance of a sleepy village basking in the early morning sun. Hemily's (left) is open for business. Next door is Lagasees Jewelry Store, then Bracy's Photo Shop (in the Graves building), Henning Bait Shop (later Shepherd's), an attorney's office, Thompson Grocery (later a parking lot), and Lemire's Drugs (later J. F. A. Raider).

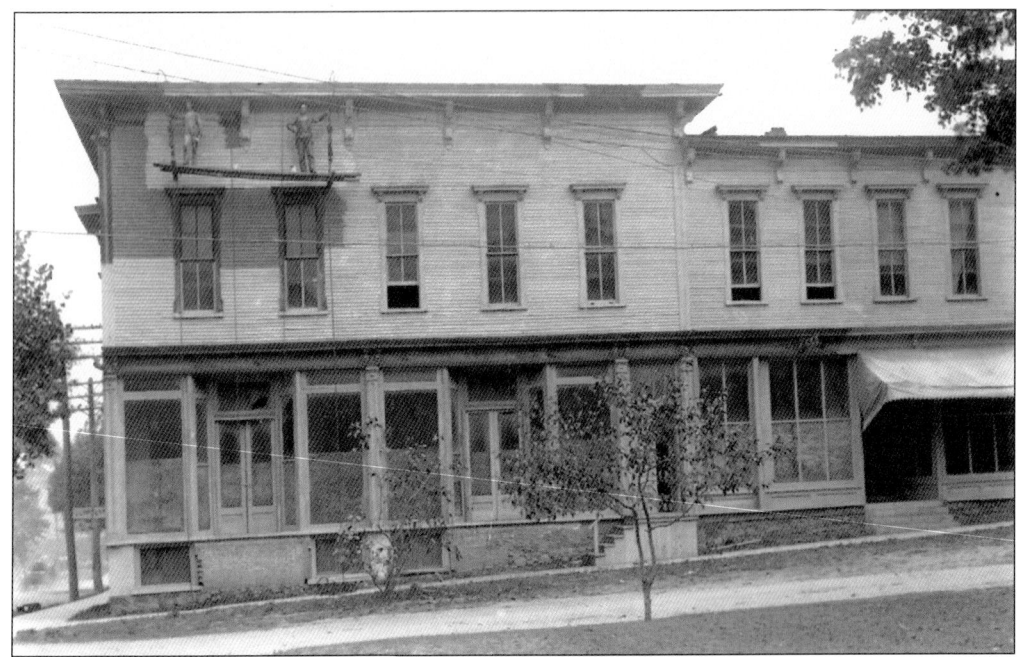

The D. P. Clay Company store was constructed in 1879 during the lumber era. It underwent a remodeling job for use as an uptown office for the Newaygo Portland Cement Company.

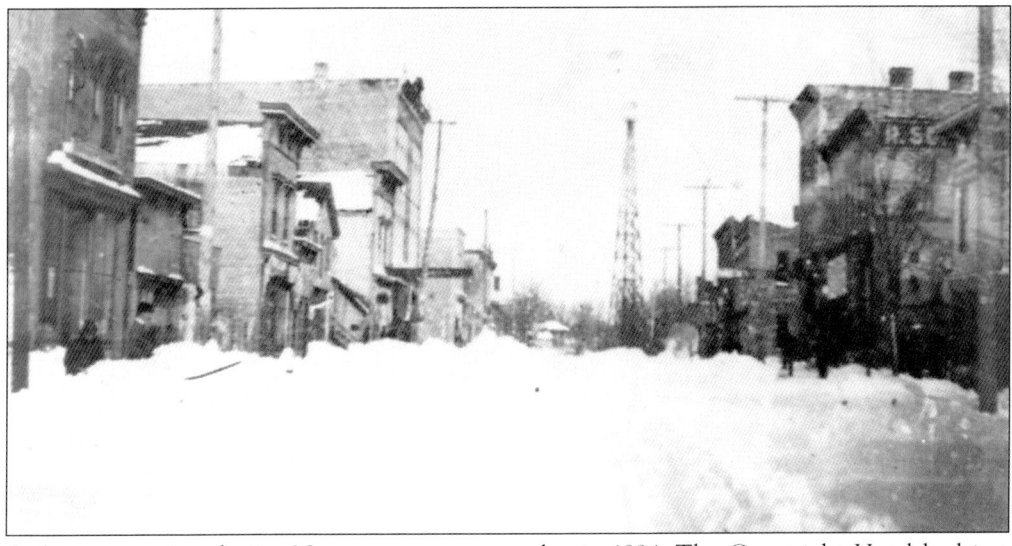

A downtown view depicts Newaygo on a snowy day in 1894. The Courtright Hotel had just completed a light tower at the end of State Road, in Brooks Park, or Court House Square. The hotel owner had a contract with the village council to light the village from a plant he had installed in his barn behind the hotel. This resulted in the first electric lights.

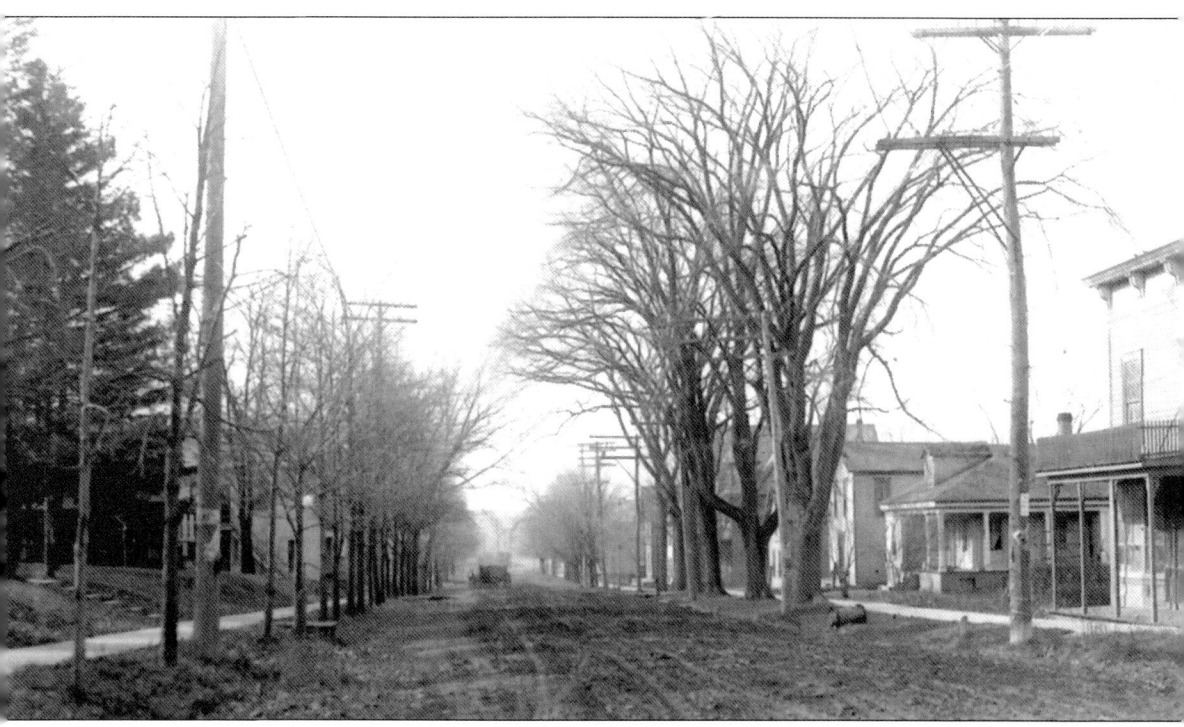

In the spring, State Road in Newaygo is a sea of mud in the 1900s. From left to right are stately elm trees, planted by S. D. Thompson, which were destroyed for the new M-37 road, the Burtons residence, the Cameron residence (supermarket), and the Heron building, which later was occupied by a grocery store and owned by Seymour Gauweiler, who later moved to Oak Grove Corners. The Riblet and Thompson residences are across the street.

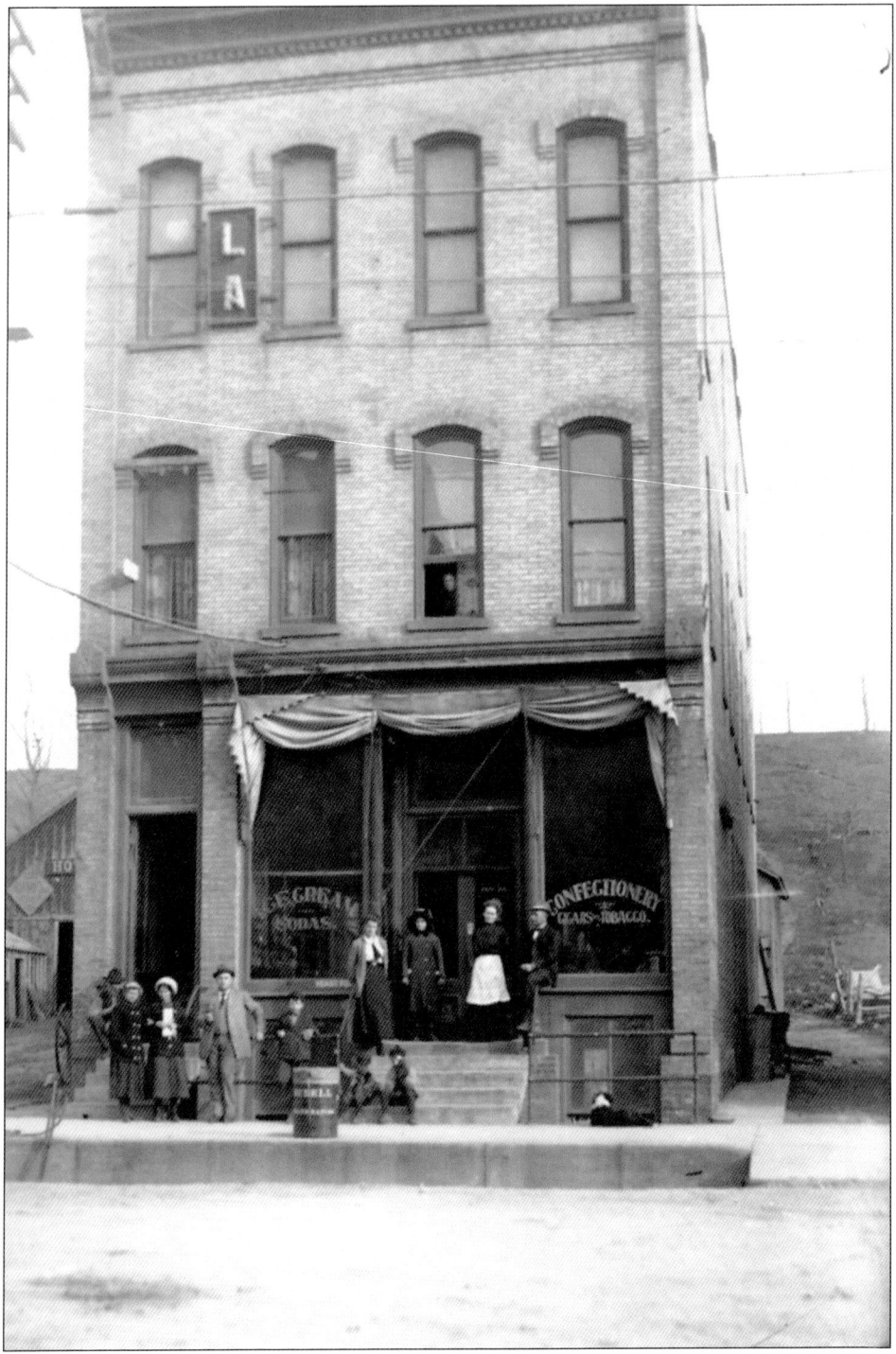

The I. N. Robinson block was built shortly after the fire of 1883. The next owner was George Day, who then sold to Art Dysinger in 1903. Among those pictured are Henry Barrons, Anna Virgis, Art Dysinger, Ruby McKinley, and Mrs. Durand. After many years, the building was purchased by Russell Shepherd, a Newaygo attorney.

*Five*

# Four Seasons of Family Fun

People in Newaygo County have always known how to relax and have a good time. No matter how difficult the times were, people have always found a way to relax and leave their worries behind. Newaygo County is blessed with 234 natural lakes and ponds and 356 miles of rivers and streams covering 12,543 acres; its 349,132 acres of forestlands make it a wonderland for recreational use and family fun.

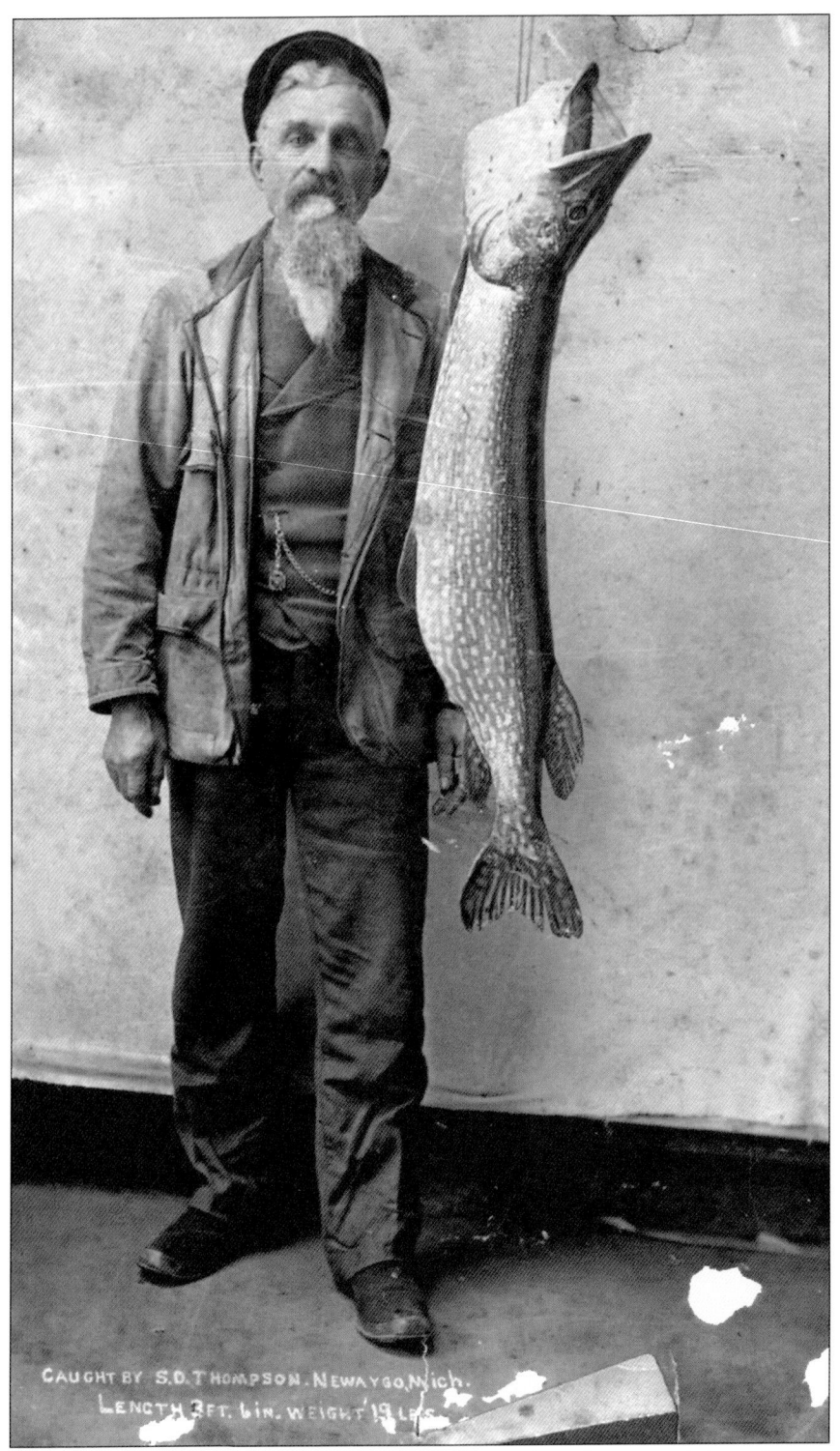
S. D. Thompson holds his prized fish that weighed 19 pounds and measured three feet six inches. Newaygo County was a popular place for sport fishing in the 1900s and still remains so today.

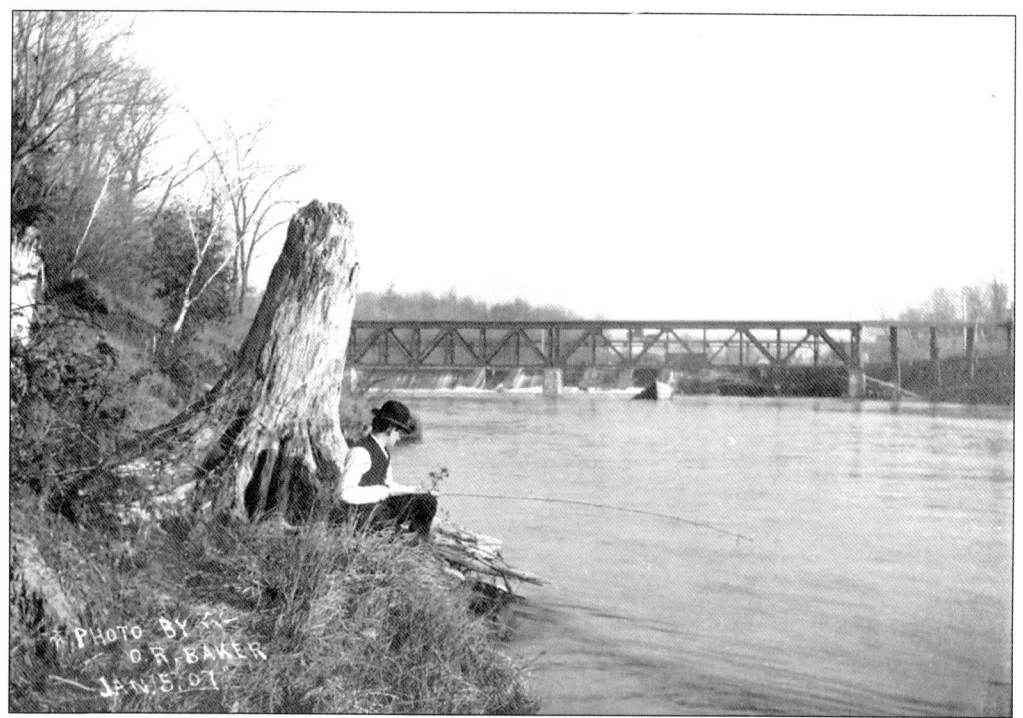

Henry Rowe takes advantage of a nice, quiet Sunday afternoon to go fishing across from the powerhouse. This picture was taken about 1907.

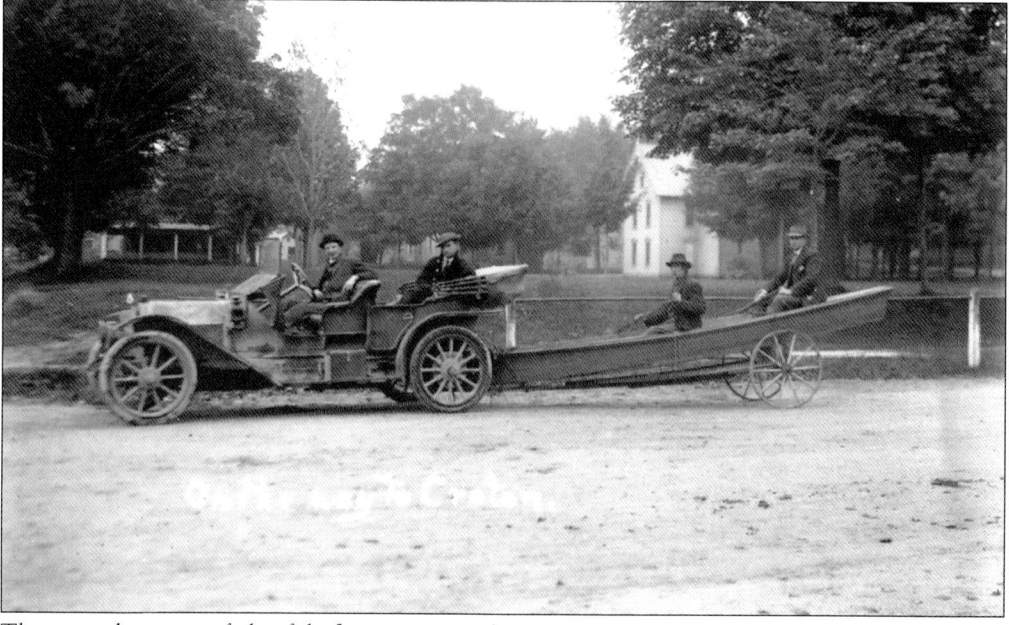

This was the start of the fish float trips on the Muskegon River. The boat was loaded on a homemade wooden trailer with woody buggy wheels with iron tires and hauled to Croton by Ben Bullis using his Buick. Archie McKinley is seated in the back of the car. In the boat are a Newaygo Portland Cement Company employee by the name of Mr. Tillipaugh (left) and guide Dave Joslin.

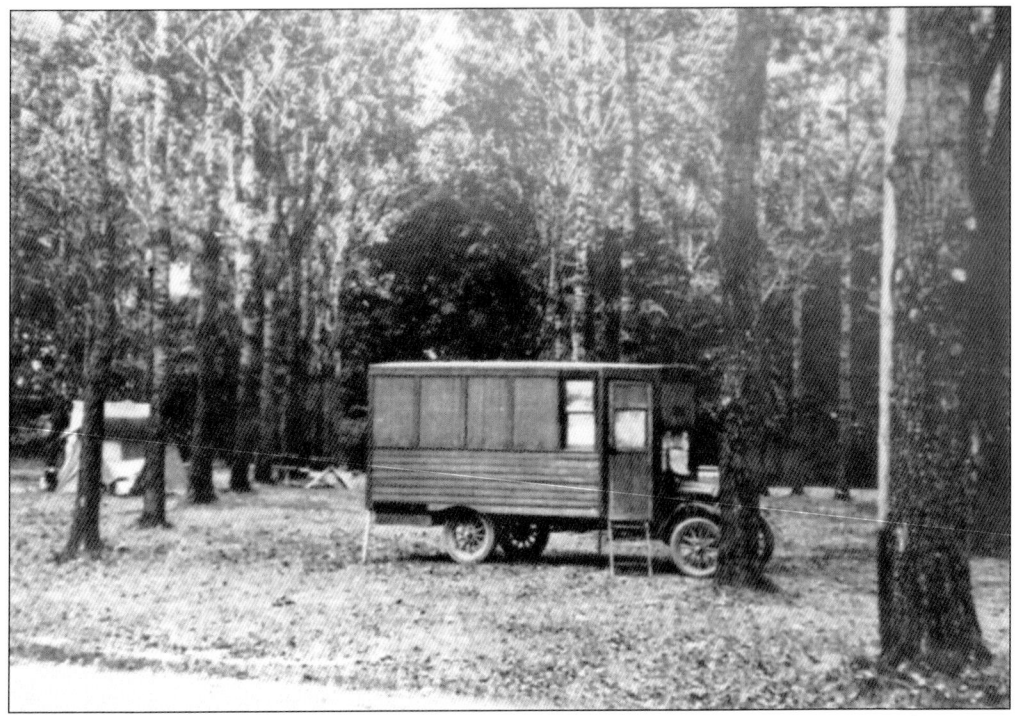

When camping at Fremont Lake in the new fashion, people became very inventive and came up with ways to bring the comforts of home with them to the lake.

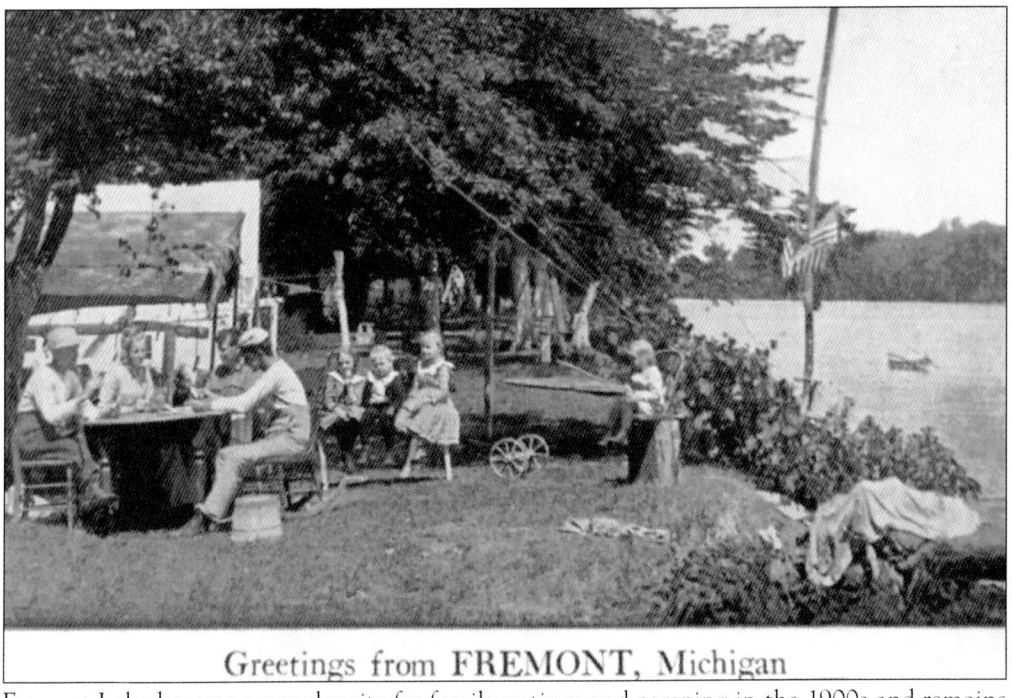

Greetings from FREMONT, Michigan

Fremont Lake became a popular site for family outings and camping in the 1900s and remains so even today. The Grand Army of the Republic held yearly reunions at Fremont Lake for many years.

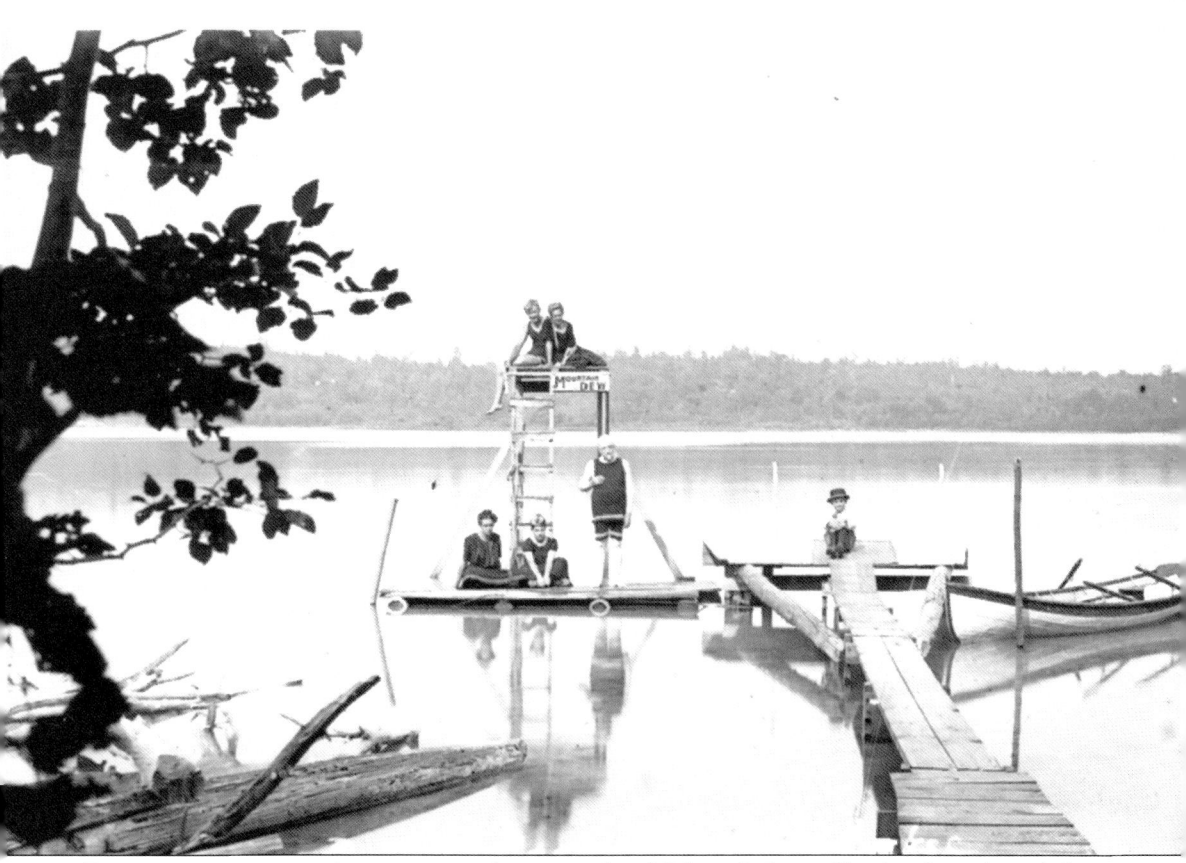

Pioneer resorters rented cottages on the west side of Sylvan Lake at Shepherd's and used the boat dock and diving raft for recreation. Zella Shepherd, her friends, and Grandpa Shepherd are shown enjoying a swim on a hot summer day. Note the extensive wilderness behind the lake shore as it appeared about 1908.

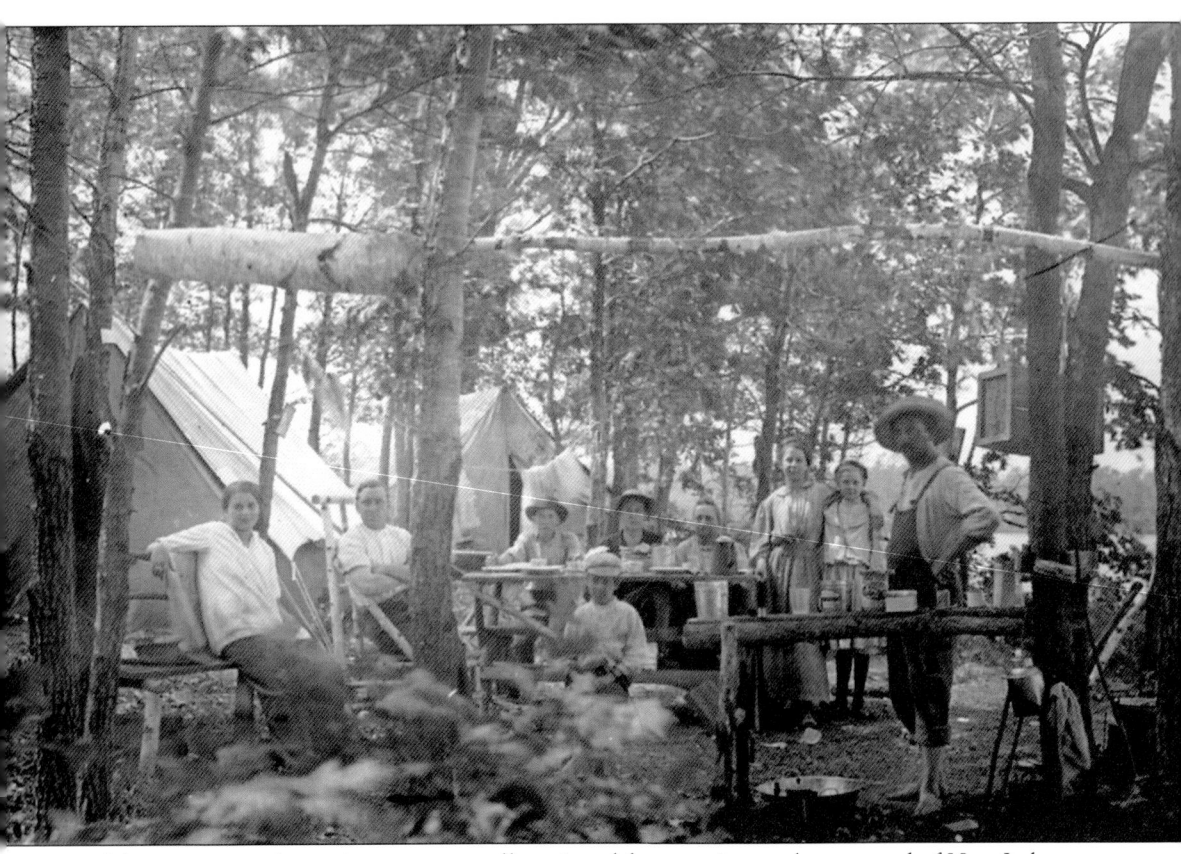
A happy group of vacationers came well equipped for camping at the east end of Hess Lake.

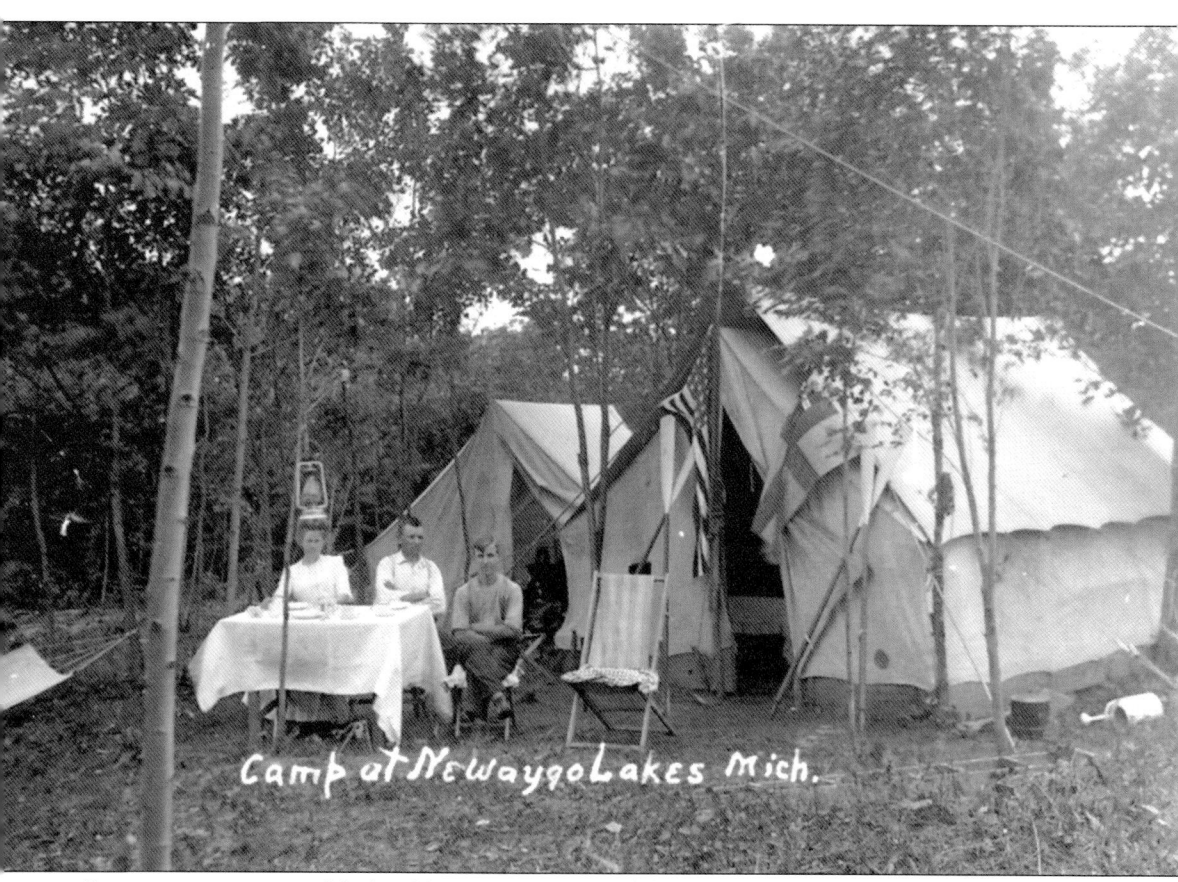

Campers are enjoying Mother Nature at Newaygo lakes in this early-1900s picture. Tents are set up for a kitchen and sleeping quarters. A picnic table is located under the trees along with a restful hammock. A lantern is hung on a pole to provide light.

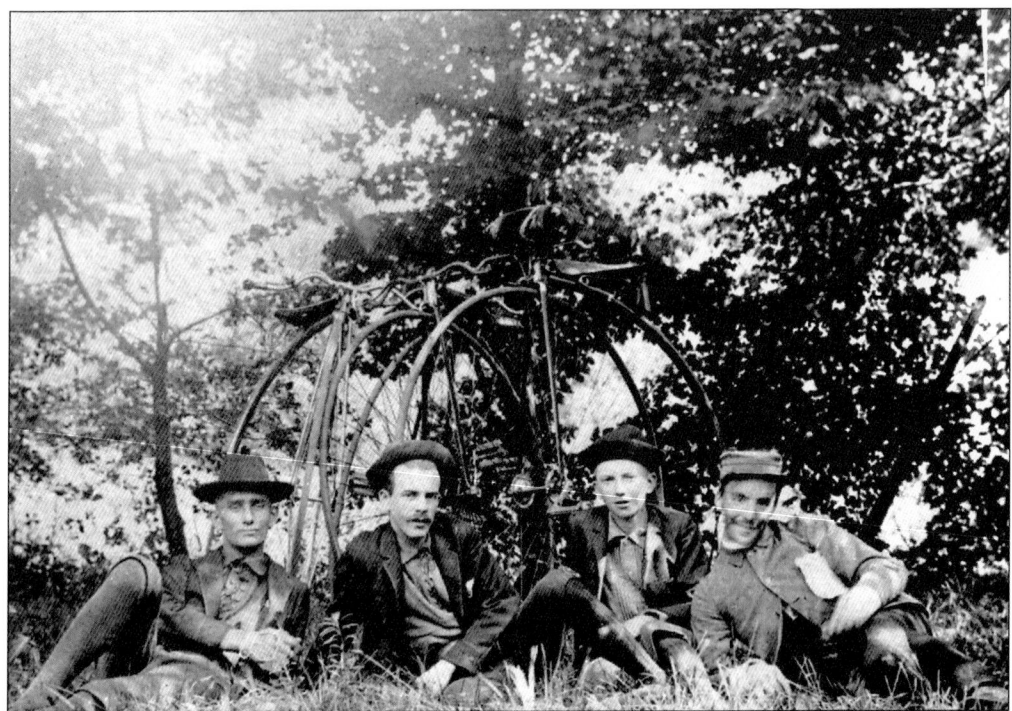
A high-wheel bicycle group from Newaygo poses for this picture in 1888. Pictured are, from left to right, Frank VanLeuven, Lou Thompson, Fred Riblet, and Fred Jacobi. A bicycle path from Newaygo to Hess Lake had been started, and this group was helping to complete it. The path was later clayed to make it a speedway. It was heavily traveled until the automobiles took over.

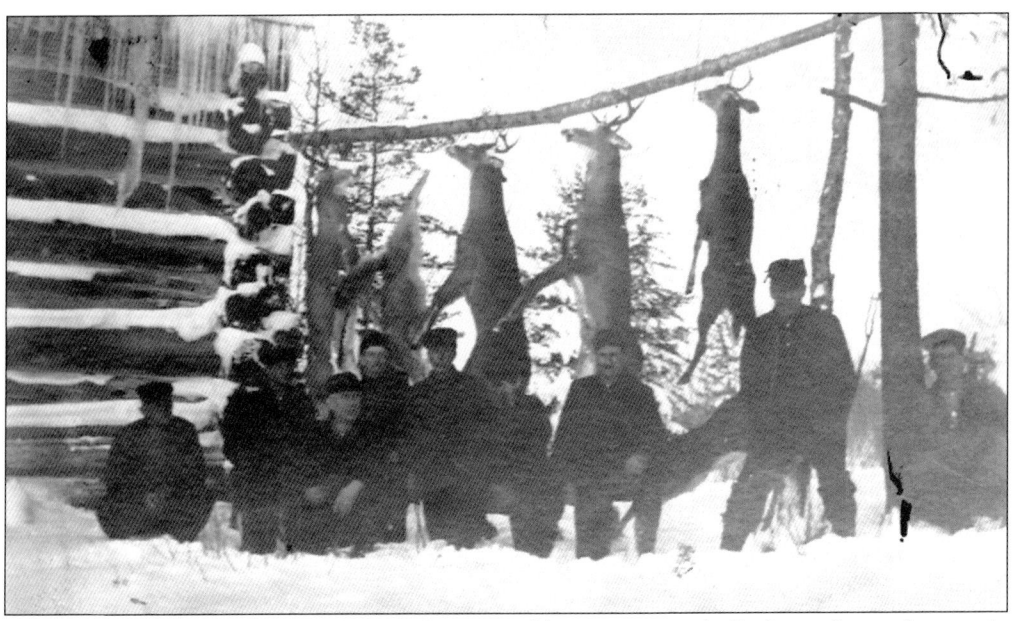
Newaygo County has long been known for its good hunting grounds. Early residents often made it through long winters by feeding their families wild game. In later years, hunting became a popular sport.

# Six
# THE MELTING POT

Many people came to Newaygo County looking for cheap fertile land for farming and raising livestock. The climate and rich soils made it ideal for the farmers who brought their knowledge of farming with them. These settlements gave the businessmen a new area to expand their trade. Many men brought their families and settled in Newaygo County, and many of those old family names still live on today throughout the county.

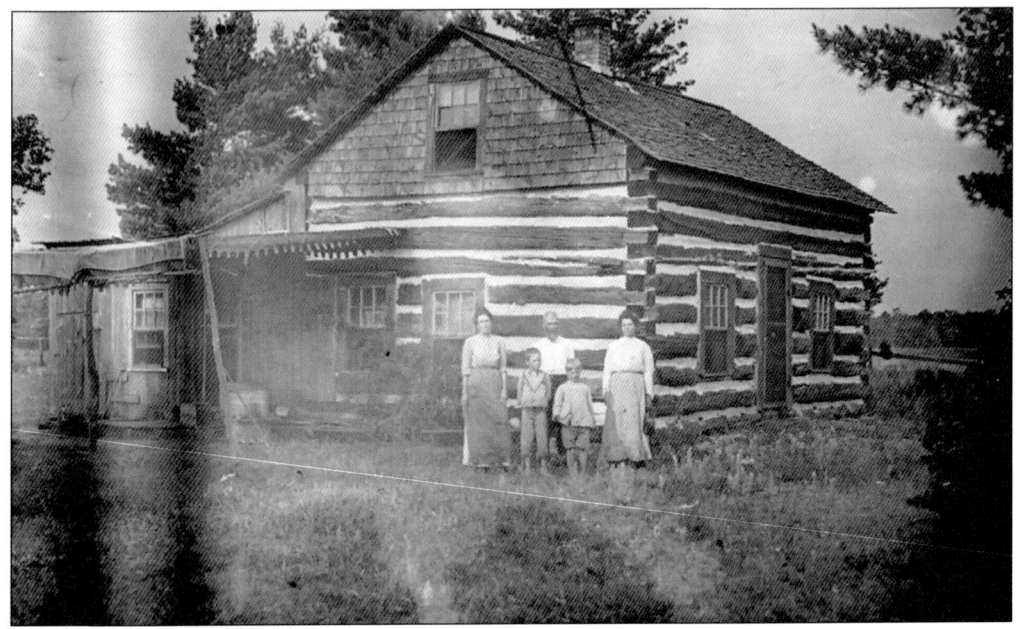
Cabins were a common shelter for pioneer settlers in Newaygo County. This cabin was located on Croton Road.

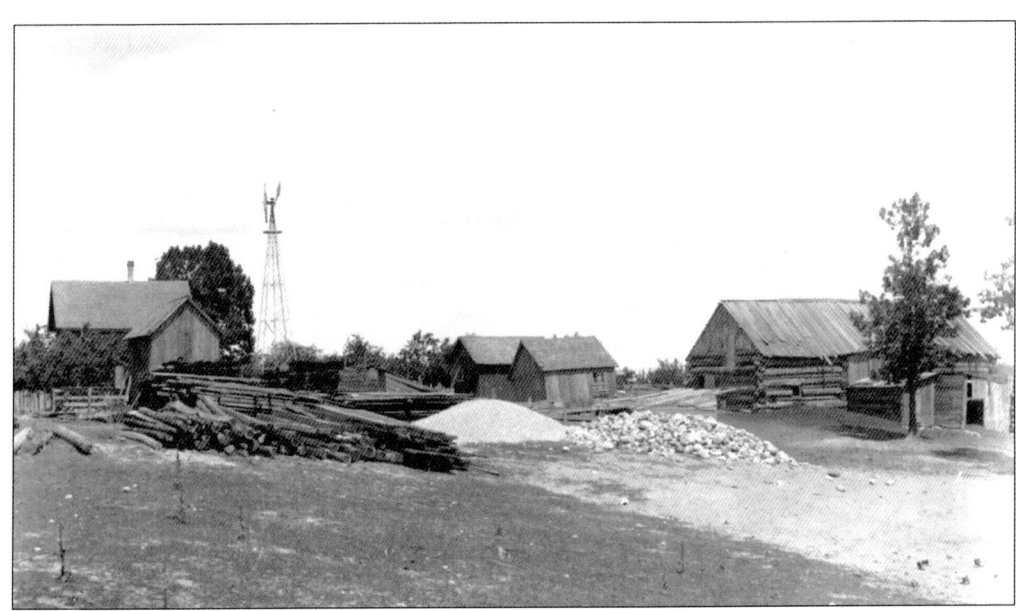
A pioneer farm in Ensley Township is pictured here. The prosperous farmer is getting ready to build a large barn to replace the old log buildings. Note the large pile of stones and sand for the foundation and lumber and timber for the upright.

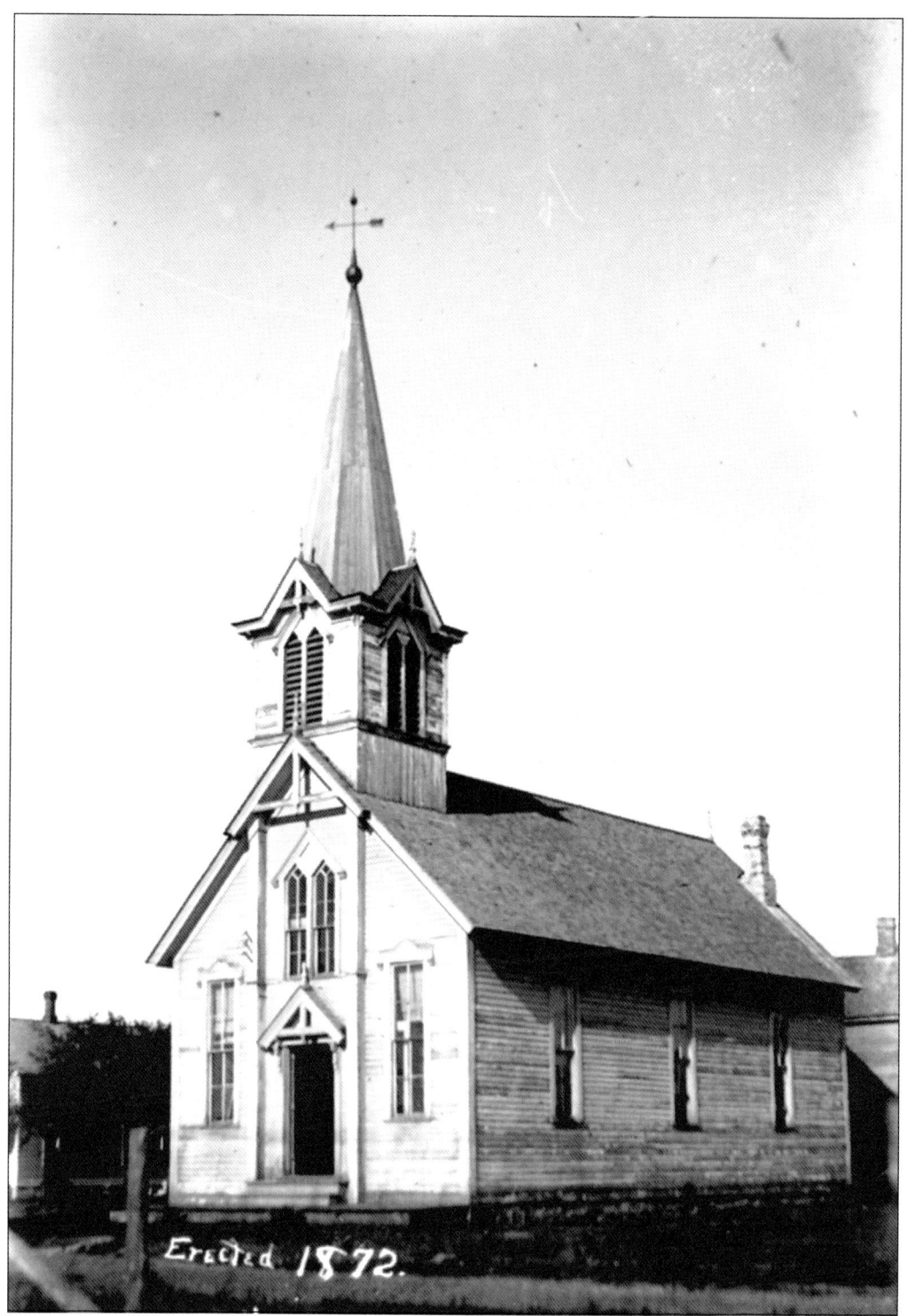
The Congregational Church of Croton was erected in 1872 and is still at the same location.

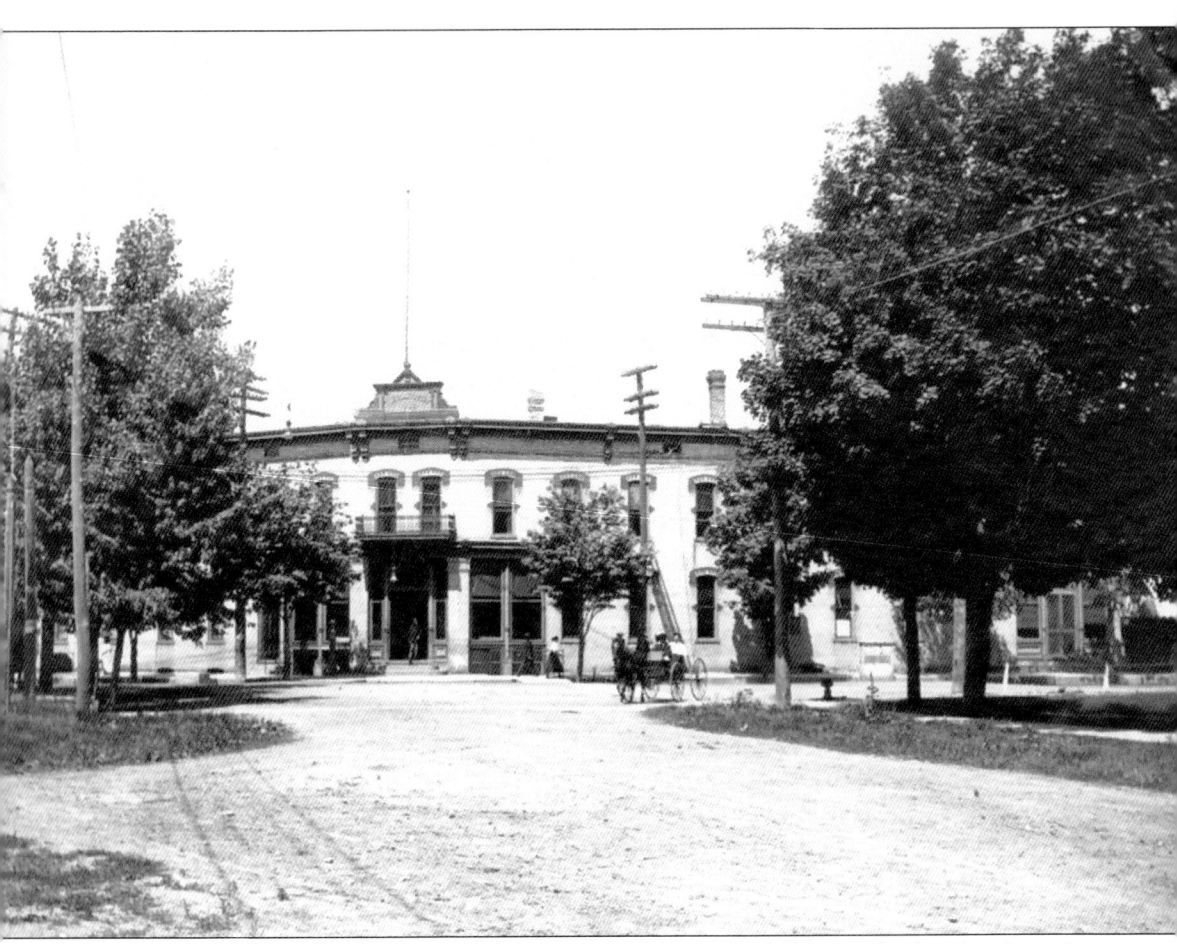
The Courtright Hotel was built by Aaron Courtright in 1883 following the big fire. Later his son, Will, joined the management and eventually took over the business. It continued to be a first-rate establishment for many years.

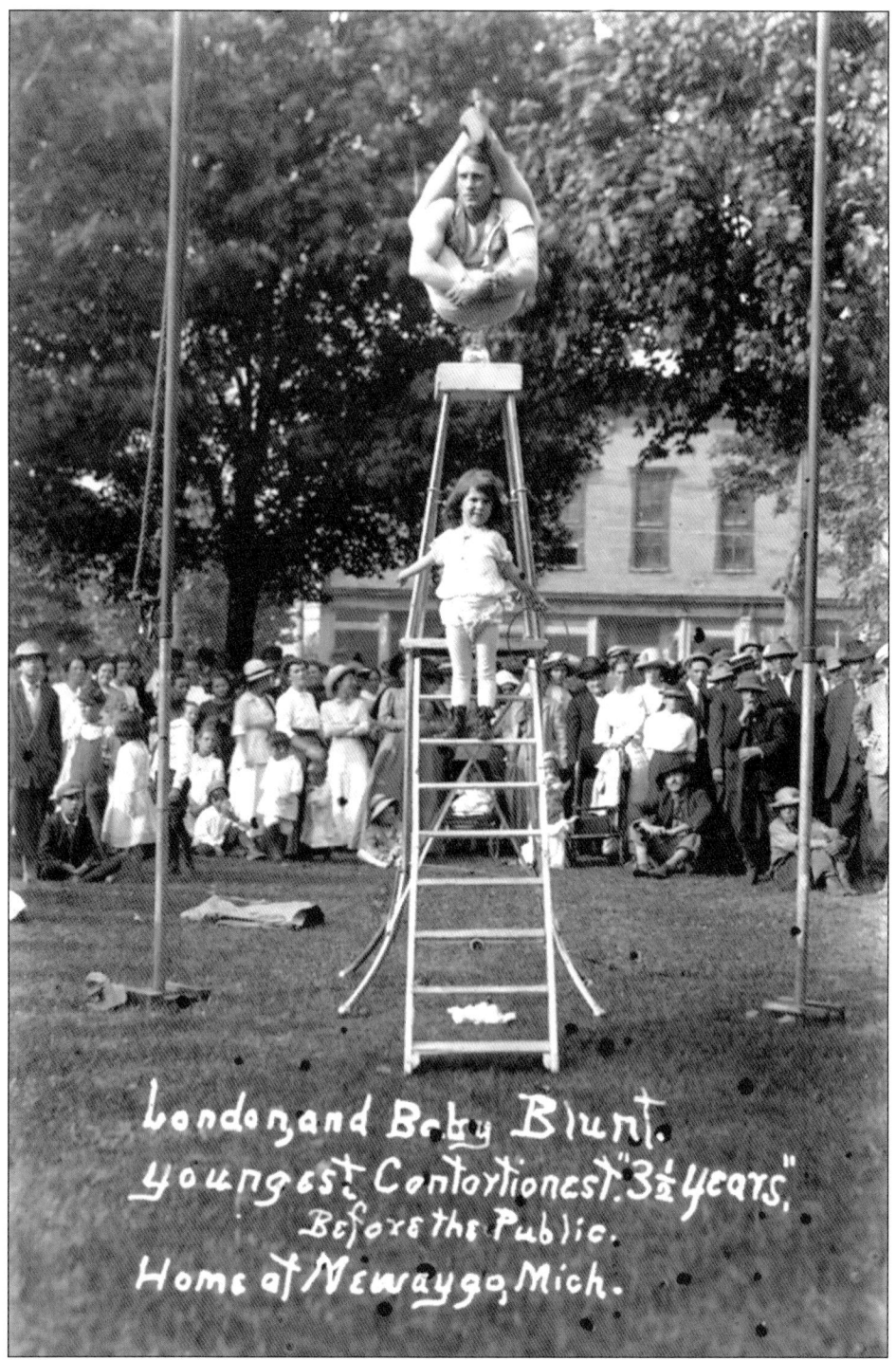

London and baby Blount entertain the crowd at Newaygo's annual Labor Day picnic, which was held in Brooks Park. It was first a homecoming affair, featuring a potluck at noon with free coffee, cream and sugar, and watermelon. All the acts were free. London owned a farm on the river road below the lower bridge.

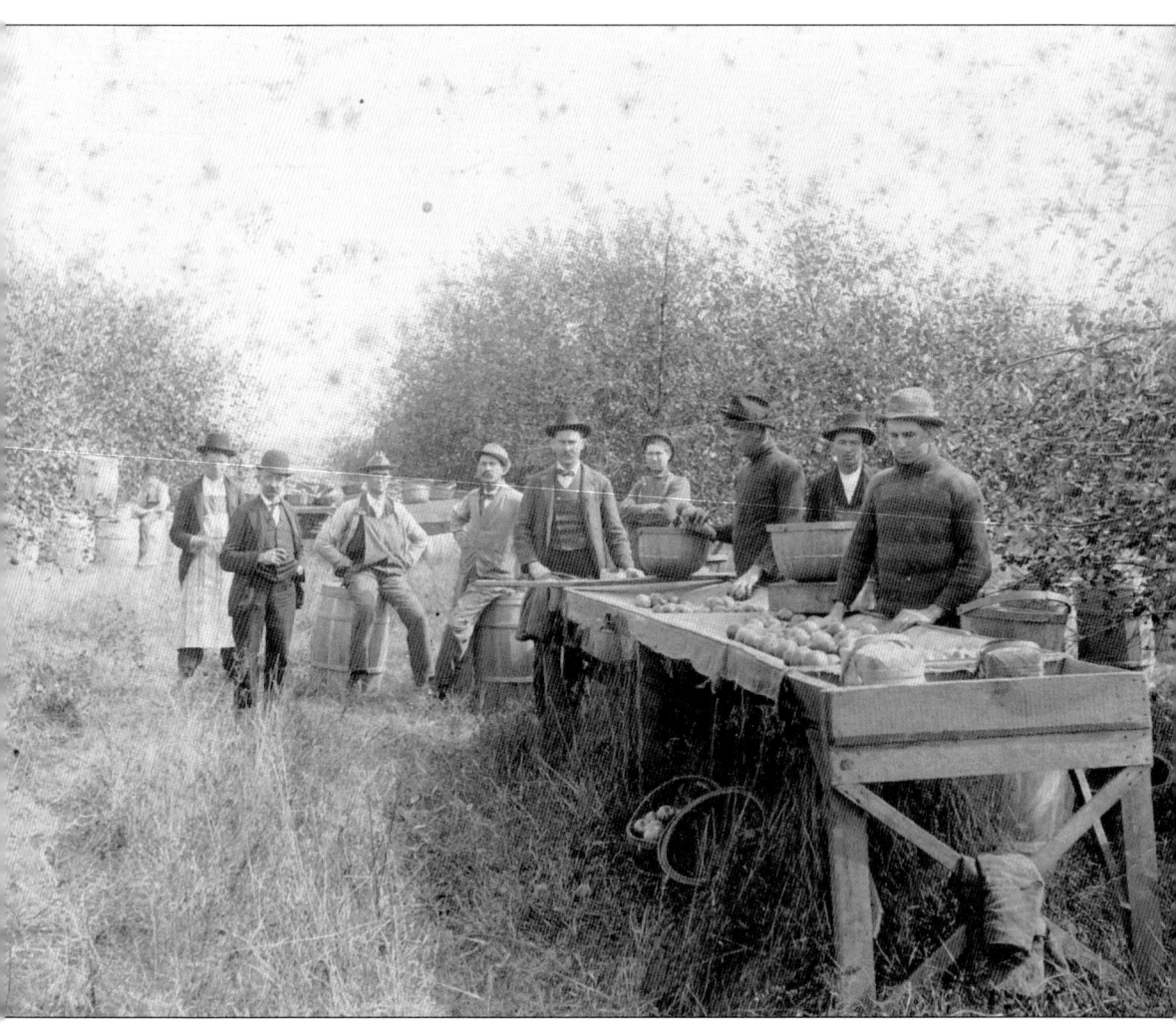

At first, dairy farms of the area supplied the local lumbering camps and mills with vegetables, fruits, meats, milk, and butter. The farms had a market at the tannery for the cow hides, to be made into leather. The land was cheap, and the soil was good. As the large pines were depleted and the lumber companies moved on to other areas, the farmers needed to find a new market. They found there was a market in the larger cities for their products, so with the aid of the railroads that had been built for shipping lumber to the cities, a new market was opened up to them. The farmers did not have time to milk the cows, separate the cream, make the butter, take it to the depot, and wait for the train, and the need for creameries arose. After the farmers completed their milking, they dropped their milk off at the creameries, which separated the milk and cream, made the butter and cheese, and shipped it off to the cities.

Many people provided services as needed in Newaygo County. This gentleman brought a cart full of wood into Fremont Center daily to sell.

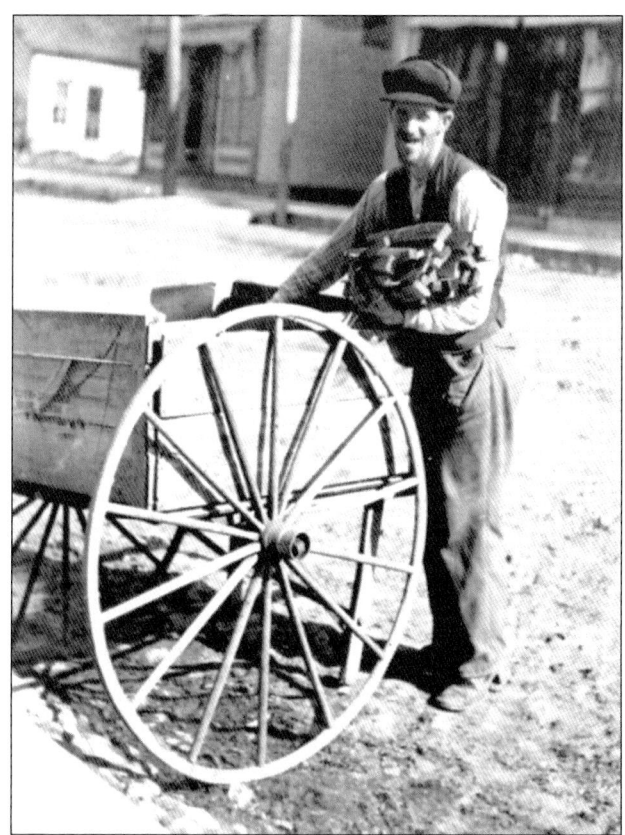

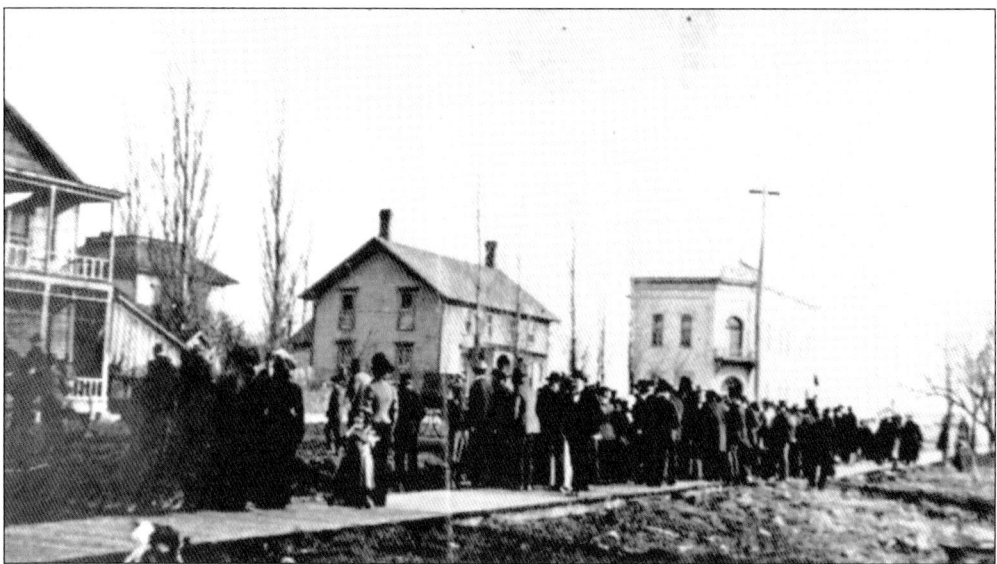

The first Cow Testing Association in the United States was organized in the Fremont Grange Hall on December 6, 1905. A bronze plaque was put on the hall near the west door in 1956. The plaque inscription read, "In the hall on December 6, 1905, there was organized the first Cow Testing Association in America, to the Dairymen of this community whose vision made this organization possible, this plaque is dedicated."

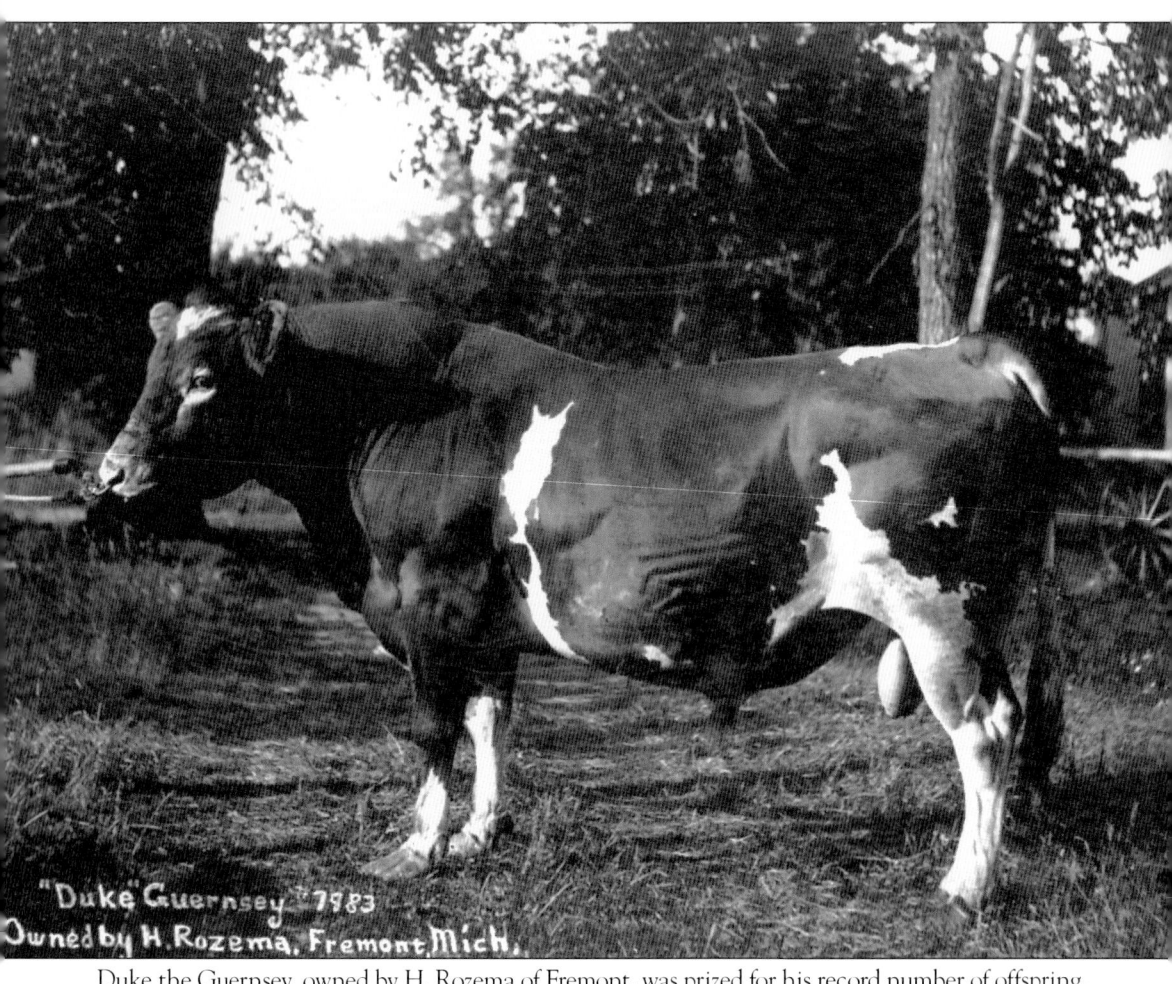
Duke the Guernsey, owned by H. Rozema of Fremont, was prized for his record number of offspring.

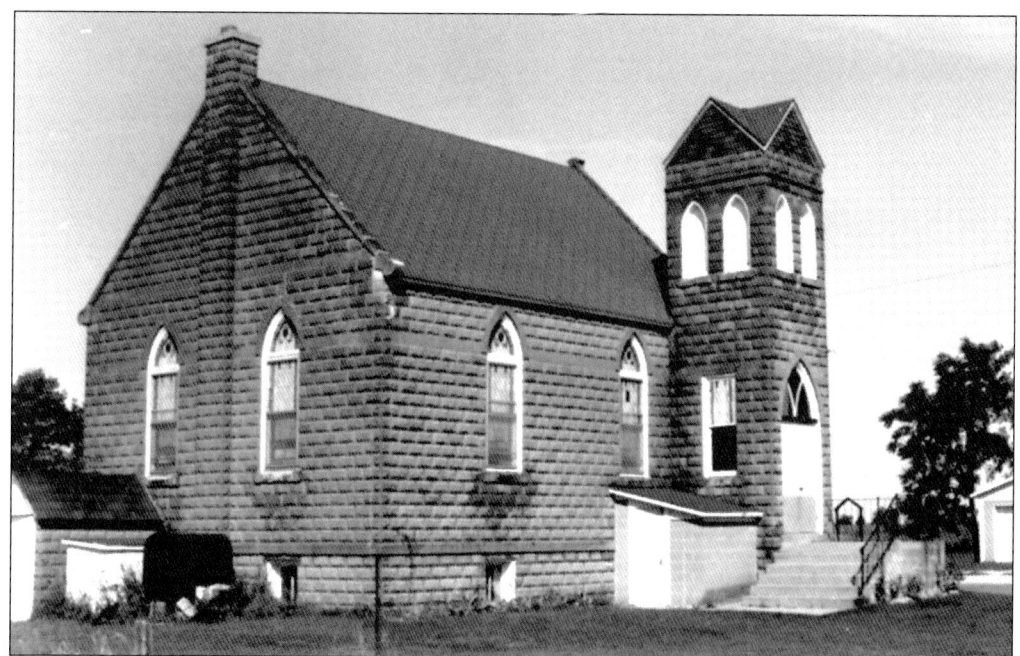

Sitka is located on the township line between Sheridan and Bridgeton Townships. The settlement was first called Sugar Bush because of the existence of a forest of hard maple trees, which made sugar, both regular and maple. A post office was established there one year after the Alaska purchase in 1867. The office was named Sitka after Sitka, Alaska.

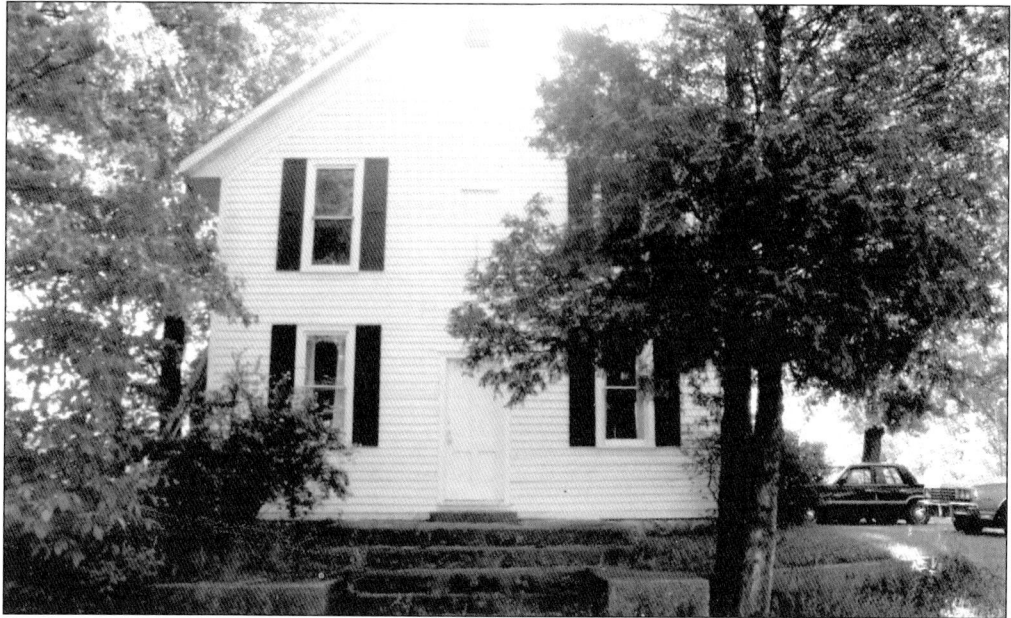

The Big Prairie Grange No. 935 was formed on November 1, 1901, by 44 citizens from the Big Prairie area. After meeting in renovated quarters for several years, the Big Prairie Grange No. 935 agreed in 1903 to join with Big Prairie Township to construct a township hall building that the Grange could also use for its meetings. Old logging buildings 10 miles from the site were taken down, and the materials were used for building the new structure.

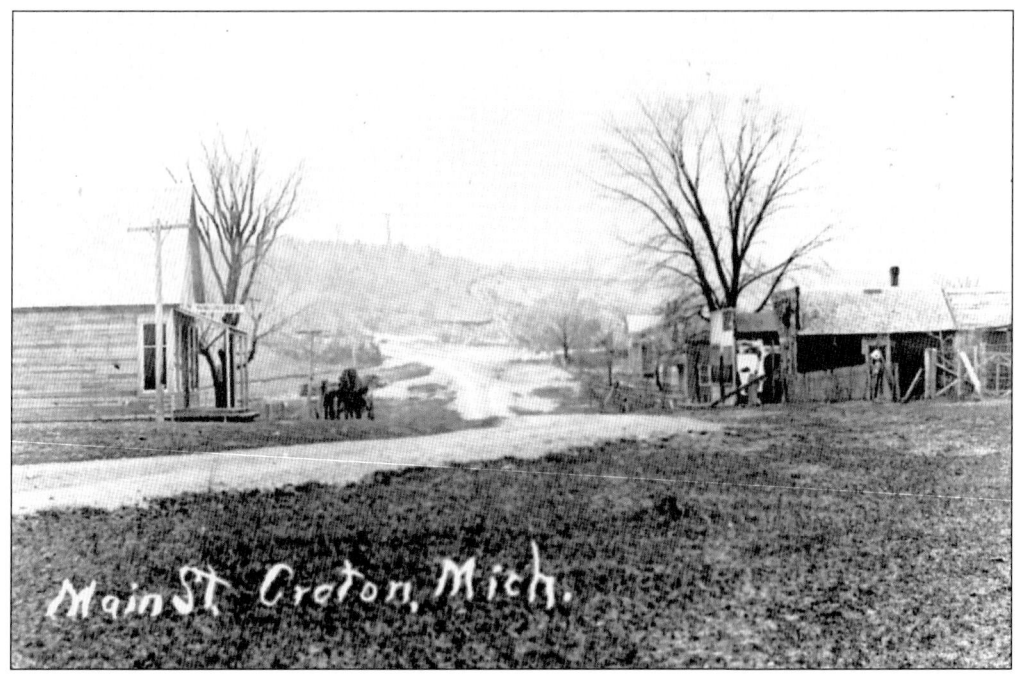
Main Street in Croton is pictured before the flooding of the town in April 1907, when the Croton Dam was put into place. The community was left intact and flooded over.

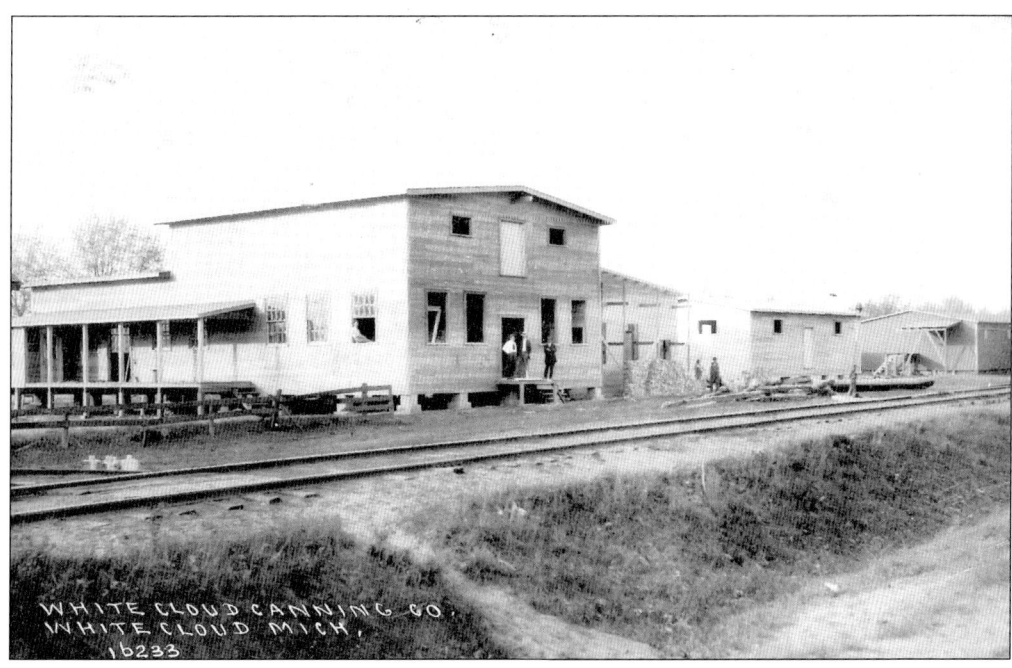
The canned produce made by the White Cloud Canning Company was shipped by the railroad, which was located next to the canning company.

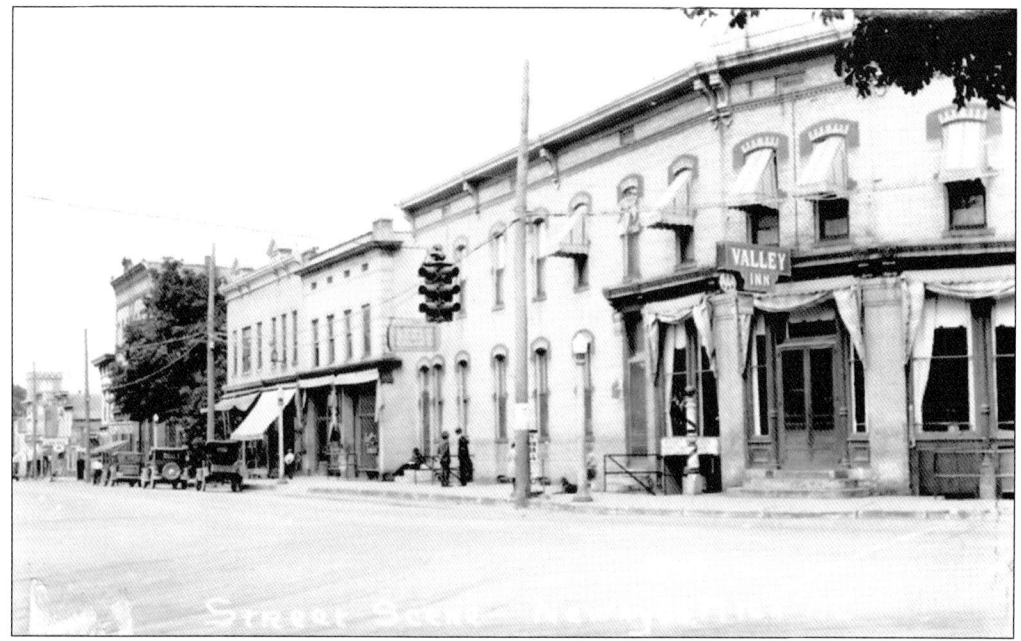

The first stop-and-go traffic light was installed in front of the Valley Inn in Newaygo. The light was later replaced by a flashing caution light, which remained in use until recently, when a new stop-and-go traffic light was installed.

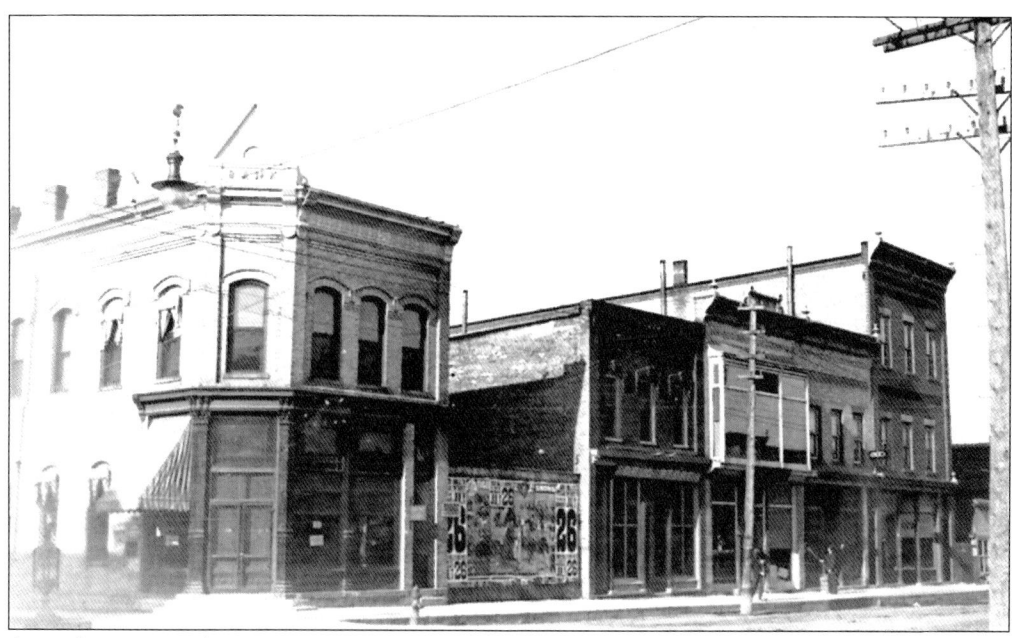

A southwest view shows Main Street in Fremont around the dawn of the 20th century. The Old State Bank (now Huntington Bank) building is on the left, and the Eagle Drug Store is the next building. Notice the sign on the wall indicating that the circus is coming to town.

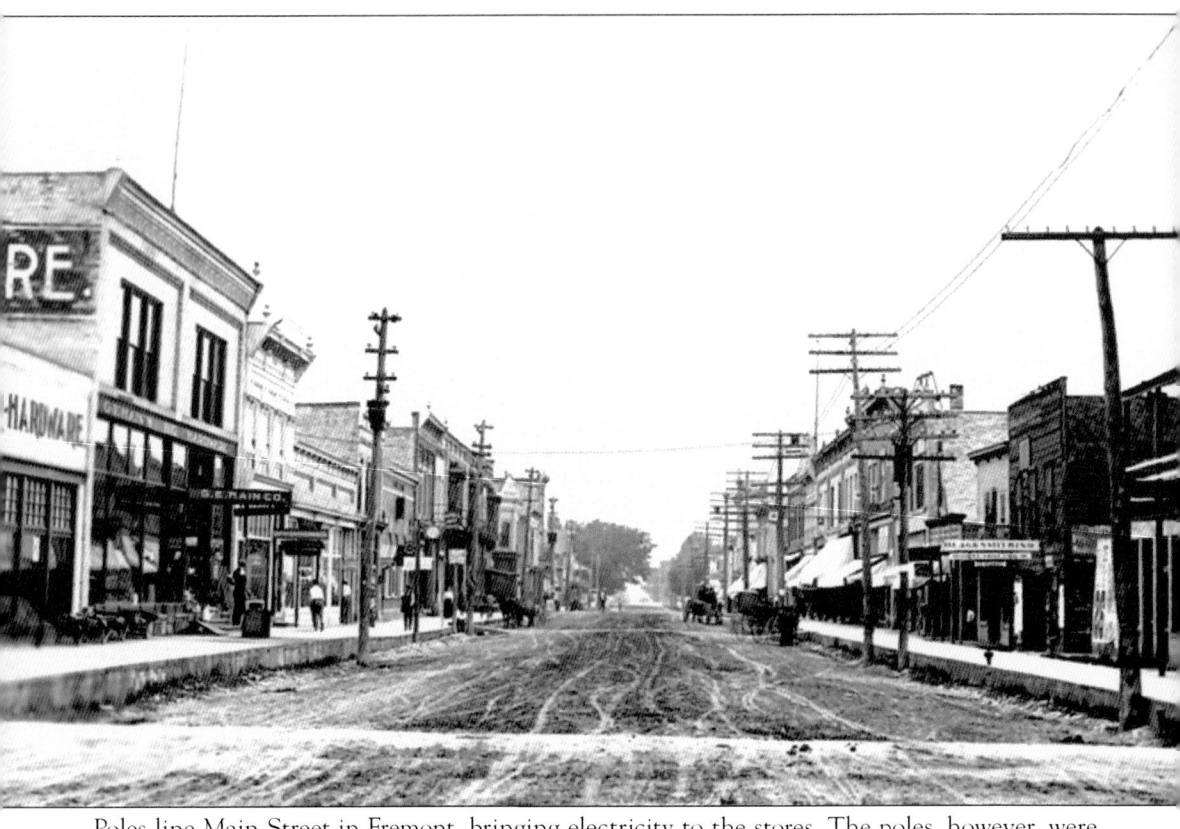
Poles line Main Street in Fremont, bringing electricity to the stores. The poles, however, were not very attractive, and it was decided to move the poles to the alleyways behind the stores.

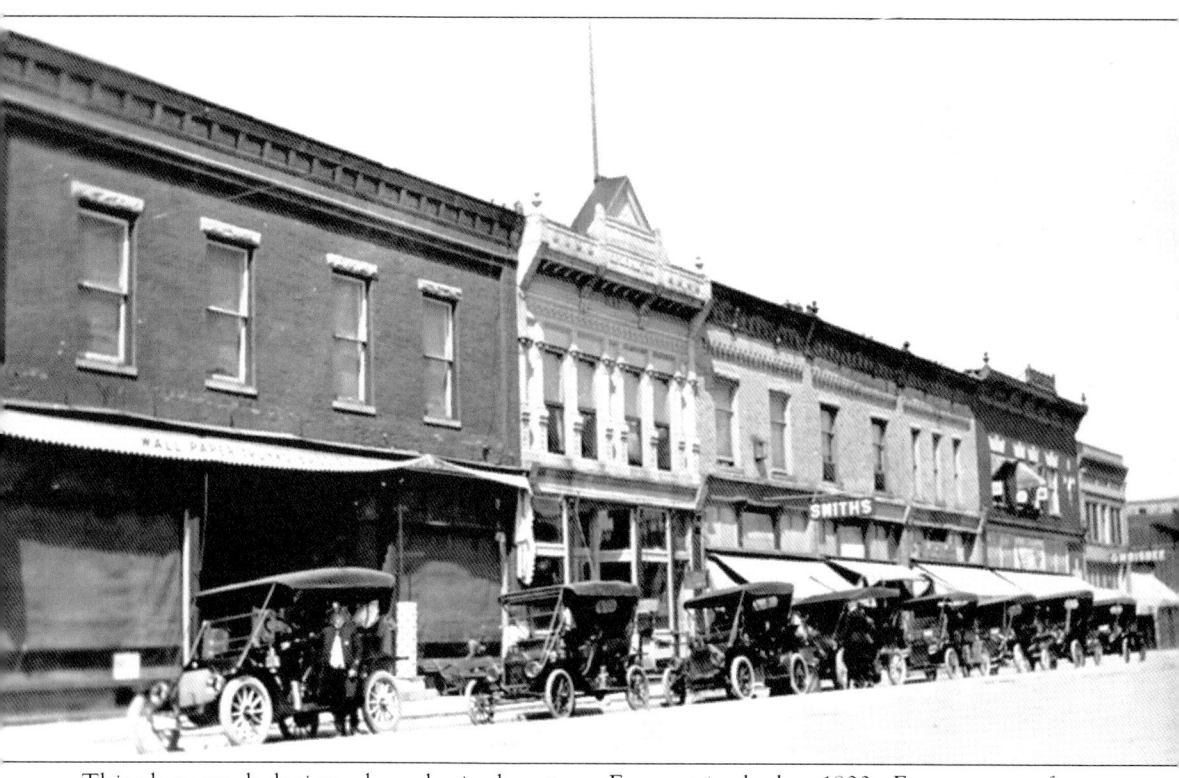

This photograph depicts a busy day in downtown Fremont in the late 1800s. Fremont was often the hub of activity and became a rapidly growing community.

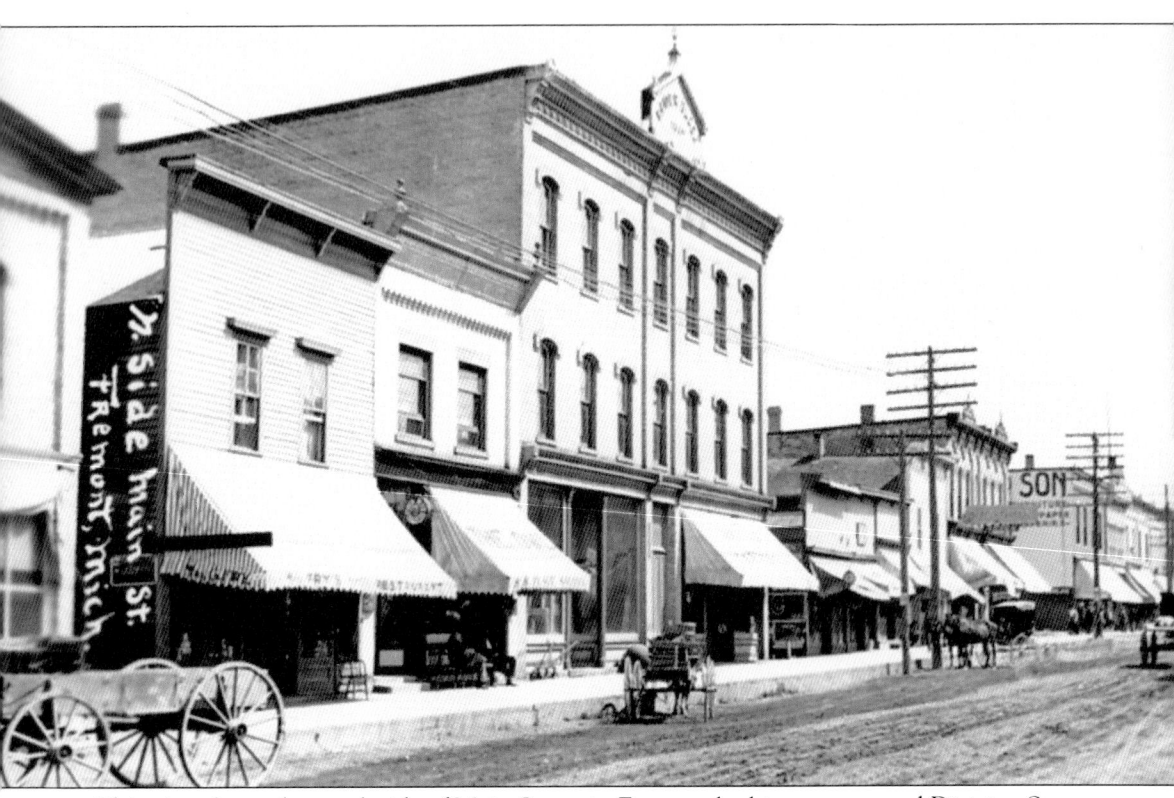
This view shows the north side of Main Street in Fremont looking east toward Division Street. The first building on the left with the awning is Fry's Restaurant.

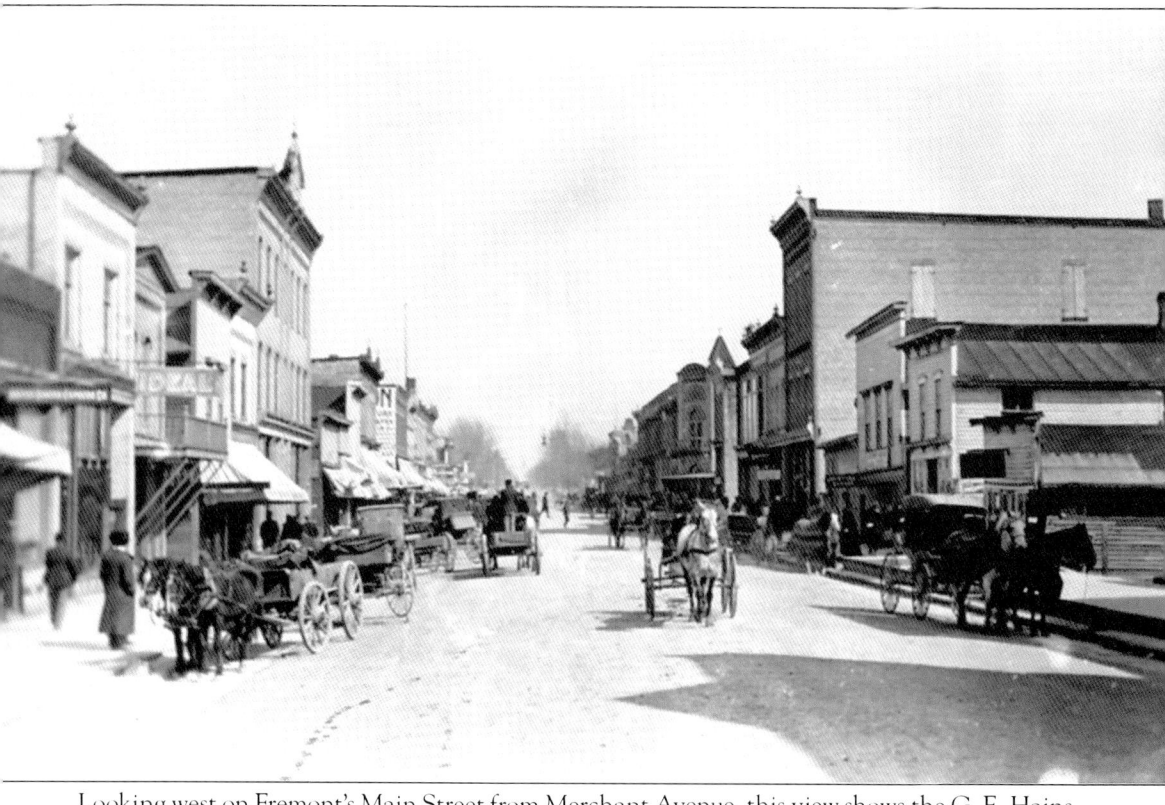
Looking west on Fremont's Main Street from Merchant Avenue, this view shows the G. E. Hains Hardware Store, located at 34 East Main Street (on the left) from 1888 to 1912.

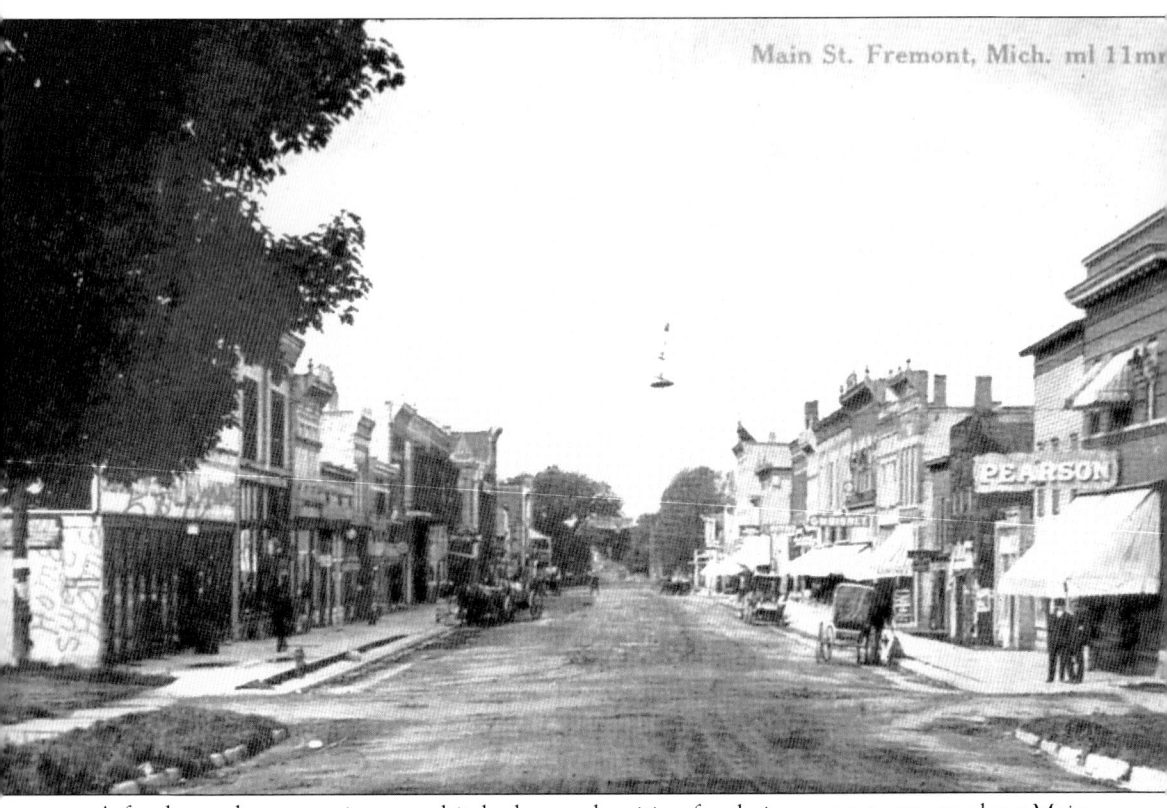

A few horse-drawn carriages are hitched up and waiting for their owners to return along Main Street in Fremont.

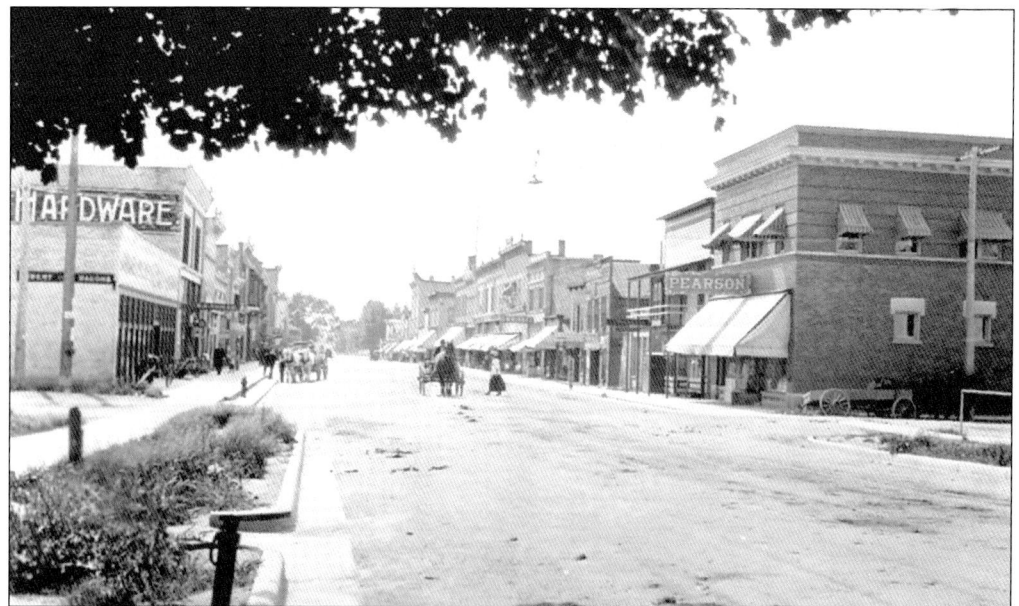
Looking west from Merchant Avenue in downtown Fremont, Pearson's Dry Good Store is on the right.

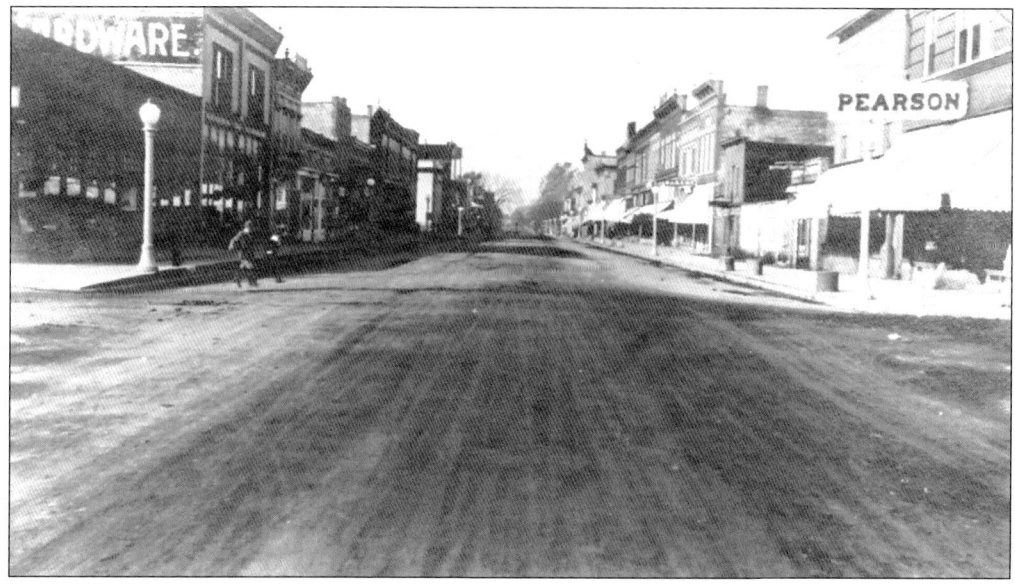
Night lamps appear along the edge of the sidewalks along Main Street in Fremont to light the way.

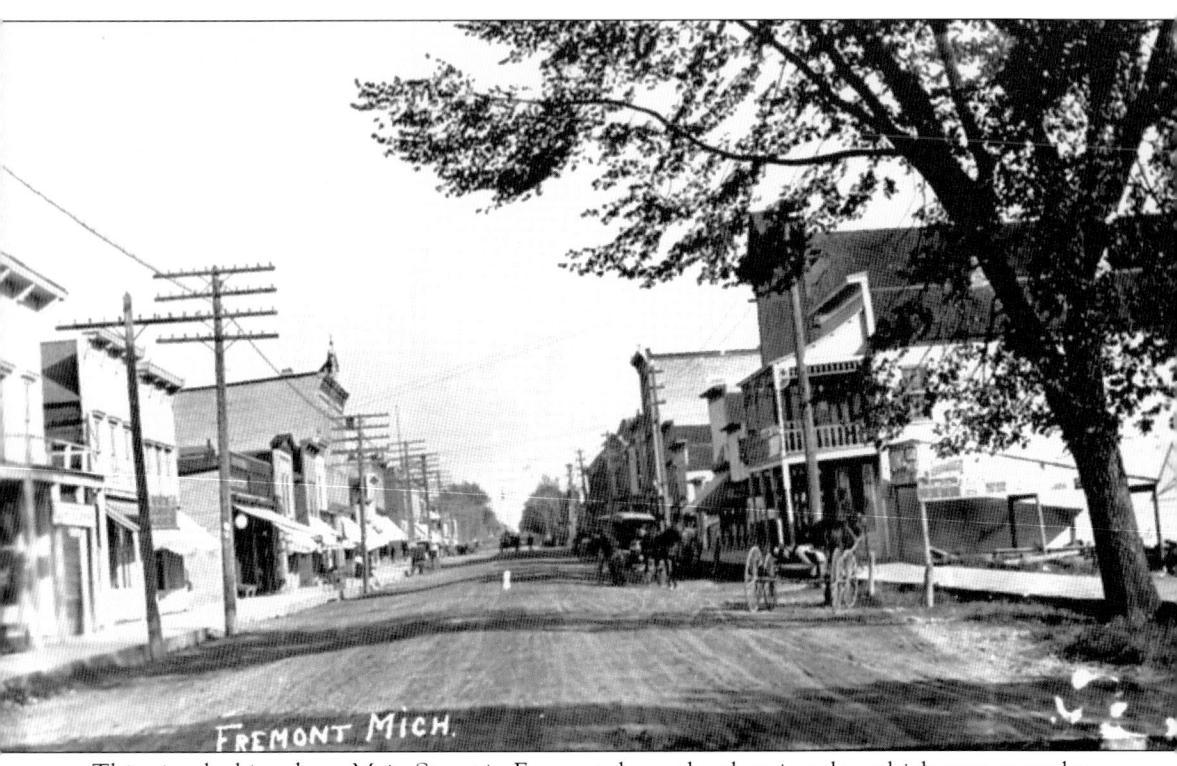

This view looking down Main Street in Fremont shows the electric poles, which were moved to the back alleyways.

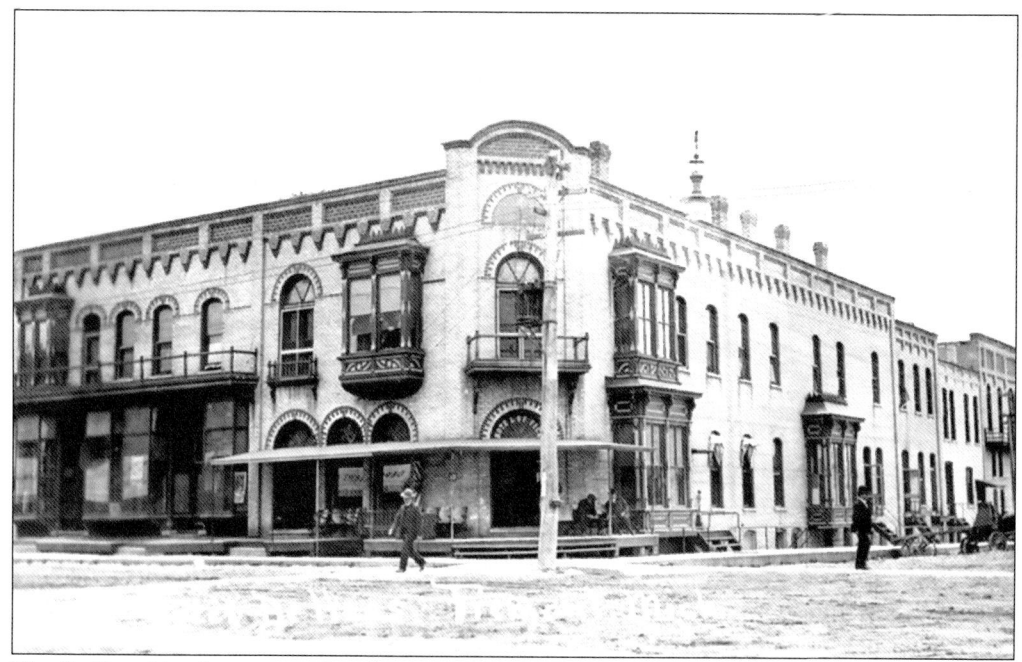

The DeHaas Hotel was owned and operated by John DeHaas from 1888 to 1923 and was located at 2–4 Main Street on the southeast corner of Main and Division Streets in Fremont. The DeHaas Hotel was a hub of activity in Fremont Center and was visited by many people.

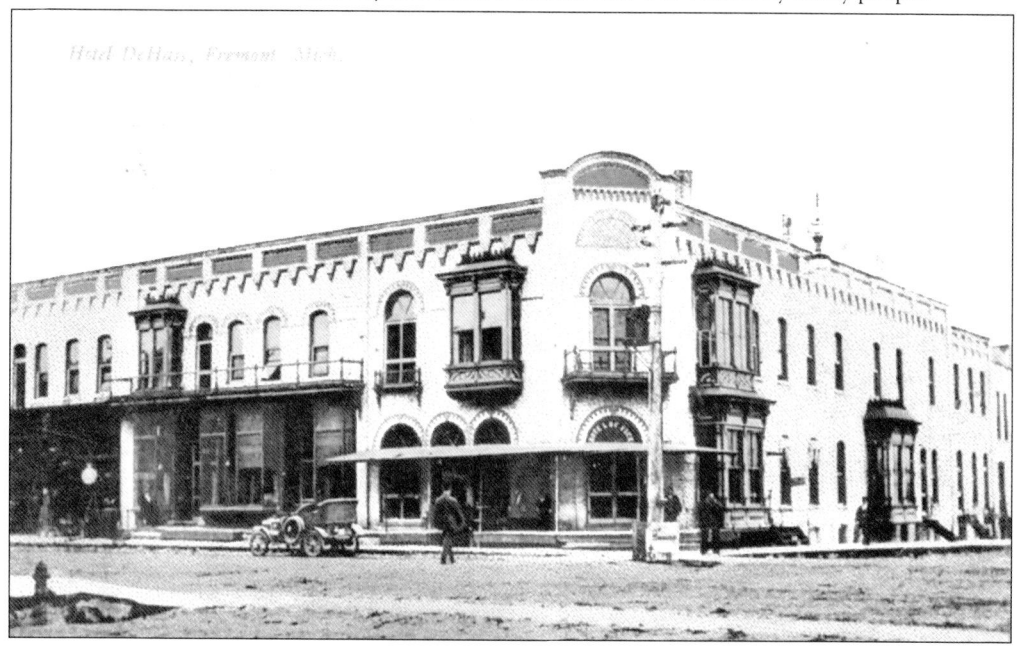

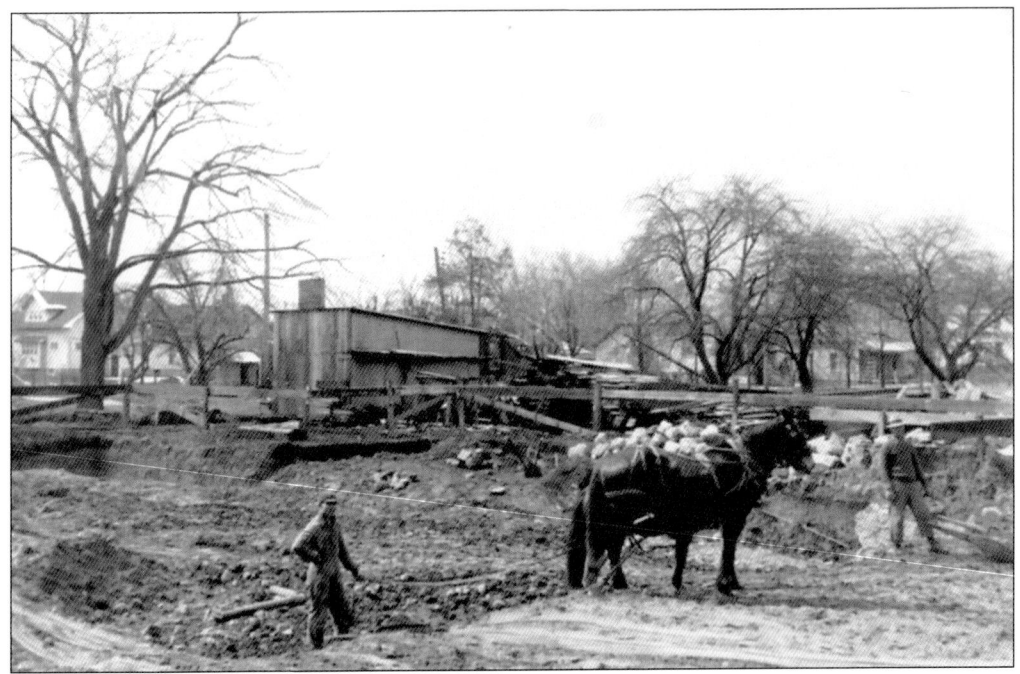
Construction of a new post office building in Fremont began in the 1930s on South Division Street, where it is located today.

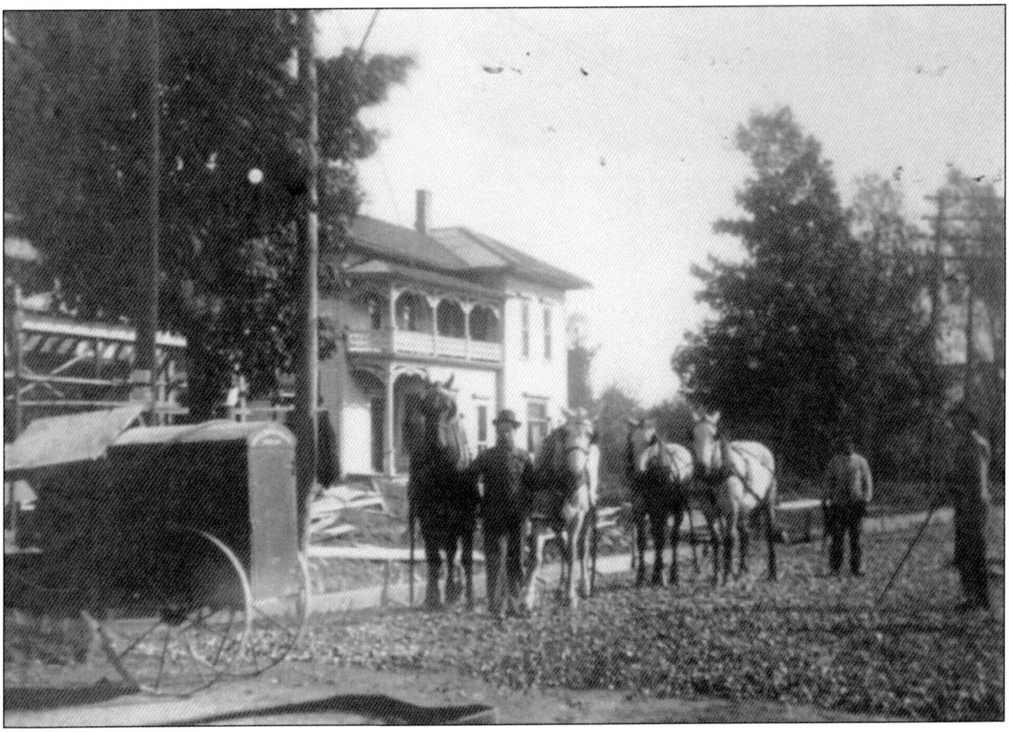

A road construction crew works on Main Street, east of Stewart Street.

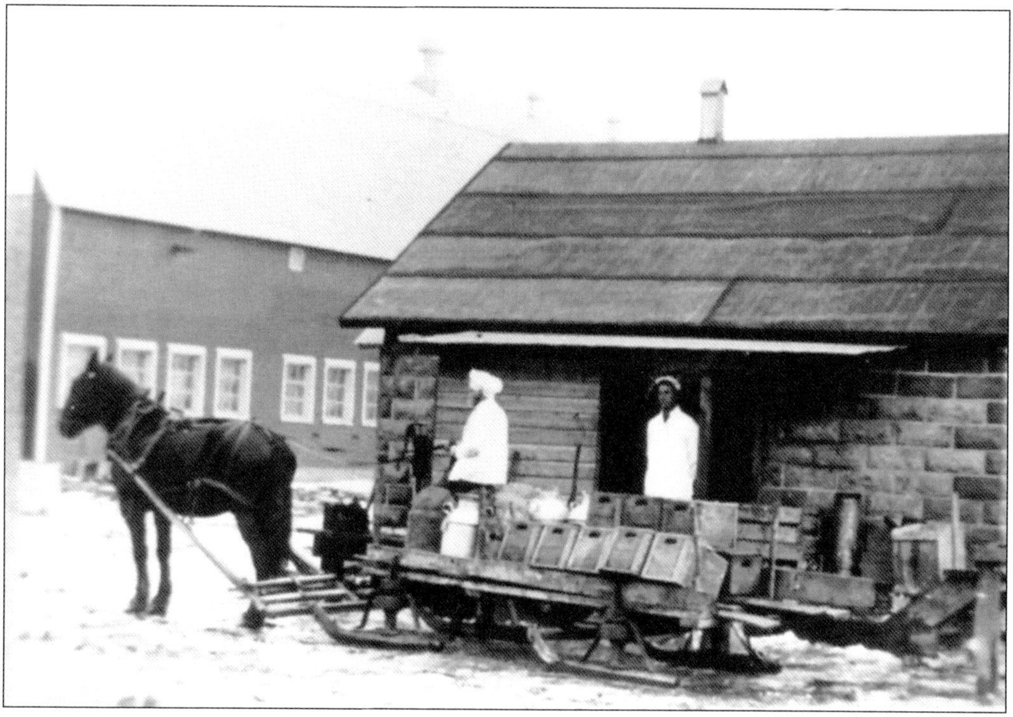

A sleigh is loaded and ready to make its deliveries.

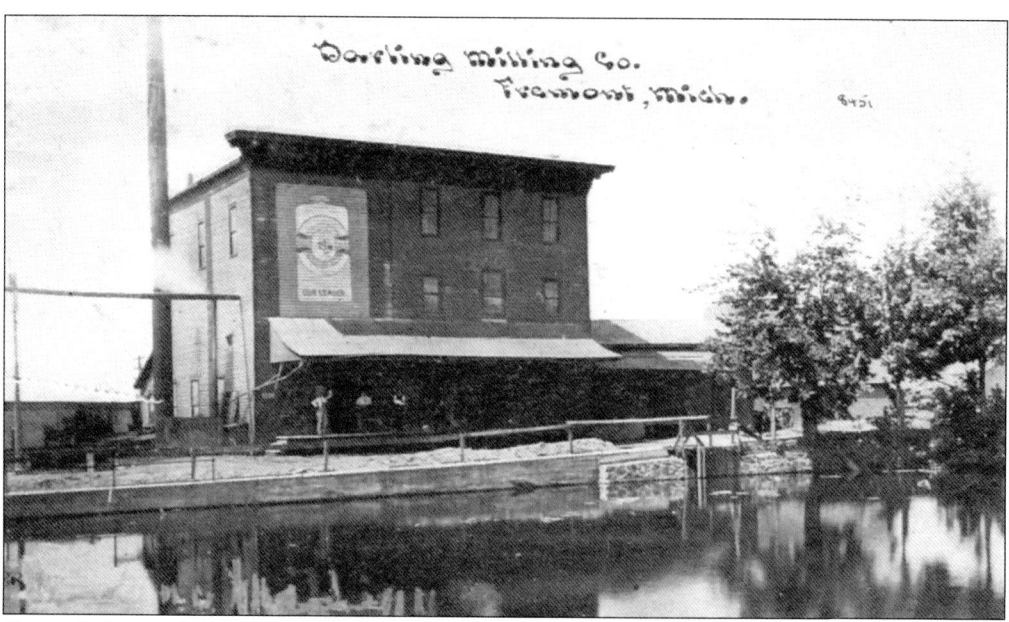

One of the early businesses in Fremont was the Darling Milling Company, located on the old millpond.

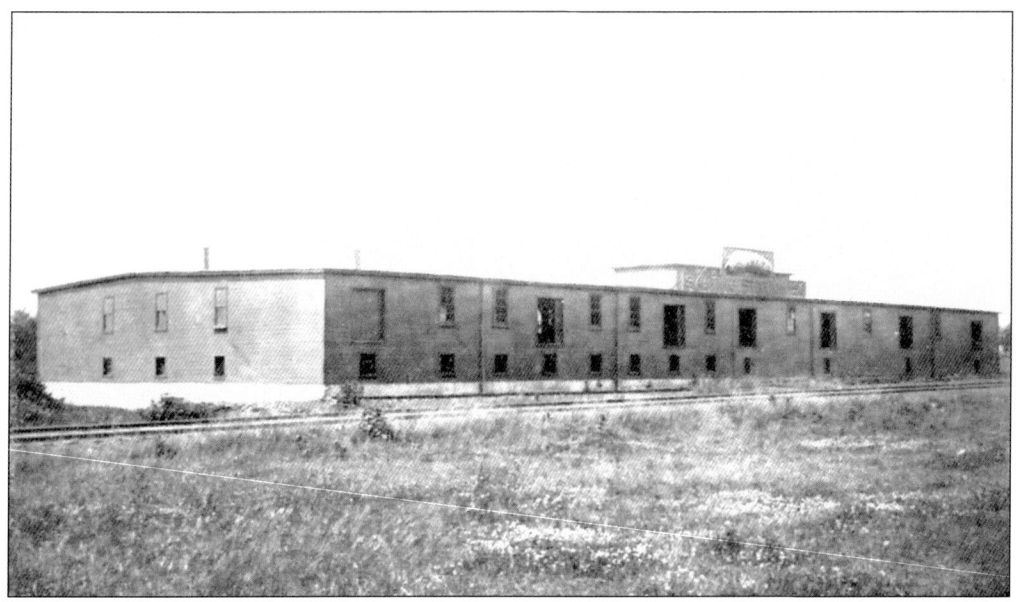
The Heinz Pickle Factory in Fremont was located at 221 North Mechanic Street. It was in operation from 1901 through 1963.

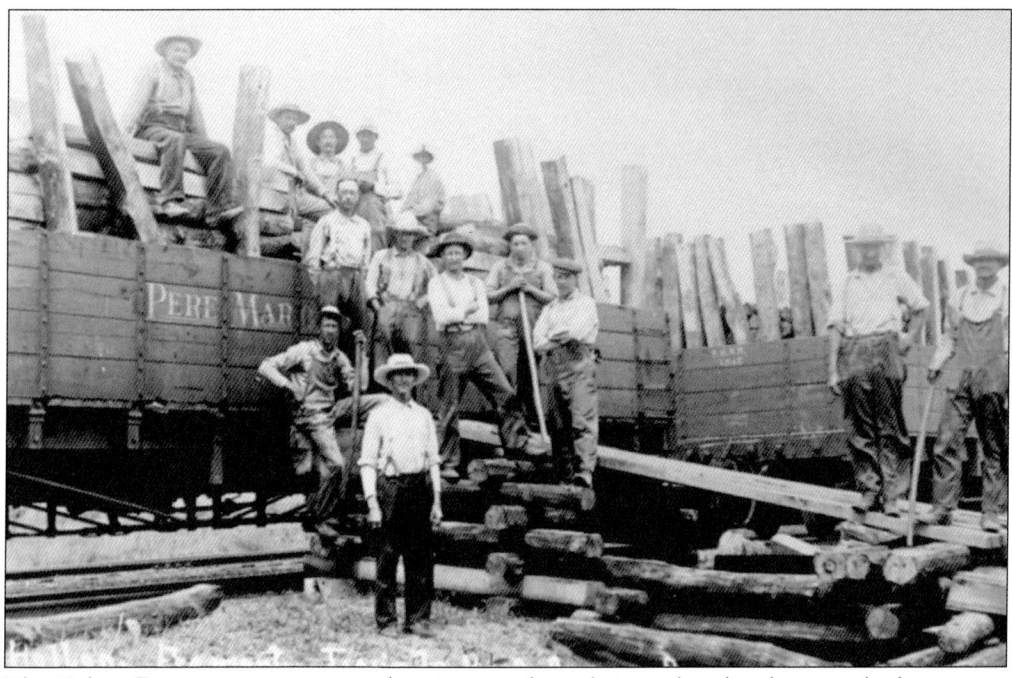
The Holton-Fremont section crew takes time out from their work to be photographed.

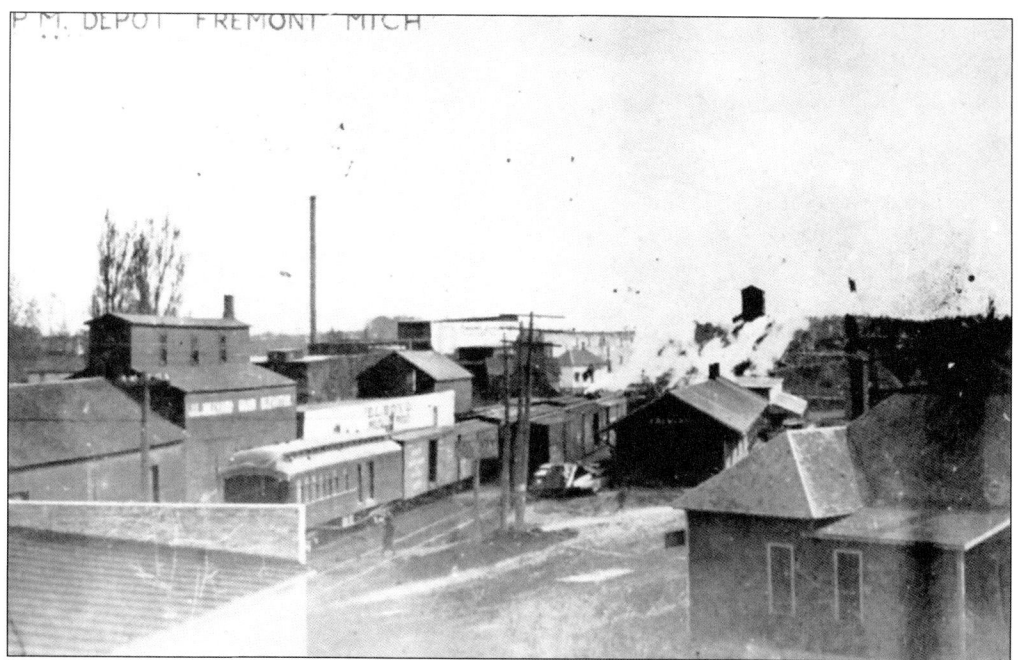
The afternoon train makes a stop at the Fremont depot.

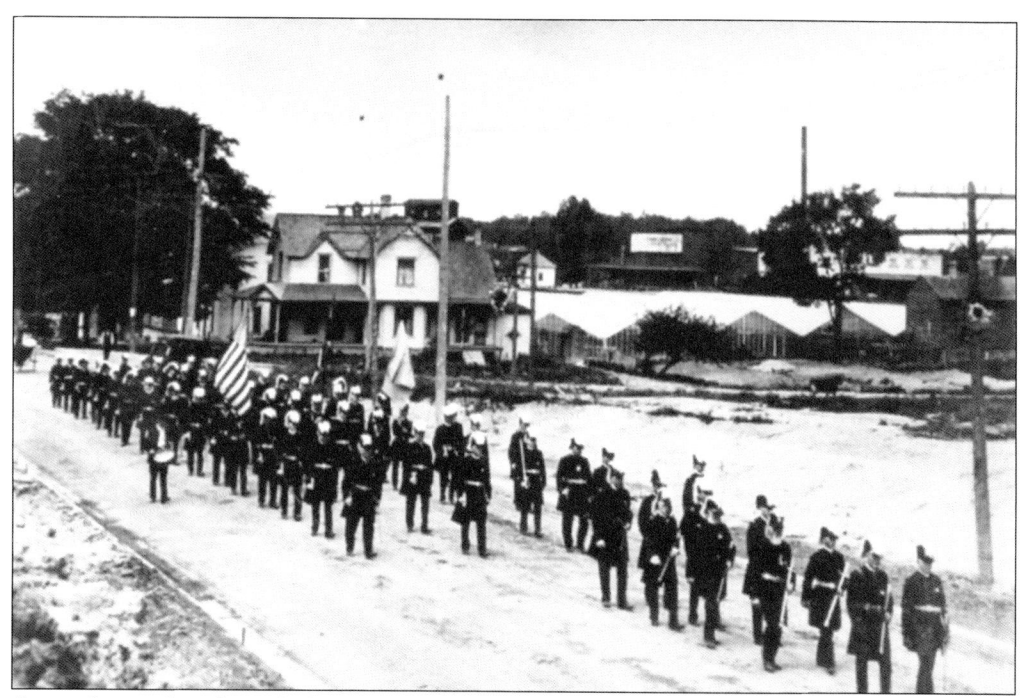
A parade marches through the streets of Fremont. Notice the greenhouses in the background.

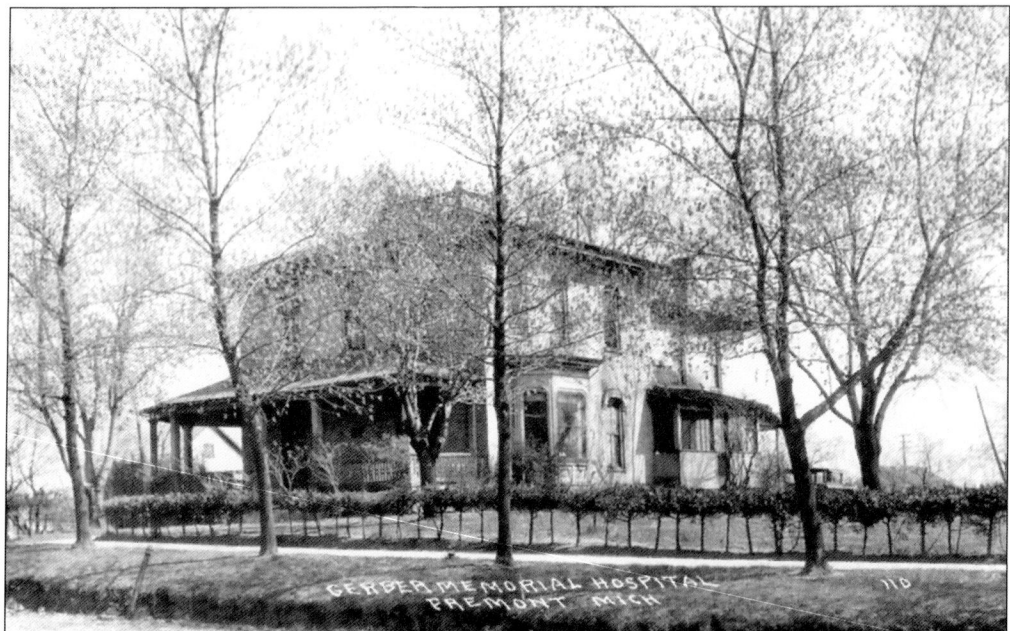

As the village of Fremont grew, there became a need for a hospital. The Gerber family donated a house that became the first Gerber Hospital building, opening in 1919.

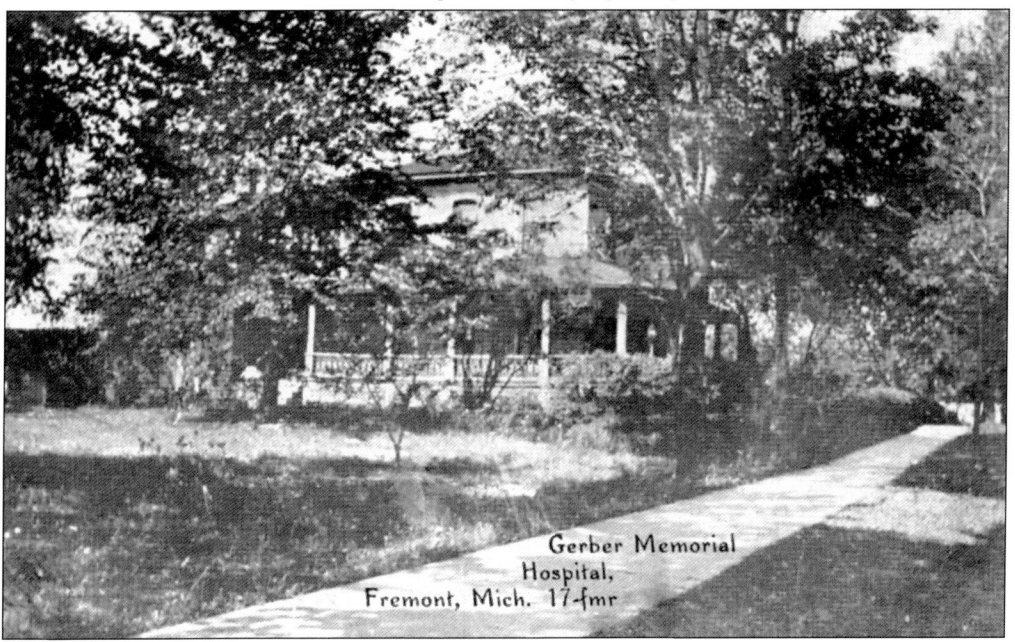

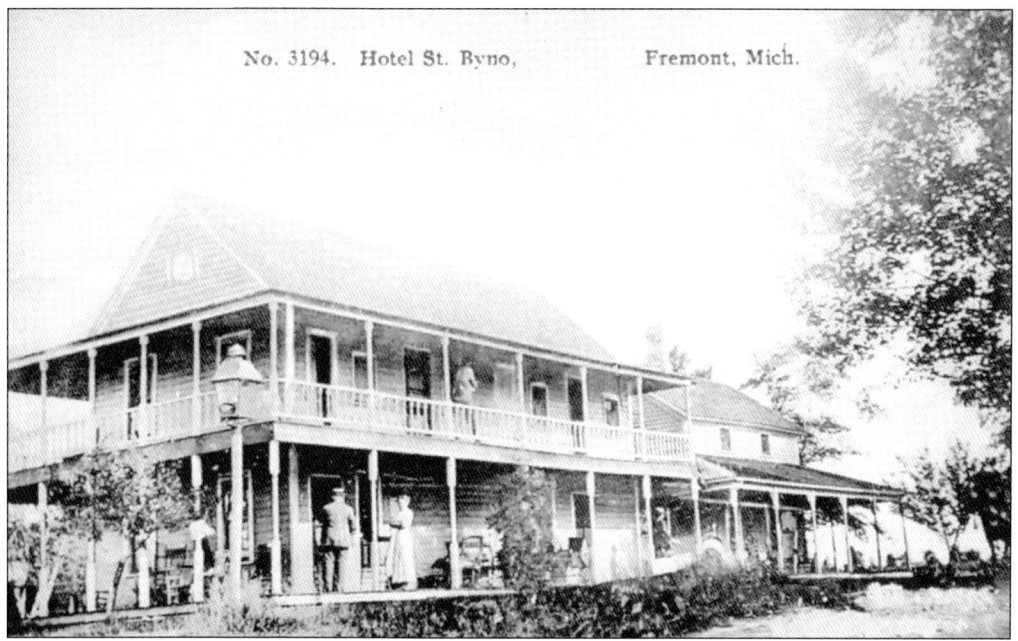

Hotel St. Byno was a popular resort on Fremont Lake. It opened for business in 1903, and it closed its doors in 1922. It was owned and managed by Thomas Mullins. It was a popular destination for vacationers to visit and enjoy the beauty of Fremont Lake.

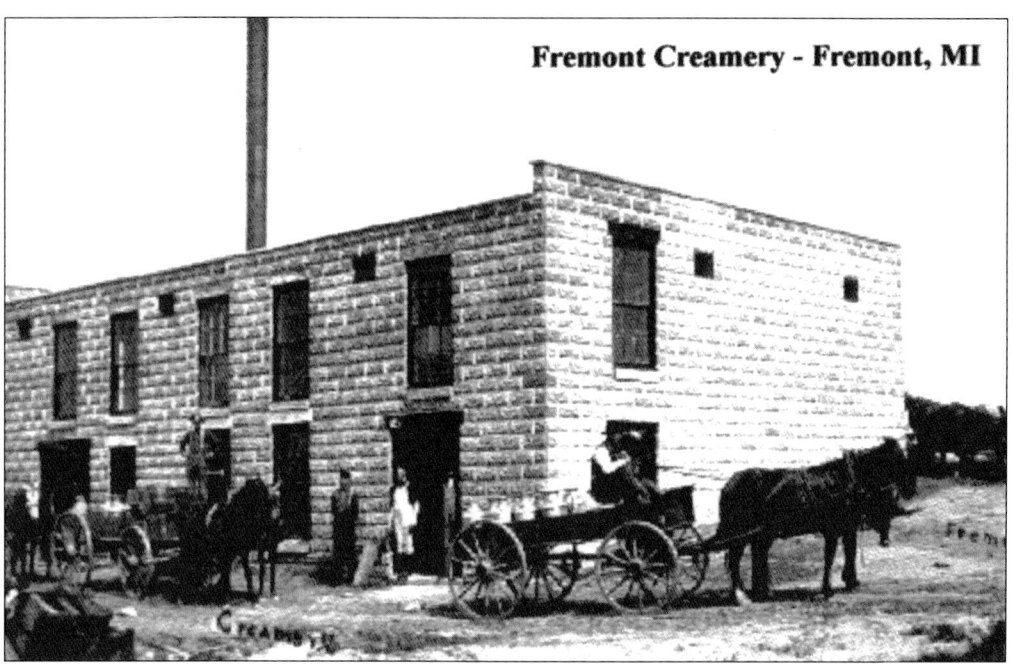

Shown here is the Fremont Creamery, located at 511 South Division Street, which opened in 1904 and closed its doors in 1946.

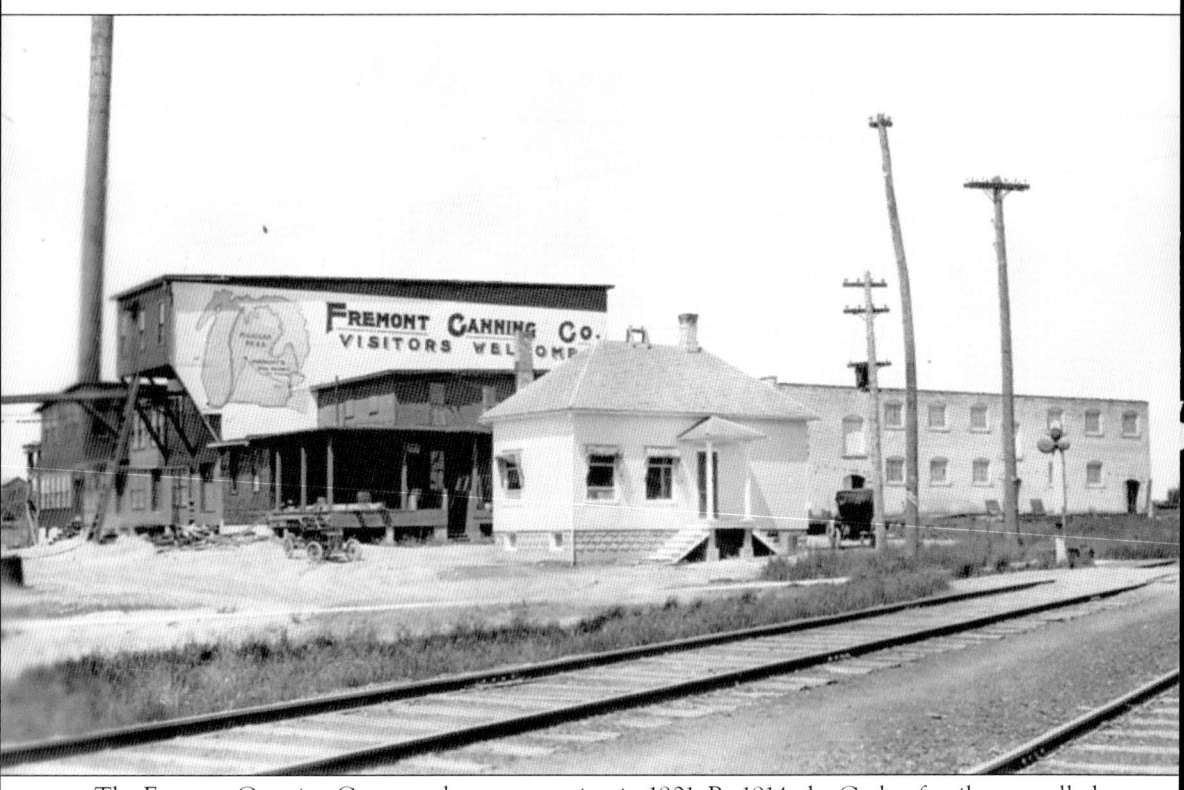

The Fremont Canning Company began operation in 1901. By 1914, the Gerber family controlled the company, and it became Gerber Products Company.

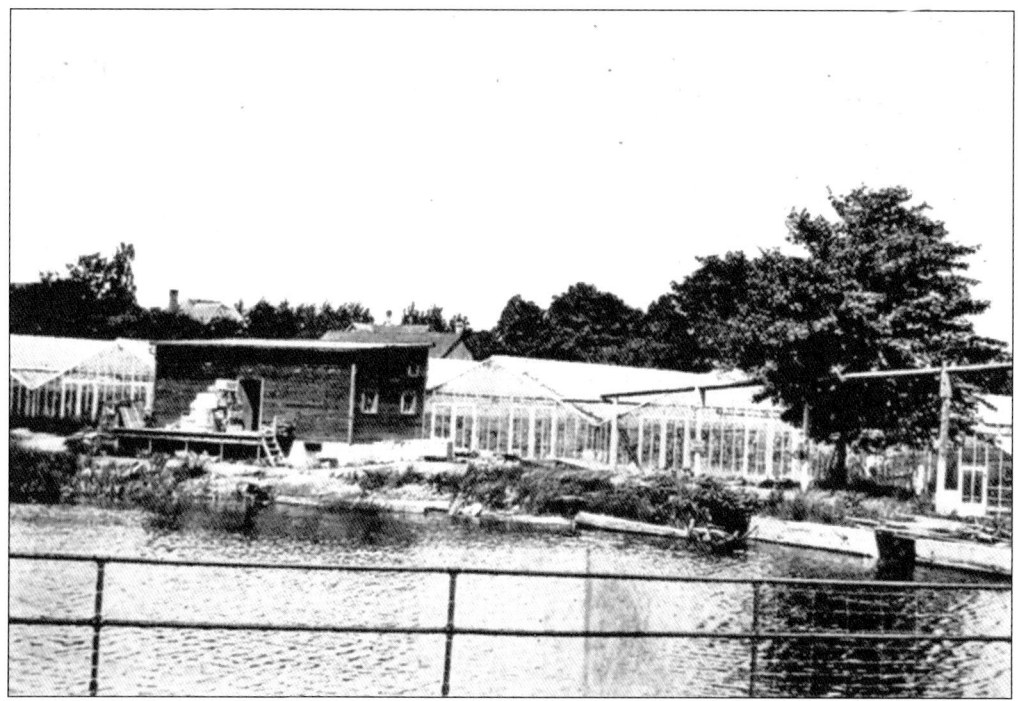

A greenhouse was located on Main and State Streets in Fremont. It was a large operation providing many plants to farms and gardeners all over. The location near the train tracks helped with the shipping.

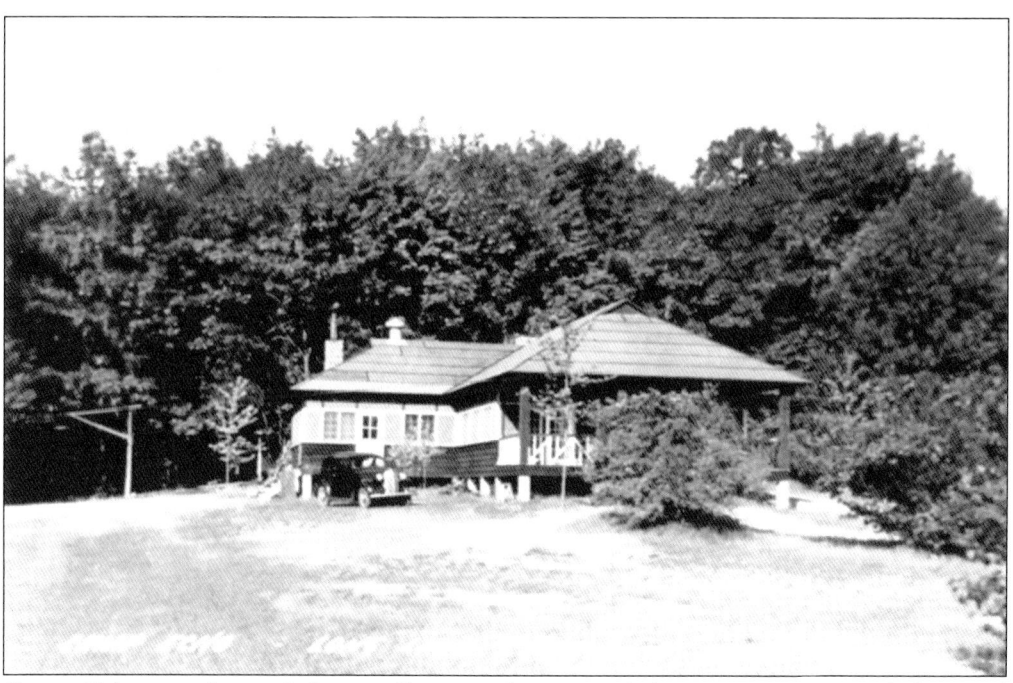

Camp Echo on Long Lake in Fremont has provided many summers of fun and recreation for campers.

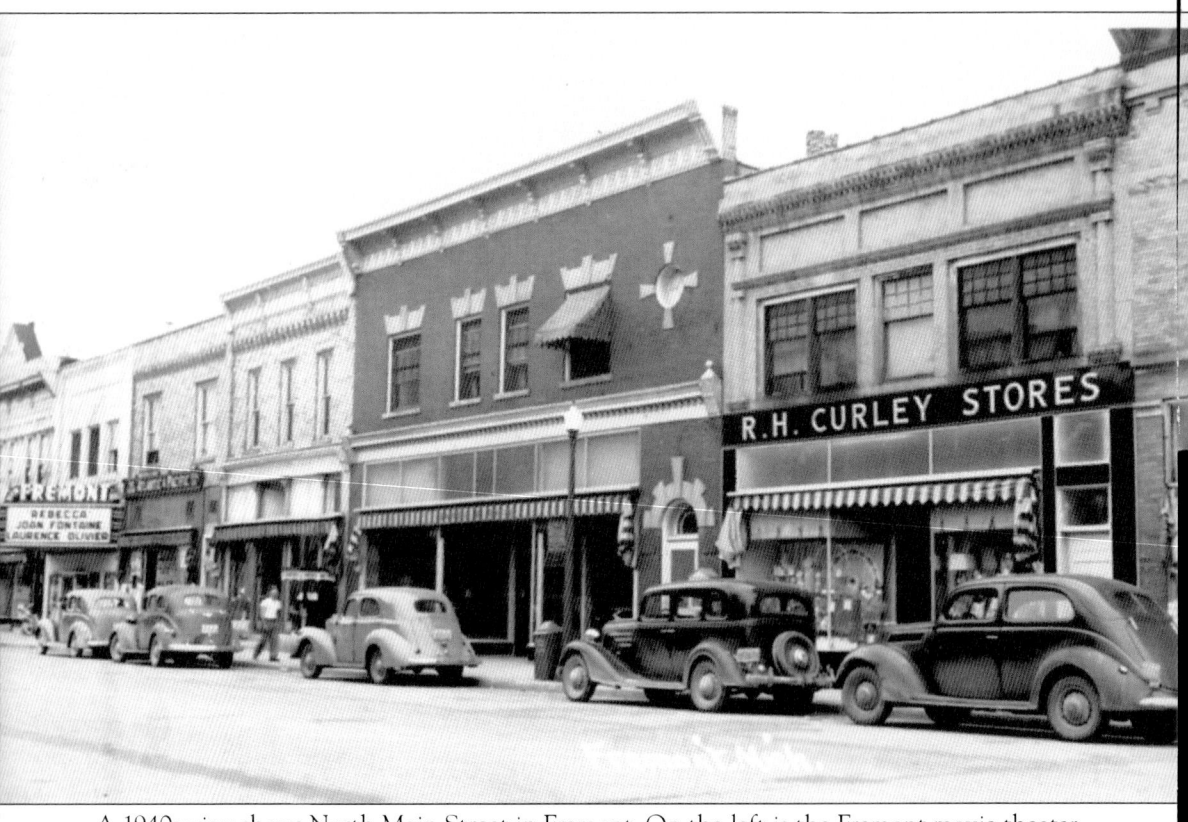

A 1940s view shows North Main Street in Fremont. On the left is the Fremont movie theater.

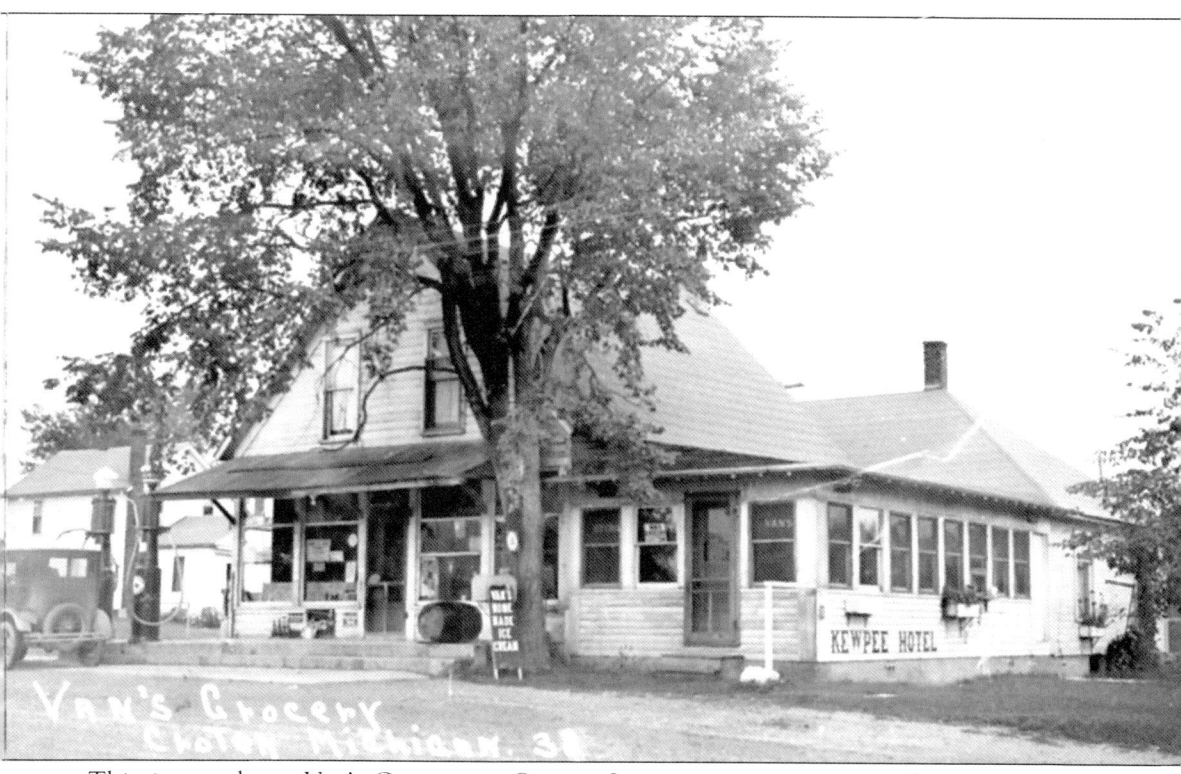

This image shows Van's Grocery in Croton. It was a convenient stop for sportsmen to stock up on supplies and a popular place for residents to purchase their groceries and gather local information.

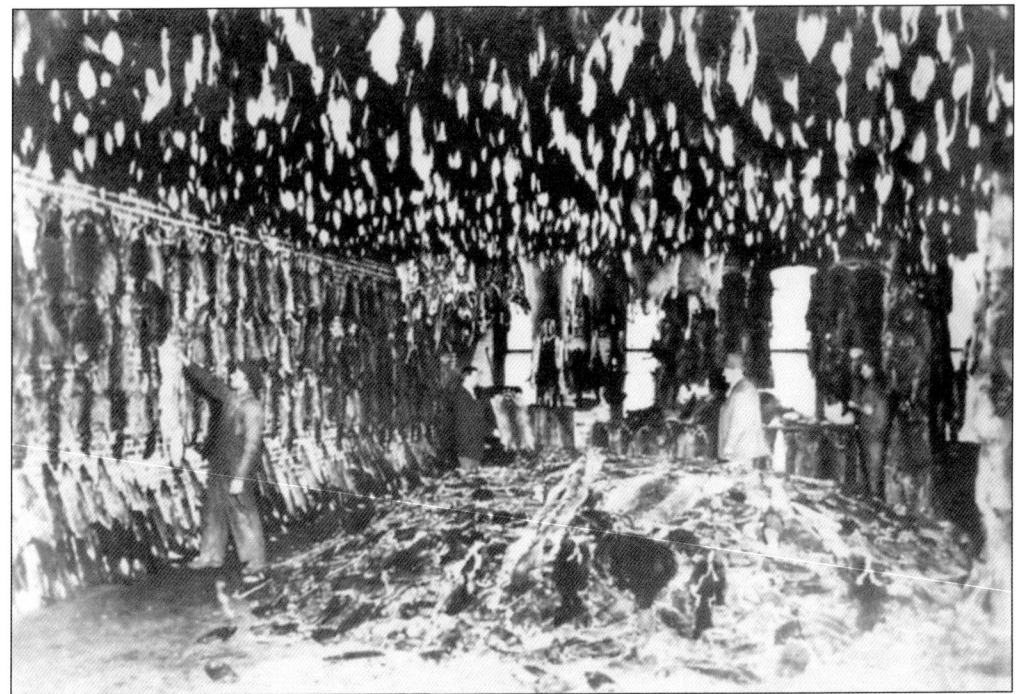

Fur pelts were a big business in the late 1800s and early 1900s, as seen in this photograph from about 1913.

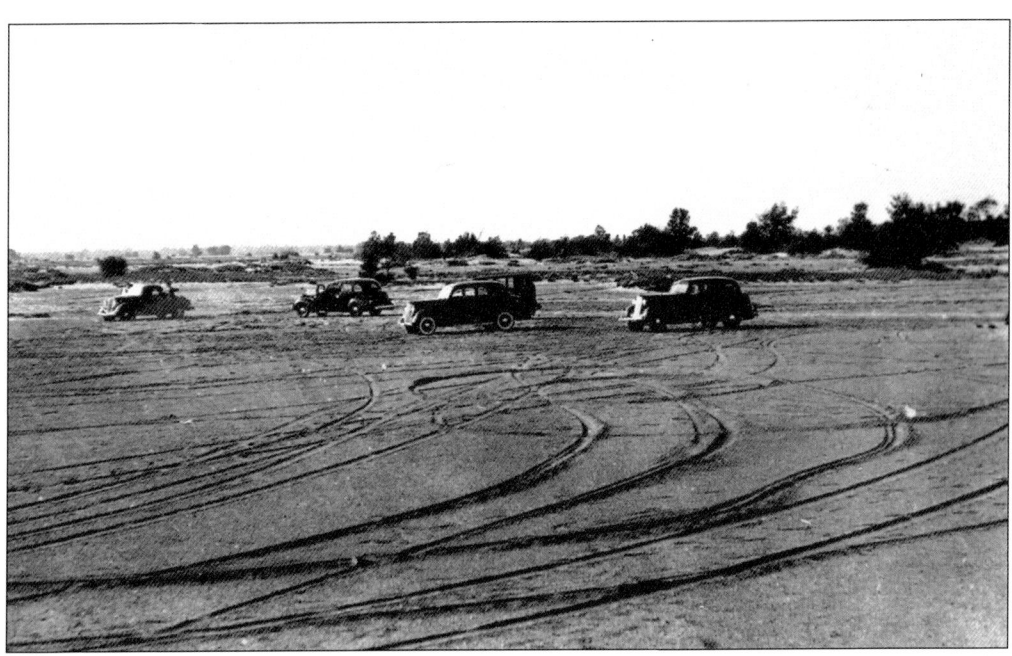

A dust bowl was created after the clear-cutting of the trees in Big Prairie Township. Within the span of one century, a part of Big Prairie Township has changed from fertile farmland to a desert, and then to a young forest. Perhaps this little corner of Newaygo County is so unique there is no other place like it in the United States.

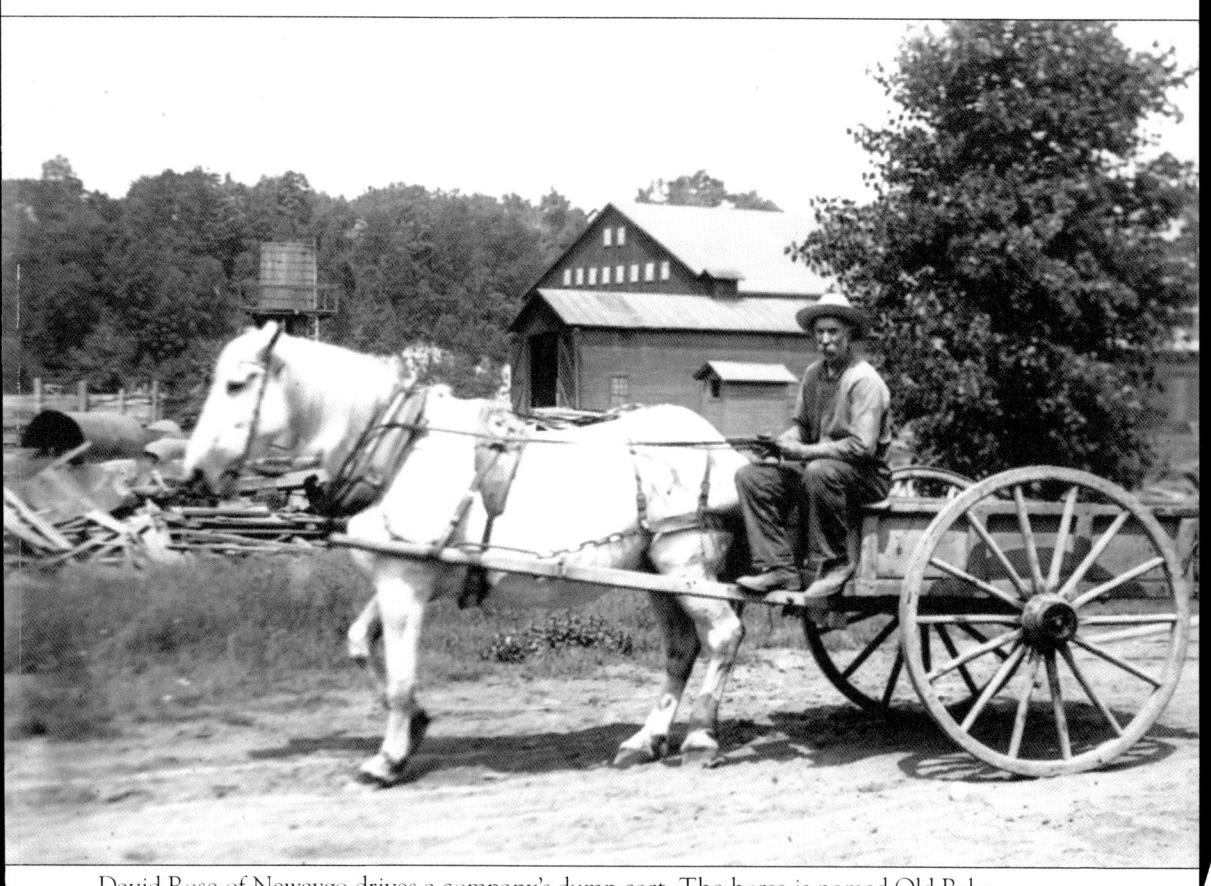
David Rose of Newaygo drives a company's dump cart. The horse is named Old Babe.

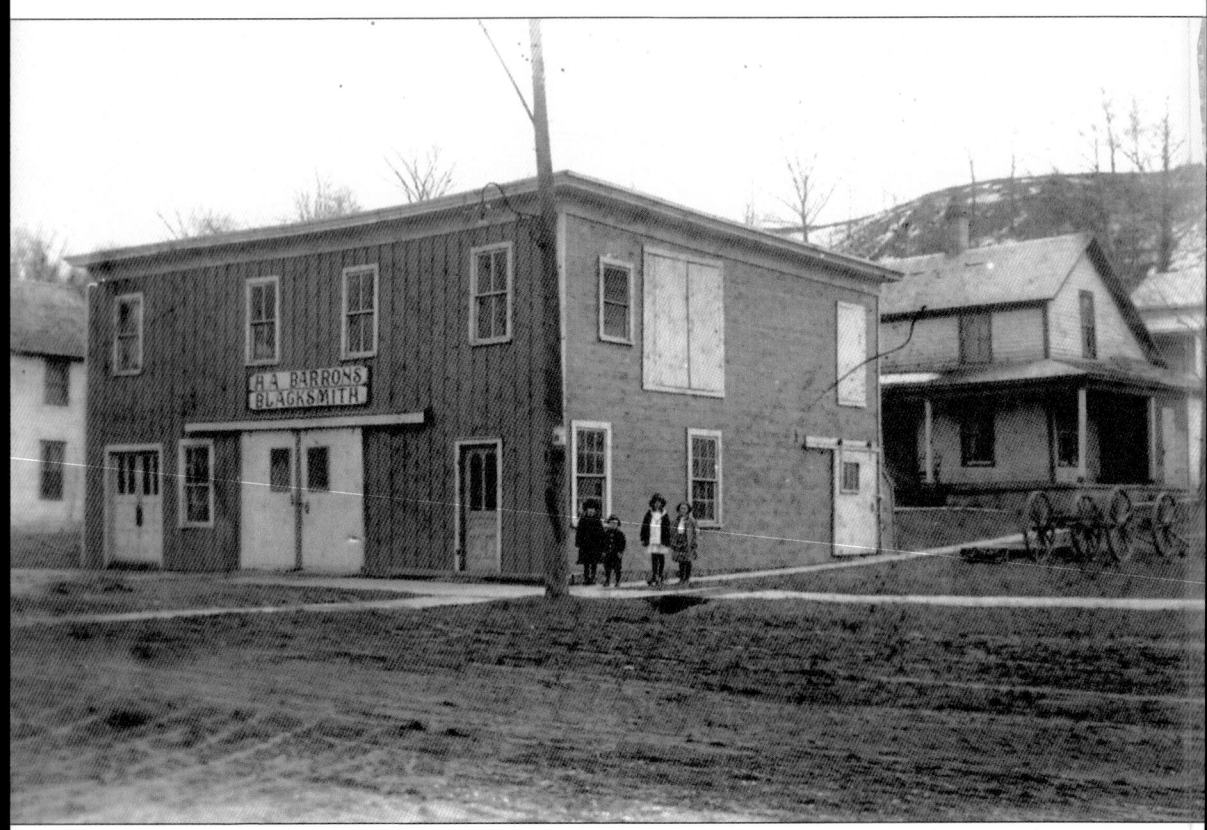

A new business block, Newaygo, is occupied by Henry A. Barrons, blacksmith. It was located on the south corner of West State Road and River Street. The house directly in back is the Barrons family's home.

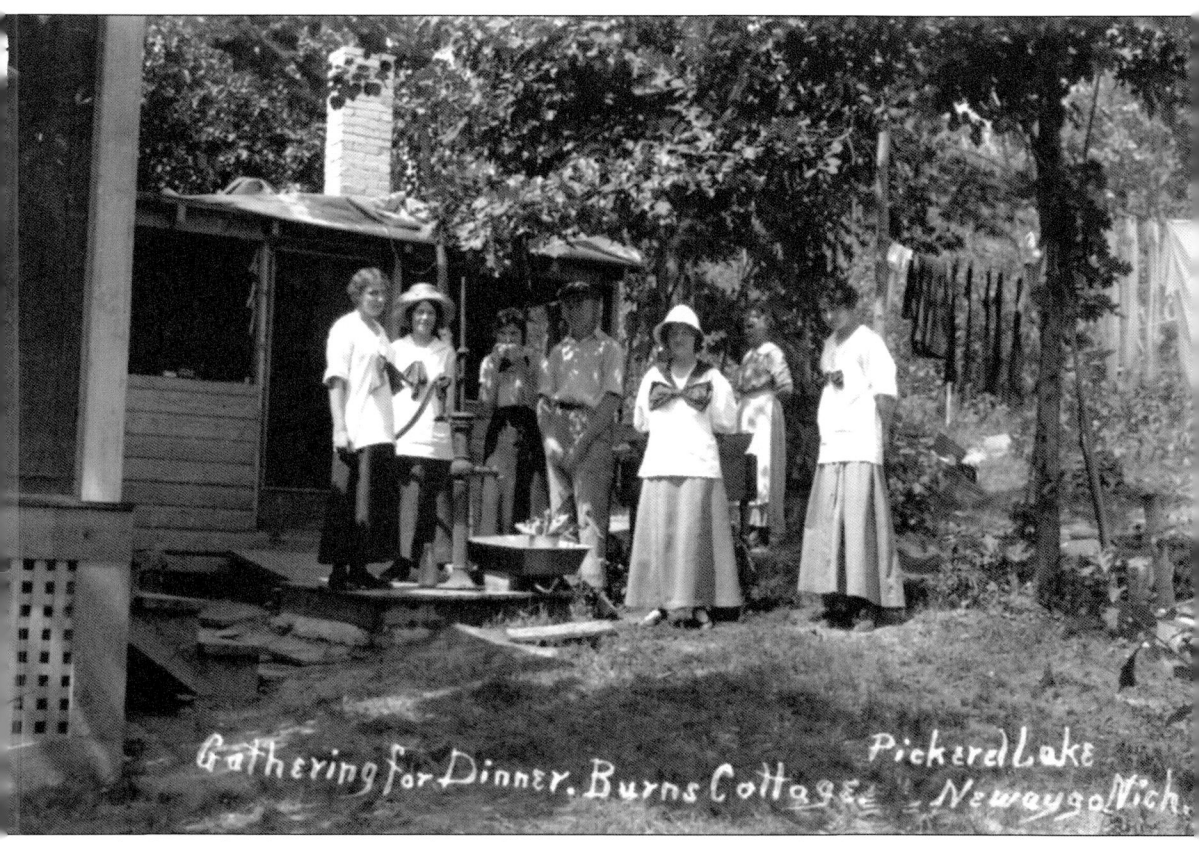

Gathering for Dinner. Burns Cottage Pickeral Lake Newaygo Mich.

The Burns family's cottage was located on the north side of Pickeral Lake, near the east channel. The family gathering for dinner includes Anna Leddy, a friend. Groceries were ordered from Thompson Brothers Newaygo and delivered to a piano box on the south side near J. Hildreth for pick up.

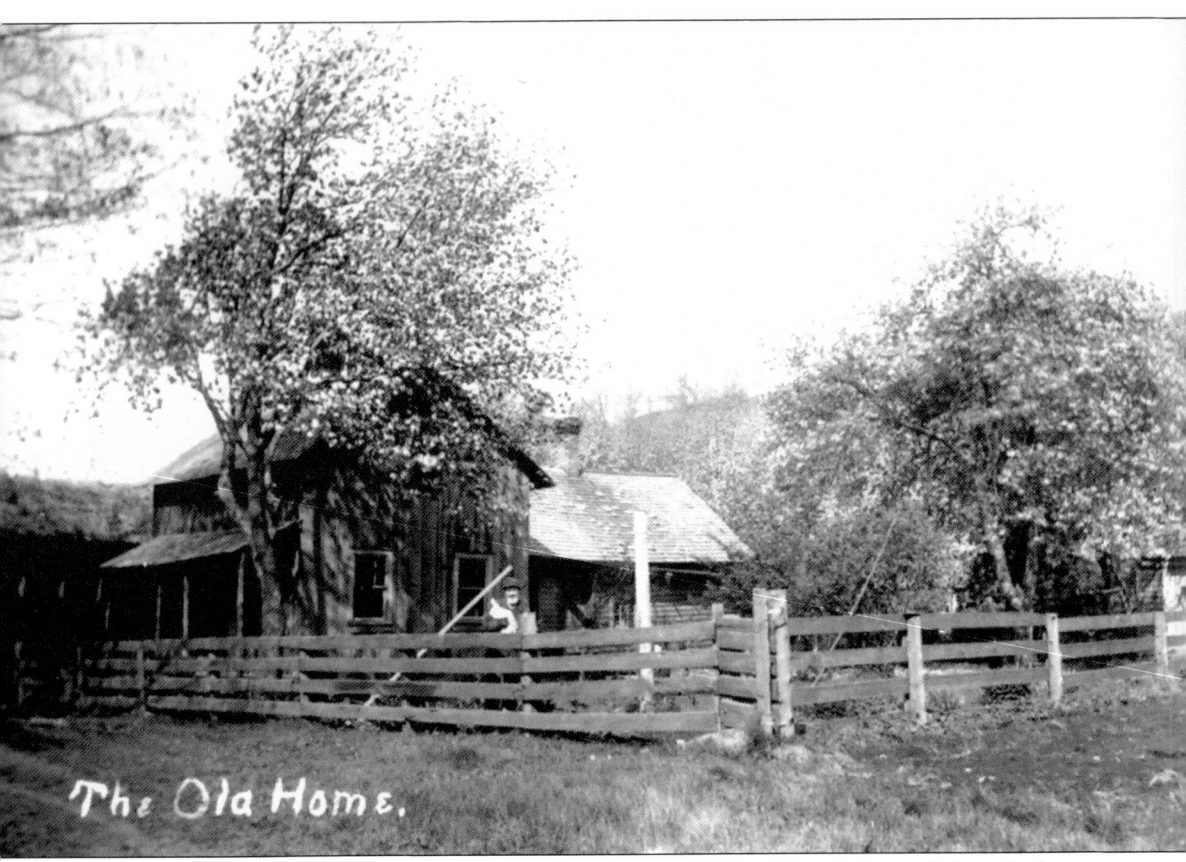

The home of Joseph C. LaMoore was located on the north side of Sarrel Street, below the lower bridge in Newaygo and across from the Muskegon River. His son, Capt. James E. LaMoore, was owner of the gasoline cruiser *Helene C. LaMoore*. There were plans to establish a freight line between Newaygo and Muskegon.

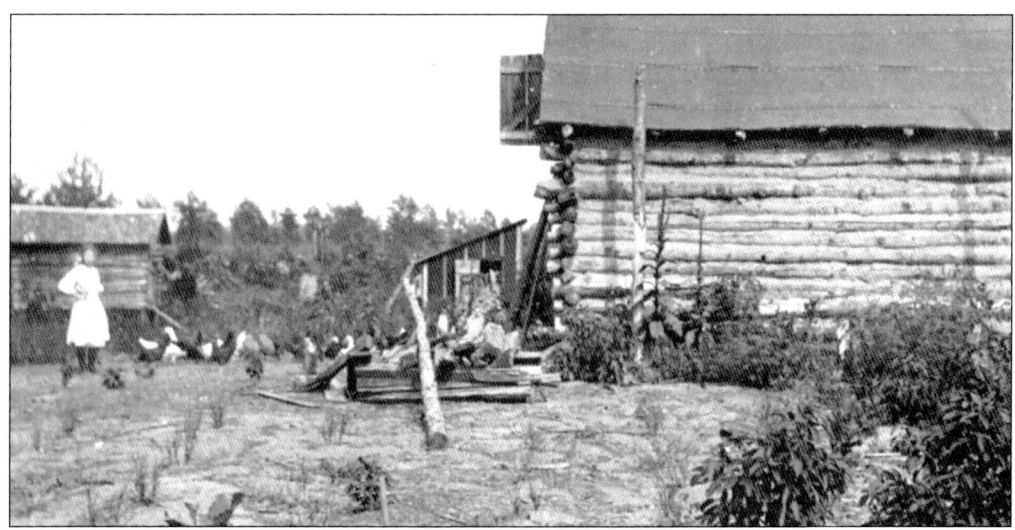
George Warren's log cabin was located on the east side of the road across from Hess Lake and Division Street. He worked for people at Hess Lake and sold cleaned bullheads in the village.

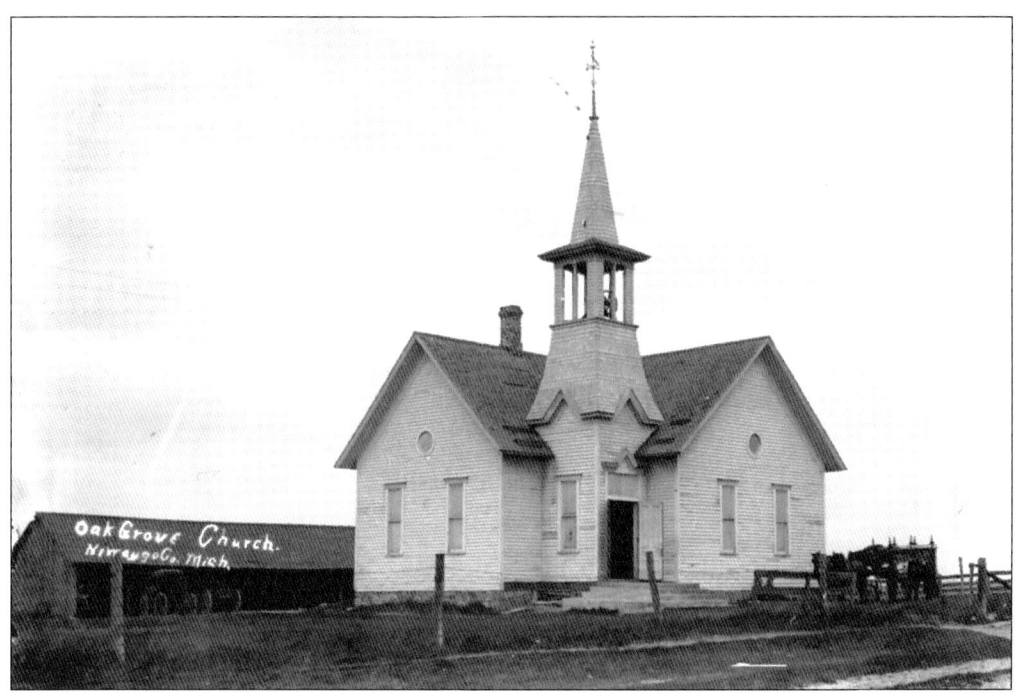
The Oak Grove Church was located at Oak Grove Center near the early Thomas Tavern in the Croton area.

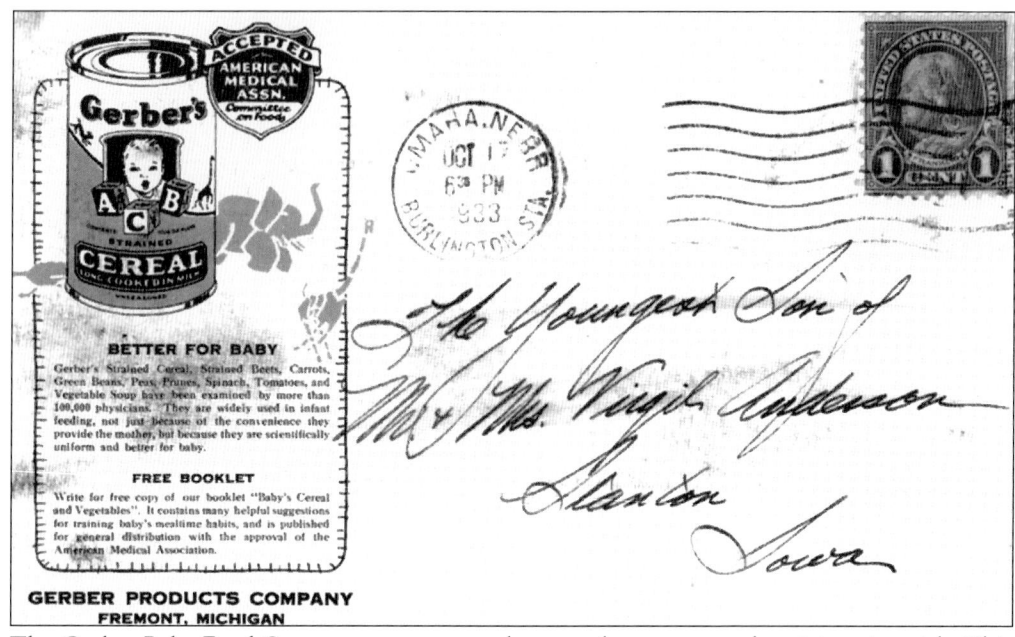

The Gerber Baby Food Company sent out cards to newborns as an advertising gimmick. This campaign helped introduce new parents to the benefits of buying Gerber baby food. This card was sent out in October 1933.

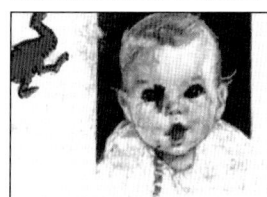

WEL—COME STRANGER · AND i hopE you LikE us ALL · tHis iz A most EX-tRA-ORD-iN-ARy WORLD. you wiLL HAVE LoTz oF EX-ciTE-mENT EX-pER-i-MENT-iNG witH it · GERBERs zTRAiNED CEREAL wiLL BE oNE oF the Firzt REAL foods you wiLL ENjoy AND A FEW months LATER you wiLL Diz-coVER VEG-ET-AbLES · RE-miND your MOtHER tHeN to Ask your docTor AbouT GERBER'S zTRAiNED VEGETAbLES · thEy ARE zpECiALLy madE FoR you to CoN-sERVE viTAmiNs, miNERAL SALTs AND thiNgz · AND thEy zAVE your mothER two oR thREE HouRz OF WoRK A DAy · WE HAVE to zAVE OuR MoTHERs oR ELSE TheyfeeL Too tiRED to pLAy. You'LL HAVE LoTz oF fun with CEREAL-CARROTs, spiNACH, pEAs AND THiNgz GooD LucK ·

FROM your FRiEND
ThE GERBER BAby

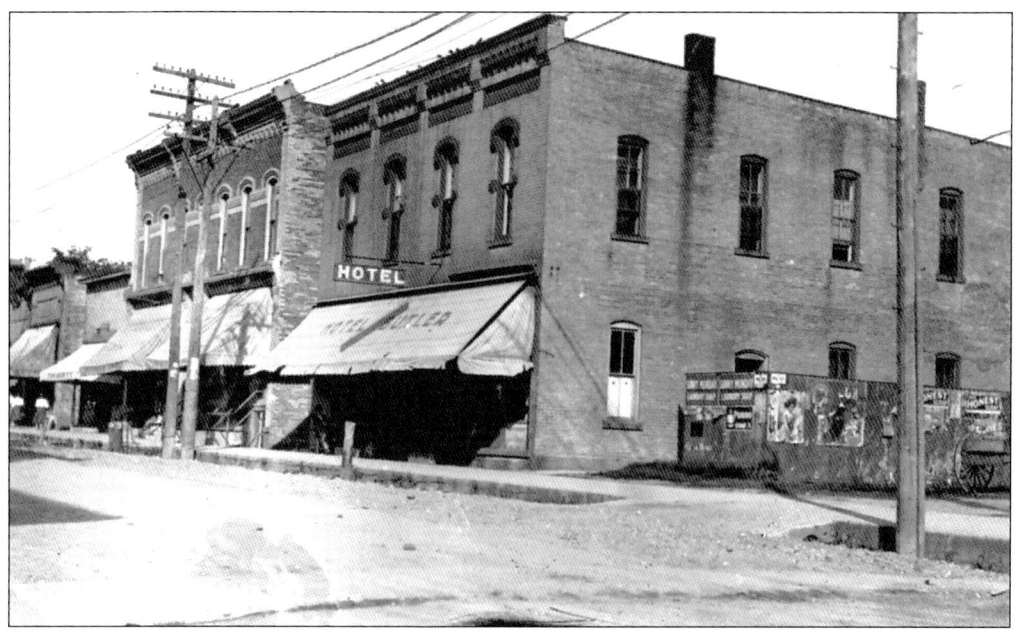

This photograph, taken in early 1900, shows State Road and the Newaygo Butler Hotel. At Bailey's Tavern on the left, a high board fence hides the view of the entrance to the saloon.

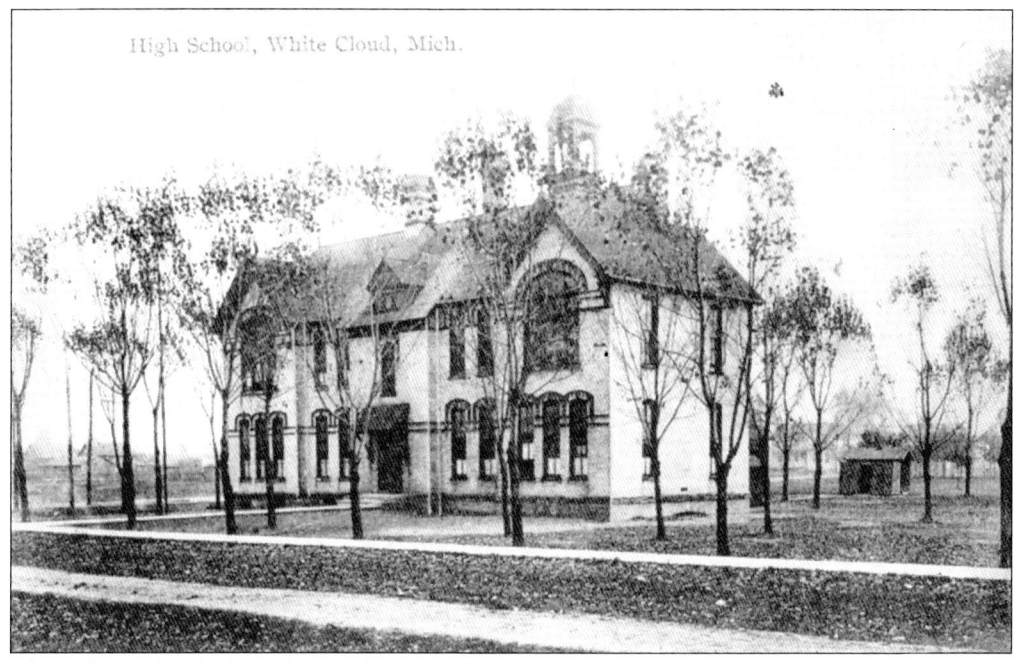

The White Cloud school has undergone many changes through the years. This photograph is an early picture of White Cloud High School.

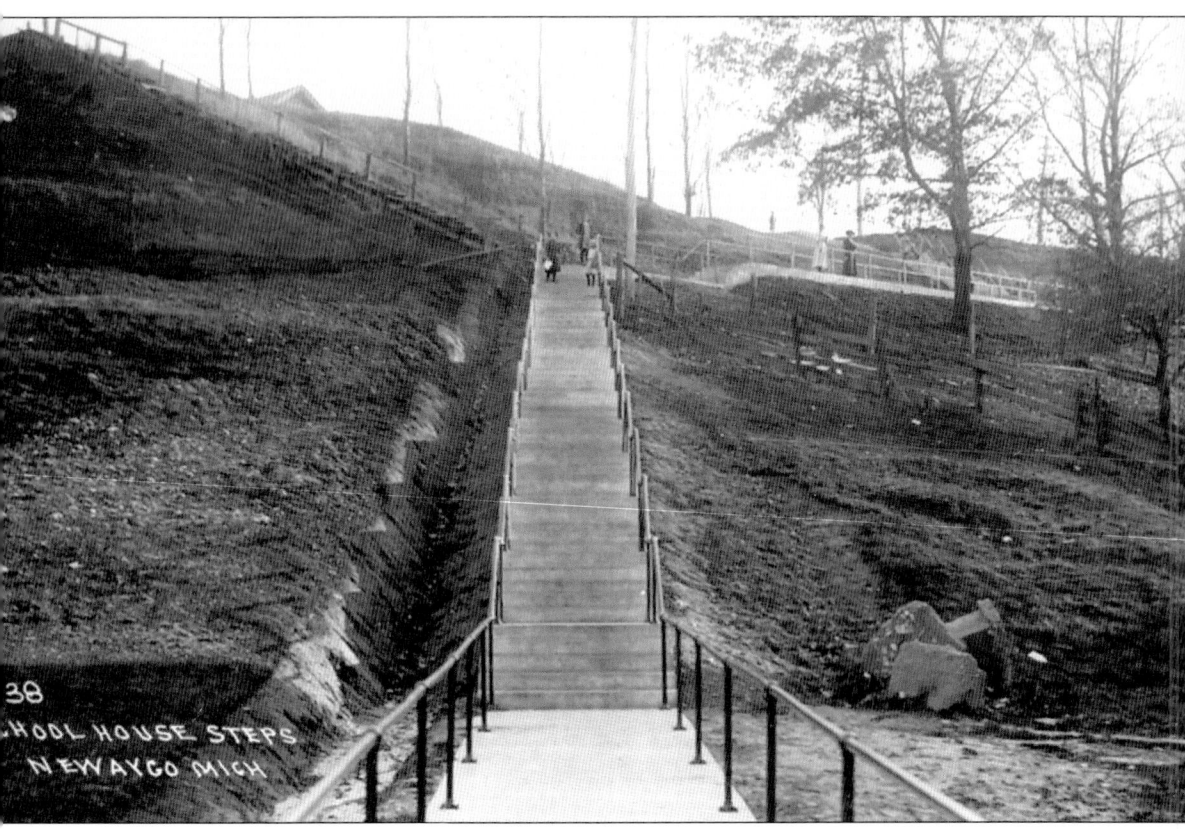
The wooden steps leading up from the town of Newaygo to the school have become a landmark in Newaygo. Many generations have climbed these steps to attend the school on the hill.